'The book's major contribution is to sho̶̶̶w̶̶̶
tions of theory, such as posthumanism, d̶̶̶̶̶̶̶̶̶̶̶̶̶̶̶̶̶̶̶̶̶̶̶̶̶̶̶̶̶ spatiality
studies. This very fine collection of essays will be of use to a wide range of
students as well as to established scholars.'

Kenneth Kidd, *Associate Professor of English, University of Florida*

'A volume like this is long overdue: a single work that not only talks about
liter   **Die**   other without making either seem the
poo   **College**   theory work in a practical, productive,
and even (dare I say it) pleasurable manner. Students, and the rest of us,
should benefit hugely.'

David Rudd, *Professor of Children's Literature, University of Bolton*

Bringing together the voices of leading and emerging scholars, *Contemporary
Children's Literature and Film* provides critical approaches for reading children's literature and film. The book argues for the significance of theory for
reading texts written and produced for young people and integrates a wide
range of critical perspectives, including schema theory, theories of space
and place, cultural globalization, feminism, ecocriticism, adaptation theory,
postcolonialism, and posthumanism.

The book accessibly introduces the very latest thinking in the field and is
attuned to contemporary issues and contexts. Individual chapters demystify theory and show how it can open up alternative ideas, challenge basic
assumptions, and unsettle the taken-for-granted with respect to authorship,
literary conventions, and the contexts in which texts for young people are
produced and consumed. This will be vital reading for anyone studying or
researching children's literature and film.

Kerry Mallan is Professor in Education at Queensland University of
Technology, Australia. Her co-edited book, *Youth Cultures: Texts, Images and
Identities*, is an IRSCL Honour Book (2003). She is a co-author of *New World
Orders in Contemporary Children's Literature* (2008). Her most recent book is
Gender Dilemmas in Children's Fiction (2009).

Clare Bradford is Professor of Literature at Deakin University, Australia. Her
2001 book, *Reading Race*, won both the ChLA Book Award and the IRSCL
Award. She is a co-author of *New World Orders in Contemporary Children's
Literature* (2008). Her most recent book is *Unsettling Narratives: Postcolonial
Readings of Children's Literature* (2007), which was a Children's Literature
Association Honor Book.

Contemporary Children's Literature and Film

Engaging with Theory

Edited by

Kerry Mallan
and
Clare Bradford

palgrave
macmillan

First published 2011 by
PALGRAVE MACMILLAN

Palgrave Macmillan in the UK is an imprint of Macmillan Publishers Limited, registered in England, company number 785998, of Houndmills, Basingstoke, Hampshire RG21 6XS.

Palgrave Macmillan in the US is a division of St Martin's Press LLC, 175 Fifth Avenue, New York, NY 10010.

Palgrave Macmillan is the global academic imprint of the above companies and has companies and representatives throughout the world.

Palgrave® and Macmillan® are registered trademarks in the United States, the United Kingdom, Europe and other countries.

ISBN: 978–0–230–23149–8 hardback
ISBN: 978–0–230–23150–4 paperback

This book is printed on paper suitable for recycling and made from fully managed and sustained forest sources. Logging, pulping and manufacturing processes are expected to conform to the environmental regulations of the country of origin.

A catalogue record for this book is available from the British Library.

A catalog record for this book is available from the Library of Congress.

10 9 8 7 6 5 4 3 2 1
20 19 18 17 16 15 14 13 12 11

Printed in China

Contents

List of Figures

Notes on Contributors

Raffaella Baccolini teaches English and American Literature and Gender Studies at the University of Bologna at Forlì. She has published extensively on women's literature, modernism, the Shoah, science fiction, and utopian studies. Her publications include *Tradition, Identity, Desire: Revisionist Strategies in H.D.'s Late Poetry* (1995); *Dark Horizons: Science Fiction and the Dystopian Imagination* (2003) and *Utopia Method Vision: The Use Value of Social Dreaming* (2007, both with Tom Moylan); *Le prospettive di genere: Discipline, soglie, confini* (2005); *Constructing Identities: Translations, Cultures, Nations* (2008, with Patrick Leech), *Gender and Humor, Humor and Gender* (forthcoming, with Delia Chiaro). She is currently working on the representation of trauma in literature and film.

Clare Bradford is Professor at Deakin University in Melbourne, Australia. Her publications include are *Reading Race: Aboriginality in Australian Children's Literature* (2001), *Unsettling Narratives: Postcolonial Readings of Children's Literature* (2007), and *New World Orders in Contemporary Children's Literature: Utopian Transformations* (2008, with Kerry Mallan, John Stephens, and Robyn McCallum). She is President of the International Research Society for Children's Literature and, in 2009, was awarded the inaugural Trudeau International Fellowship.

David Buchbinder holds a Personal Chair in Masculinities Studies at Curtin University of Technology in Perth, Western Australia, where he teaches in the Department of Communication and Cultural Studies in the School of Media, Culture and Creative Arts. He has edited *Essays in Masculinities Studies 2002* (2003), a collection of undergraduate essays on masculinity; he has published two books, *Masculinities and Identities* (1994) and *Performance Anxieties: Re-presenting Men* (1998), and has published widely in the area of masculinities studies focusing on the cultural representations, across various genres and media, of men, masculinities, and male sexualities. He has begun work on a third book on masculinity, *Studying Men and Masculinities*, to be published by Routledge.

Elizabeth Bullen is Senior Lecturer at the School of Communication and Creative Arts at Deakin University in Melbourne, Australia. Her published research centres on child and youth texts and cultures in the context of globalisation, consumer capitalism, and identity. In 'Inside Story: Product Placement and Adolescent Consumer Identity in Young Adult Fiction', *Media, Culture & Society* (2009), she shows how consumerism, gender, and class become mutually constitutive. Her forthcoming book interrogates representations of social class in contemporary children's fiction.

Kerry Mallan is Professor in Education at Queensland University of Technology is the author of numerous articles, book chapters, and books on children's literature, including *Gender Dilemmas in Children's Fiction* (2009). Her book, *Youth Cultures: Texts, Images and Identities* (co-edited with Sharyn Pearce) won the Honour Book Award from the International Research Society in Children's Literature (2003). With Clare Bradford, she edits the refereed journal *Papers: Explorations into Children's Literature*. In 2006 she received the Dame Annabelle Rankin Award for Distinguished Services to Children's Literature.

Geraldine Massey worked as a teacher–librarian in government and non-government schools before tutoring in courses in children's literature and primary literacy at Queensland University of Technology. She was a research assistant for the Australian Research Council funded grant 'Transformative Utopianism: Contemporary Children's Literature Responding to Changing World Orders from Glastnost to 11 September, 2001', with Clare Bradford, Kerry Mallan, John Stephens, and Robyn McCalllum. In 2010, her doctoral study, entitled *Reading the Environment: Narrative Constructions of Ecological Subjectivities in Australian Children's Literature*, was awarded by *Queensland University of Technology*. She is the co-editor of *The History of Teacher-Librarianship in Queensland* (2010).

John Stephens is Emeritus Professor in English at Macquarie University, Sydney. He is author of *Language and Ideology in Children's Fiction*; *Retelling Stories, Framing Culture* (with Robyn McCallum); *New World Orders in Contemporary Children's Literature* (with Clare Bradford, Kerry Mallan, and Robyn McCallum); editor of *Ways of Being Male*; and author of about a hundred articles and two other books. He is a former IRSCL President, and currently Editor of *International Research in Children's Literature*. In 2007, he received the 11th International Brothers Grimm Award in recognition of his contribution to research in children's literature.

Maria Takolander is Lecturer at Deakin University, Melbourne. She is the author of a book of literary criticism, *Catching Butterflies: Bringing Magical Realism to Ground* (2007), and a book of poetry, *Ghostly Subjects* (2009). Her current research project involves an interdisciplinary examination of the transformative nature of literary experience, with one focus being on children's culture.

Christine Wilkie-Stibbs is Associate Professor and Reader in Children's Literature and Criticism at the University of Warwick, England. Her publications include *The Feminine Subject in Children's Literature* (2002) and *The Outside Child In and Out of the Book* (2008).

Introduction: Bringing Back Theory

Kerry Mallan and Clare Bradford

> The Latest Theory is that Theory Doesn't Matter
>
> (Eakin, 2002)

In a report in the *New York Times* about a public symposium on the future of theory held at University of Chicago in 2002, staff writer Emily Eakin suggests that theory appears to have taken a back seat to more pressing current affairs – the Bush Administration, Al Qaeda, Iraq. Further, she reports that the symposium's panel of high-profile theorists and scholars, including Homi Bhabha, Stanley Fish, Fredric Jameson, seemed reticent to offer their views on what is often touted as the demise or irrelevance of theory. The symposium and other commentaries on the topic of theory have prompted the view that the 'Golden Age of Theory' has passed and we are now in a 'Post-Theory Age'. Given these pronouncements, we need to ask – Does theory matter any longer? Is it time for its obituary? Or are reports of the death of theory greatly exaggerated? The question remains whether to mourn or celebrate the demise of theory, and whether the body has in fact breathed its last. The title of this Introduction – 'Bringing back theory' – suggests a resurrection, or perhaps a haunting, as if the funeral has passed and, like Banquo's ghost, theory returns to unsettle or disturb the celebration. It also suggests an entreaty, or perhaps a return performance. Rather than settle on one meaning, one interpretation, we are happy for all possibilities to coexist. The coexistence of different theories, different approaches, different interpretations also reflects the state of literary and cultural studies generally and children's literature criticism in particular. No single theory or viewpoint predominates or vies for hegemony. Yet, one further question lingers – what is theory?

'Theory' written with a capital 'T' is an encompassing term which gathers a number of theories under its umbrella. Perhaps we might define 'Theory' as so-called 'High Theory' – structuralism, post-structuralism, Marxism, psychoanalysis, and so on, and lower case 'theory' as a minor player. But this kind of hierarchical division serves little purpose, especially when theory in one form or another influences our daily lives. Theory is not solely the domain of adults; children too are quite capable of coming up with a theoretical proposition about everyday phenomena and surprises – rainbows, thunder, why bubbles burst. As Jonathan Culler observes, 'we are ineluctably in theory' (2007: p. 3). Theory, regardless of its status as high or low, sophisticated or simple, offers a supposition or a system of ideas explaining something. However, our interest here is not with everyday theory, but with critical theory and what it can offer the study of children's literature and film.

Since the time of Aristotle's *Poetics*, theory has informed readers about the nature of literature, its affects, genres, and functions. However, the birth of critical theory is relatively recent. Critical theory arose from its early proponents' dissatisfaction with the 'practical criticism' that characterized approaches to literature study from the 1920s. Pioneers of practical criticism, such as I. A. Richards, F. R. Leavis, and Cleanth Brooks, advocated a close reading of literature without regard to history or context. Undoubtedly, 'close reading' of texts remains an important aspect of criticism today, but simply analysing the 'words on the page' in isolation fails to take account of the theoretical or ideological assumptions on which such analysis is based. This kind of reading in a theoretical void pertains to liberal humanist practice, which operates from a set of uncritical assumptions about the value of literature, the constancy of human nature, the transcendence of an essential individuality over cultural and other influences, and so on. However, approaches to criticism have always been characterized by peaks and troughs, with each decade of the twentieth century riding on a new wave of critical theory ready to wipe out the liberal humanist consensus (Barry, 2002: p. 32). Peter Barry, like others who provide a chronology of the development of critical theory, maps these new waves, noting both the turn away from and the return towards a particular theory. For example, Marxist literary criticism, first introduced in the early twentieth century, returned with renewed vigour and political agency in the 1960s. From the 1970s, other theories which railed against liberal humanist orthodoxies began to make their presence felt, namely, feminist criticism and linguistic criticism. In the 1970s and 1980s, both structuralism and post-structuralism foregrounded language and philosophy, rather than history or context. This prompted a 'turn to history' which was ushered in by New Historicism (USA) and Cultural Materialism (UK). Finally, in the 1990s, the move from grand universalizing theories to more specific forms of criticism and theory emerged from postcolonialism, post-modernism, and postfeminism (Barry, 2002: p. 33). The twentieth century was undoubtedly an important period in the history of critical theory. Now in the twenty-first century we may well ask – 'Is the party over?'.

For and against theory

This book seeks to demonstrate how theory informs readings of children's literature and film. Rather than writing off theory as irrelevant, we argue that theory is alive and well, and its prognosis promises a long and healthy life. We have briefly noted the genealogy and high points of theory; now we want to engage with some of the arguments put forth by its detractors and consider the value and weaknesses of these positions.

One claim is that theory fails to take account of 'real readers' and 'real viewers'. Now that reader-response theories and audience studies have fallen out of favour with proponents of critical theory, those who insist on empirical evidence claim that theory is unable to explain the experience that reading a book or viewing a film offers 'real' people. Stephen Prince (1996) asserts that film theories construct spectators within the theory, but that 'real' spectators are missing. The absence of real readers is often noted by assessors when children's literature scholars apply for grants or discuss their work outside their field; a recurring question is – 'But what do the children think?'. In responding to this question, we need to consider the assumptions that are behind it: namely, that only real readers can offer 'authentic' interpretations about a text's content or assessments of its worth. Presumably these unbiased accounts are immune from any ideological predispositions on the part of readers, and the responses are therefore untainted by the stain of theory. Assumptions about 'real readers' are often based on the liberal humanist tenet that there exists a universal reading experience. While proponents of reader-response theories claim the benefits of learning from real readers, critics of this approach point to its potential for making generalizations about readers and particular texts which fail to take account of the diversity of readers, cultural contexts, and reading practices.

A second claim is that theory uses a lexicon or stock of words and phrases that is often obscure or elitist, but which nevertheless carries critical currency in specialist scholarly contexts. Valentine Cunningham (2002) illustrates this point with reference to what has become known as 'the Sokal hoax', where a spoof article, 'Transgressing the Boundaries: Toward a transformational hermeneutics of quantum gravity', replete with references to cultural theory, sociology of science, post-modernist views about quantum physics, and so on, was published (after peer review) in the journal *Social Text*. While Sokal's hoax focused more on deriding cultural theorists and sociologists by demonstrating that they couldn't distinguish the genuine 'article' from a false one, it also mocked the way theoretical language, especially that which proposes post-modern ideas about science, and the characteristically slippery, allusive, and paradoxical discourses of post-modern theories, can be easily mimicked, becoming prey to its own cleverness. However, there is another side to this claim which Culler takes up with reference to Paul de Man's *Resistance to Theory* (1986). As Culler puts it: 'a certain resistance to reading and to theory is not just a lapse or a failure of theory but is inherent in the theoretical enterprise' (2007: p. 83). This observation comes from de Man's argument that the language that theory speaks is 'the language of self-resistance' (1986: pp. 19–20). In other words, the point of theory is to resist the reading it advocates. While theory provides us with concepts and metalanguage as part of its systematic approach to understanding phenomena, it also makes mastery impossible, 'since theory is itself the questioning of presumed results and of the assumptions on which they are based' (Culler, 2007: p. 79). Consequently, criticisms concerning the language of theory work to remind us of the questioning and sceptical nature of theory. This characteristic of theory is easily forgotten in what can sometimes become a single-minded endeavour to advocate a theoretical point of view without either attending to its internal paradoxes and dilemmas or accepting its methods as provisional and self-critical.

A third claim with particular relevance to literary studies is that theory fails to take literature as its object. This claim argues that we have become distracted by other texts and discursive practices and that literature (and reading) is now passé or elitist. Eagleton's thinly veiled lament at young scholars' interests in 'vampirism, and eye-gouging, cyborgs and porno movies' is an example of this kind of distraction (2003: p. 3). Children's literature scholarship has similarly developed an interest in a wide range of topics (including cyborgs and vampires). The field is marked by inclusiveness, ranging across 'literary' texts in different forms and formats (picture books, novels, graphic novels, comics, film, videogames) and including adaptations from one form to another. This inclusiveness has contributed to a broadening of the idea of 'literature' as an object of study. The variety of texts also points to the interdisciplinary nature of literary studies, which draws on a wide range of cultural theories. Culler's observation that 'literary and cultural studies take place within a space articulated by theory or theories, theoretical discourses, theoretical debates' (2007: p. 2) applies also to children's literature studies.

While Culler suggests that the turn from a narrowly defined and elite strand of literature has been in progress for the past two decades, he concedes that there is 'evidence of a new centrality of the literary' (2007: p. 14), which has seen the return of aesthetics and of the propensity for scholars (often outside literary studies) to use literary works to 'advance and to question theoretical assumptions'. In support of Culler's first point, texts written for teachers, such as *Critical Literacy and the Aesthetic* (Misson and Morgan, 2006), argue that secondary English classrooms can profit from an engagement with post-structuralist theories and aesthetics in teaching literature. Culler's second point is demonstrated by Judith Butler's (2004) use of *Antigone* in theorizing models of kinship, and David Baggett and Shawn Klein's (2004) edited book, *Harry Potter and Philosophy: If Aristotle Ran Hogwarts,* published in Open Court's Popular Culture and Philosophy Series. Baggett and Klein's text is one example of how this children's book in particular has prompted interest and criticism from both inside and outside children's literature studies, attracting the attention of other disciplines (including philosophy) as well as religious communities. It would seem that once the doors were opened many chose to enter what was once a closed community. Frank Kermode makes the point that when theory became not theory of literature but Theory, it became inclusive of other interests and a loss of 'intimate contact with literary texts' occurred (2003: p. 58). Thus, the assertion that literature is no longer the main object of literary studies is true, but not in a totalizing way. What this claim fails to consider is the concomitant effect of theory on literature and of literature on theory, a dual project that Culler describes as 'bringing theory *to* literature and bringing out the literary in theory' (2007: p. 5).

A fourth claim is that theory encourages poor reading. Poor reading in this instance refers to the ways in which theory is said to misdirect readers into distorting the text to suit a particular theoretical point, or what Cunningham terms 'interpretative excess' (2002: p. 79). Of course, theory cannot be anthropomorphized into a force which directs the hand that writes or the mind of the one who reads. The argument is, however, not as simple as this. While Cunningham argues that theory 'distorts reading' (p. 88), and offers several accounts of blatant misreading of texts, he also concedes that theory 'has massively enriched reading by precisely inducing readers to pursue its multi-directional potentialities' (p. 39). A problem with the kind of mixed-blessing argument about theory is that it fails to consider readers as active in the process of interpretation. Readers do not come to texts as innocents (neither are texts ever innocent). Even when young children encounter picture books for the first time, they bring to the text, unless they have been living in an isolated environment, a sense of story, experience of human actions, desires, motivations, and a functioning language. Their lived experience in the world has already shaped them so that they arrive at a text with a predisposition towards a story, certain expectations, and so on. So too scholars and students carry their own repertoire of competencies, assumptions, knowledge about texts and intertexts, as well as a critical tool kit of theoretical concepts, interpretative rules about genre, symbol, language, beliefs, and assumptions. Theory, therefore, is only one element in the reading of texts, but it can be a significant element.

Related to the claim that theory produces poor readers is the argument that readers influenced by theory may fail to grasp the 'right' meaning of a text or to divine what the author intended it to mean. As Culler notes, theory seeks to 'adjudicate' among various sources, practices, discourses, conventions, habits, and so on that come into play when a reader interprets the meanings of a text. Poor reading, then, is not simply a matter of being led by the nose by theory or of failing to get into the head of the author. Rather, it is about failing to take account of other factors that comprise valid evidence for determining a justifiable meaning or interpretation of a text.

While these four claims (and there are more) may not necessarily constitute arguments against theory *in toto*, they nevertheless highlight the ways in which theory has been used and abused and the potential traps that await

those who head off like fearless knights errant determined to prove themselves worthy of any theoretical challenge they encounter. They also offer
us a way of taking stock, by considering how children's literature scholars
and students are best served by a critical reflexiveness, exemplified by a
willingness to scrutinize the value of theory they wish to deploy and a pre-
paredness to locate themselves in relation to theoretical discourses. Perhaps
most importantly, contemporary work in children's literature requires novel
combinations of theories and the adoption of new fields of enquiry as the
forms and modes of textual production change.

Children's literature and theory

Scholarship in children's literature began to develop in the 1970s, when academic courses in the field were established and key journals were instituted,
including *Children's Literature, Children's Literature Association Quarterly,
Signal, Children's Literature in Education,* and *The Lion and the Unicorn.* These
developments coincided with the rise of literary and cultural theory in the
1970s and 1980s.

While scholars in the fields of literary and cultural studies quickly
responded to the theoretical turn which dominated literary and cultural
studies until the mid-1990s, children's texts, and the critical discourses
associated with them, continued to rely to a large extent on liberal humanist notions of individual growth and maturation, often expressed in terms
of an individual who recognizes or accepts an identity which constitutes
the core of being. As noted earlier, these liberal humanist traditions are to a
large extent at odds with post-structuralist, post-modernist and postcolonial
theories which contest notions of a fixed, stable identity and of the univer-
sality of (Western) human experience. Moreover, children's literature scholarship has always paid close attention to the readers (and implied readers)
of texts which are implicated in processes of socialization; in critical work,
this emphasis has often found its expression in reflections on what might be
confusing or unsettling to child readers, or in the idea that children 'need'
narratives which give them hope. Many children's literature scholars have,
of course, drawn upon various forms of critical theory such as feminist,
post-structuralist, psychoanalytic, and postcolonial theories.

In the 1990s a rich collection of scholarly texts emerged which brought
a wide range of theoretical perspectives to children's literature. Significant
works include: Jacqueline Rose's *The Case of Peter Pan or the Impossibility of
Children's Fiction* (1992); *Language and Ideology in Children's Fiction* (1992)
by John Stephens; Peter Hunt's edited collections, *Children's Literature: The
Development of Criticism* (1990) and *Understanding Children's Literature* (1999);
Rod McGillis's *The Nimble Reader* (1996) and *Voices of the Other* (1999); and
Ideologies of Identity in Adolescent Fiction (1999) by Robyn McCallum. These
texts provided sustained, scholarly discussions of how theories drawn from

a variety of fields – psychoanalysis, linguistics, critical theory, stylistics, literary theory, cultural studies – could be employed to the study of texts produced for young people.

The first decade of the twenty-first century has seen other scholarly works contribute to the critical discussions begun in many of these earlier works (and others). Often these new works consider texts from within a new millennial context of a world characterized by increasing cultural, political, and social flux. These include: Clare Bradford's work on postcolonial theory and children's literature *Reading Race* (2001) and *Unsettling Narratives* (2007); Perry Nodelman's *The Hidden Adult* (2008) which engages with the ongoing problematic relation between adult and child that haunts children's literature. Gender and its discontents continue to inform children's literature criticism in works such as John Stephens' edited volume *Ways of Being Male* (2002), Christine Wilkie-Stibbs' *The Feminine Subject in Children's Literature* (2002), Victoria Flanagan's study of cross-dressing fiction in *Into the Closet* (2007), and *Gender Dilemmas in Children's Fiction* (2009) by Kerry Mallan; psychoanalytic theory and its application to popular texts is deployed in Karen Coats' *Looking Glasses and Neverlands: Lacan, Desire, and Subjectivity in Children's Literature* (2004). The gothic returns in *The Gothic in Children's Literature* (2007) co-edited by Anna Jackson, Karen Coats, and Roderick McGillis; the aesthetic and social vision of children's literature is the subject of Kimberley Reynolds' *Radical Children's Literature* (2007); and the impact of changing world orders and the utopian impulse in children's fiction is taken up in *New World Orders in Contemporary Children's Literature* (2008) by Clare Bradford, Kerry Mallan, John Stephens, and Robyn McCallum. This listing is not exhaustive; rather, it is indicative of the activity that is apparent in the field. In addition to these authored and edited collections there are also handbooks, guides, textbooks, and encyclopedias that tease out the significance of theory to children's literature.

Given all this lively scholarship, one could be forgiven for asking why we need another book on children's literature and theory. One answer is that the field continues to evolve and respond to changing times. Hunt noted two decades ago that children's literature criticism was finding 'a unique voice' (1990: p. 3). How this unique voice has been modulated and heard, particularly in the twenty-first century, is a key thematic of this book. While the preceding section made a case for the continuing value of theory, our primary concern in this book is about bringing innovative approaches to contemporary texts and theories. To this end we have included the work of familiar scholars as well as those who are new to the field so that we can take up our challenge to deliver fresh and innovative discussions that demonstrate how children's texts engage with contemporary issues and how theory can assist us in our reading of these texts.

'Children's Literature' is an inclusive term that accommodates the study of literature and other media, and extends to a wide demographic of readers from preschool to young adulthood (adults too are often drawn to children's literature for various reasons). While we have selected literature and film as the textual modes on which we focus, this is not to dismiss the significance of 'new media' such as computer games and social networking sites that rely on interactive technologies and computer-enabled devices. The work of theory in relation to new media is an important field but is beyond the scope of this book. However, the primary texts discussed in the following chapters include a wide readership across children and young adults.

While literary studies and film studies are discrete disciplines with their own fields of study and critical language, they also share some common ground, especially with respect to aspects of their narrative form and function: character, point of view, focalization, plot, and theme. Their individual styles and aesthetics are created by literary or cinematic elements that are integral to the medium, but which are often expropriated to achieve a certain mixed-form aesthetic or affect. In their discussion of the animated film *Madagascar*, Clare Bradford and Raffaela Baccolini (Chapter 2) draw attention to the film's use of cinematic techniques to signal narrative shifts, create a visual aesthetic, and achieve intertextual resonances. Picture books too use cinematic techniques – framing, 'camera' angle and distance (far shot, medium shot, close up), montage – to extend and complement conventional artistic elements, principles of composition, and use of symbol. Picture books are one example of a hybrid visual–verbal form common in children's literature which enables different theorizing of its 'literariness' – its narrative, rhetorical, artistic, performative qualities. In a related way, children's film – live action and animation – is another form which warrants our critical attention. Like literature, film does not simply reflect the world but actively constructs worlds and meanings. One such other world is vividly delineated in Maria Takolander's discussion of the film *Monster House* (Chapter 5), which she reads through a prism of gothic, feminist, and psychoanalytic theories.

Another area which is receiving renewed interest in children's literature research is adaptation (book to film, book to multimedia, film to book spinoff). In her article in *The Lion and the Unicorn*, Linda Hutcheon recognizes the value of children's literature for theorizing 'everything from postmodernism to parody, from irony to adaptation' (2008: p. 169). David Buchbinder in this collection (Chapter 7) expands on Hutcheon's points and draws on a rich and varied range of texts and discourses to consider adaptation with respect to young adult fiction.

These connections between children's literature, film, and critical theory are not limited in their significance, nor do they appeal to a small age-defined demographic (children) or to a small section of the academic community. They also reflect the way in which children's texts are caught up in wider cultural, political, and social spheres of activity. Texts and theory are performative: they *do* something, and therefore incur important ethical responsibilities. These ethical responsibilities are not narrowly conceived in terms of moral content and values (or lack of them) advanced by texts. Rather, they are concerned with larger issues of truth, representation, and being (selfhood, identity, subjectivity). Such issues form the touchstones of literature and film, regardless of age classification; they are also the enduring concerns of theory. Several chapters illuminate how different theoretical perspectives – cognitive schemas and scripts (Chapter 1), spatiality (Chapter 2), globalization (Chapter 3), gender (Chapters 4 and 5), ecocriticism (Chapter 6), and posthumanism (Chapter 8) – cast light on how texts seek to represent and validate notions of self, cultural identity, being, place, and belonging.

Our dual focus on literature and film enables us to broaden our scope in examining the performative function of theory: what theory can do and how it asks questions about meaning, common sense, and reality. We also want to put theory to the test to see how it opens up alternative ideas, challenges basic assumptions and premises, and unsettles the taken-for-granted with respect to authorship, literary conventions, and the contexts in which texts are produced and consumed. We want to explore how theory can proffer new ways of being, new forms of belonging, and new relations in a world that is increasingly affected by change, globalization, threat, and fear. How it sees the dialogical relations between history and tradition, on one hand, and the new and the fashionable, on the other. How it offers insights into the paradoxes of capitalism, consumerism, and identity politics. How it directs our attention to the layers of the palimpsest – the intertexts, sources, and constant referentiality – that constitute literature and film. How it can demystify and expose cultural forms and structures we often take as natural. These are ambitious goals and this book cannot engage in depth with all the possibilities we raise. Nevertheless, this account of the capacity of theory – to engage and stimulate our thinking, assist in our formulation of ideas, and scrutinize 'facts', discourse, and language – offers a useful conceptual framework for thinking about theory.

This book is not a survey or history of theory. Many books offer useful guides to the chronological development of fields of theory. Rather, the chapters of this book seek to consider the dynamic interplay between children's literature, film, and theory. Our aim is to elucidate the relations between theory and text by working on a select range of theoretical concepts and discourses, social and cultural issues, and texts produced for children and young adults. To achieve this aim we invited the contributing authors to address certain topics which we felt would yield a lively discussion of theory, contemporary issues, and texts. The range of possible topics is endless, but as in all works the final decision involves a degree of shared interest and preference. In the following chapters, the work of pioneering theorists (Lacan, Foucault, Appadurai, Kristeva, Baudrillard, Deleuze) mixes and mingles with more recent theoretical discourses and concepts (performativity, queer, ecocriticism, spatiality, posthumanism, monstrous-feminine, globalization, relationality, utopianism, cultural geography, technoscience).

The collection opens with 'Schemas and Scripts: Cognitive Instruments and the Representation of Cultural Diversity in Children's Literature' by John Stephens. Working with insights offered by cognitive poetics, Stephens examines a range of picture books and novels to develop his argument that the cognitive instruments of schema and script can function in texts to assist with positive representations of cultural diversity, which may transform an existing 'script' into another way of understanding the world. This chapter is followed by 'Journeying Subjects: Spatiality and Identity in Children's Texts' by Clare Bradford and Raffaella Baccolini. The authors have called on concepts and reading strategies developed across three fields of research – cultural geography, postcolonial theory, and utopian theory – to inform their analysis of the complex intersections of place and identities in children's texts. In 'Local and Global: Cultural Globalization, Consumerism, and Children's Fiction', Elizabeth Bullen and Kerry Mallan draw on theories of cultural globalization to explain some of the ways in which broader globalization processes are translated into narratives written for children and young adults. Their discussion considers the impact of globalization on the marketing of children's texts and culture and their engagements with the 'local' and the 'global'. Maria Takolander's 'Monstrous Women: Gothic Misogyny in *Monster House*' takes up perspectives from the field of gothic theory – itself a hybrid field drawing on psychoanalytical and political theories – to consider representations of women in the animated film *Monster House*. Shifting the focus to bodies, identities, and performativity, 'Splitting the Difference: Pleasure, Desire, and Intersubjectivity in Children's Literature and Film' by Christine Wilkie-Stibbs draws on a range of queer, feminist, and psychoanalytic theories to examine how identities are negotiated in a selection of Lesbian, Bisexual, Gay, Transgender (LBGT) narratives that break ranks with the heterosexual imaginary. She argues that these texts develop ideas of self that are more complex and more diverse than the standardized discourses of the child would have otherwise admitted. In 'Children as Ecocitizens: Ecocriticism and Environmental Texts', Geraldine Massey and Clare Bradford provide an overview of the field of ecocriticism from its beginnings in the 1960s, discussing the extent to which children's environmental texts mobilize concepts and approaches from this field. In 'From "Wizard" to "Wicked": Adaptation Theory and Young Adult Fiction' David Buchbinder examines the historical and contextual nature of adaptation. He argues that it is more profitable to consider the adaptation of an originary text (regardless of the medium) on the merit of what it sets out to do as an *autonomous text*, rather than being viewed simply as always-already a poor imitation of a better original. In an essay that returns to the spirit of the Introduction, Kerry Mallan concludes the volume with 'All that Matters: Technoscience, Critical Theory, and Children's Fiction'. In this final essay, she argues that science and children's fiction open up a new theoretical space to explore questions about life, death, and what matters as considerations of our posthuman existence.

1

Schemas and Scripts: Cognitive Instruments and the Representation of Cultural Diversity in Children's Literature

John Stephens

Cognitive poetics over the past couple of decades has suggested some powerful approaches to literature as a form of human cognition and communication with a specific potential for responding to social reality. The theory offers some vital insights into how readers construct mental representations in their minds, and it has the further possibility of forging connections between representations of social ideology and the various reader response theories that remained widespread in children's literature criticism long after they seemed to have disappeared from general literary theory and practice. To explore a small example of how some basic structures of cognition function in literature, this chapter argues that processes whereby the cognitive instruments of schema and script are textually modified have played a central function in positive representations of cultural diversity, as such modifications are an expression within story worlds of wider transformations of social mentalities. The contexts for these processes have been the various stages of the rise (and decline) of multicultural ideologies over the past four decades since they began to be identifiable in the 1960s – in the USA, for example, the Civil Rights movement was followed by programs in the 1970s to reorganize primary and secondary education to benefit students from minorities. However, as Will Kymlicka has recently pointed out, local processes such as this are part of a much larger process involving the conversion of 'historic relations of hierarchy or enmity into relations of democratic citizenship' (2007: p. 88). He points to strategic reasons why groups and states developed some willingness to support or accept multicultural reform, including big issues such as 'changes in the geopolitical security system of the Western democracies, and changes in the nature of the global economy' (2007: p. 88). Kymlicka thus adduces the following sequence of movements:

(i) a revolution in ideas about human rights and human equality following World War II;

(ii) processes of decolonization between 1948 and 1966, and the concomitant contesting of assumptions about ethnic and racial hierarchies;

(iii) racial desegregation initiated by the American civil rights movement, and then local adaptations of civil rights liberalism in numerous other countries (e.g., where minorities had been assimilated, losing language and culture, rather than segregated);

(iv) the establishment of 'rights-consciousness' (an assumption of equality) as an element of modernity.

Although children's literature around the world has thematized multiculturalism and cultural diversity in varied ways, the sequence referred to above has functioned as a basic ground for representing diversity in children's literature, and in many places it still does so. On the whole, children's literature has sought to intervene in culture to affirm multicultural models of human rights and human equality, and it has done this by striving to transform the schemas and scripts that were common in Western cultures up until the mid-twentieth century and are still quite pervasive today. To effect such a transformation, children's texts have primarily attempted to transform the central components of schemas, and hence the story scripts into which they are drawn. As Lyn Calcutt et al. argue, 'As clusters of ideas for thinking with, cognitive schemas can facilitate our understanding of how social categories are conceptualized' (2009: p. 171), so changes made within a cluster allow others to be conceptualized in fresh and nonthreatening ways. Importantly, this process involves a whole range of everyday schemas as well as those directly involving cultural diversity.

The transformative potential of schemas and scripts

Schemas are knowledge structures, or patterns, which provide the framework for understanding.[1] They shape our knowledge of all concepts, from the very small to the very large, from the material to the abstract. Thus schemas shape our knowledge of:

(i) objects (e.g., attributes or characteristic spatial and functional relationships – motion along a path, bounded interior, balance, and symmetry [Turner, 1996: p. 16]);

(ii) situations (personal relationships; gender roles; etc);

(iii)   genres (fantasy; realism; adventure story; a narrative about friendship; etc);

(iv)   cultural forms and ideologies.

Schemas do this because they are aspects of memory. As we read a verbal text, or look at a picture book, the data matches part of a schema in the memory and activates it. Generally, a schema consists of a network of constituent parts, and the stimulus evokes the network and its interrelations, especially what is normal and typical about that network. A schema is instantiated (a) by naming it; or (b) by citing a selection of constituent parts. Whereas a schema is a static element within our experiential repertoire, a script is a dynamic element, which expresses how a sequence of events or actions is expected to unfold.[2] One does not need to be given every event in the causal chain that constitutes a script to understand it. Rather, one infers the complete script from a core element and identifies unexpressed causal links between events (see Schank and Abelson, 1977: p. 38). A simple script informs an incident portrayed in Michelle Cooper's *The Rage of Sheep* (2007), in which the 15-year-old female narrator, Hester, is taking her dog for a walk and they encounter a cat. The *dog chases cat* script has basic components: Fred, the dog, approaches a shrub. A cat bursts from the shrub and runs away. Because a reader recognizes the script, it would be redundant to include intermediate steps such as: The cat saw the dog approaching. The cat was afraid of the dog. We understand the minimal sequence because we can draw on our store of stereotyped sequences of actions that form a crucial part of human beings' knowledge about the world. Creative works involve a further level of connectivity between the pre-stored, dynamic knowledge representations bound up with everyday life and the stereotypic plot structures that readers use to anticipate the unfolding story logic of creative works (see Herman, 2004: pp. 89–91). Of course, the logic of a created story does not follow a stereotypic script, and the process of connecting apparently deviant or merely unexpected events may involve readers in unfamiliar insights and perceptions, or may even transform the script into another way of understanding the world.

Much of the transformative potential of schema and script is evident in the ways Cooper transforms the simple script:

'Stop that,' I told him as he strained towards a quivering shrub....
'You're a horrible, disobedient dog,' I said, 'and I really don't know why I –'
The shrub exploded and a furry grey animal shot out and dashed down the footpath. Sodden leaves flew everywhere as Fred, legs skittering in all directions, hurled himself after it.
'Fred!' I shouted, trying to hang onto his worn leash and stay upright. 'Stop!'

'Woof!' said Fred. He gave a giant lunge forward and snapped the leash in two. Free at last, he streaked along the road, jaws snapping, the grey thing barely a length in front of him.

(Cooper, 2007: pp. 88–89)

Stored in the memory, previous experiences form structured repertoires of expectations about current and emergent experiences. Although Hester is myopic and cannot identify what she sees here, the schema (static repertoire) allows readers to perceive that the running 'furry grey animal' is probably a cat, while the dynamic script repertoire further enables readers to anticipate how events will unfold (a) when a dog encounters an animal that flees, and (b) when the owner is unable to control the dog. In this example, readers not only recognize a sequenced set of particular objects involved in a particular event but also a sequence of objects that belong to categories (cat/dog/hostility) involved in an event (a chasing) that belongs to a more comprehensive category (a pursuit script). A reader's process is not preordained, however, and as Raymond W. Gibbs argues, readers will decide both 'what script is relevant and how it should be modified to fit the situation in hand' (2003: p.33) – in other words, readers may understand the text creatively. When these skeletal elements of repertoire are elaborated as narrative fiction, a writer has various options beyond expressive representation of setting ('a quivering shrub', 'sodden leaves'). Schema and script can be modified for comic purposes, as when in *The Rage of Sheep* Fred's antics become a comic source of humiliation for Hester, although the further possibilities of a myopia schema are not developed at this point. The myopia schema functions rather as a recurring, characterizing motif, as Hester deals with the consequences of concealing her eye problem from parents and teachers. As such, however, it runs in parallel with other things that set Hester apart – especially her academic cleverness and her brown skin. Sustained mapping of a schema throughout a text is a key element in drawing out the significance from the story world, because once readers recognize and mentally instantiate the schema, the recurrence or addition of further components enables the schema to be modified for socially transformative purposes. This possibility is vital for representations of cultural diversity. I will further develop the argument below.

When readers recognize the beginning sequence of a script, they anticipate what is to come and derive satisfaction from how the text expands the script by completing or varying the expected pattern. Thus readers assume that Fred will not catch the cat and that Hester will face some kind of problem, but that is all the script imparts. When readers respond to the script and its further articulation, they are engaged in what Mark Turner (1996: p. 20) refers to as 'narrative imagining': readers predict what will happen and subsequently evaluate the wisdom or folly involved. Hester's attempt 'to hang onto [Fred's] *worn* leash' (my italics) does not just anticipate that the leash will break but also that Hester is victim of her own or her parents' carelessness. Second, narrative imagining is a cognitive instrument for explaining how the story moves from a normal situation (girl walking dog) to a bizarre or humiliating situation (girl trying to entice dog back out of a sewerage overflow pipe).

Modifying the variable components of a schema

In principle, if children's literature is to affect how the mind understands and structures the world, this will be most evident in picture books, which target audiences at a stage of mental development when schemas may not be fixed in memory in a particular form. To illustrate how this works in practice, I turn now to a simple example from a collection of stories published by Janet and Allan Ahlberg in 1987, at a time when children's literature in England was most optimistic about cultural diversity. In this story, 'The jackpot', a giant has a problem with boys named Jack, all of whom want to play out the *Jack and the Beanstalk* story. The giant's solution – to capture the Jacks and relocate them at a distance from his house – only serves to make them work together:

> The Jacks formed a football team ... Now the giant is plagued with Jacks, twelve at a time (eleven plus a substitute). Often they arrive roped together like climbers. (Ahlberg & Ahlberg, 1987: unpaged)

At this point, the text has introduced the schema for a cooperative group or team. The word *team* itself evokes the schema. Now, the team schema has some constant components: it consists of a group linked in a common purpose, and its members have complementary skills and coordinate their efforts. The schema also has variable components: the concept covers different kinds of teams – here a football team and a climbing team – and the background of the members may be homogeneous or heterogeneous. The team drawn by Janet Ahlberg in the illustration that accompanies the text demonstrates variables of ethnicity, class, age, and dress preferences. The text-picture interaction here has gone considerably further than exploiting illustrations to represent a multicultural society as setting for a fractured fairytale about the otherness of giants (who are not depicted as other at all). The illustration shows a heterogeneous group represented as linked in a common, mutually supportive purpose. But the illustration also impacts on the language, so that ethnicity, class, and so on are represented as normal variables. Hence the cooperative, multicultural society has the potential to change the schemas used to make sense of the world.

Practices of representation and multicultural scepticism

The problem for children's literature has been that models of human rights and human equality can be simplistic and may fail to engage with the actual politics of diversity. As far as I am aware, it has been uncommon for the literature to address the problematics of contemporary cultural diversity, and then almost only in the YA novel. Opponents of multiculturalism challenge at least two of the assumptions Kymlicka sees as positive schemas – erasure of ethnic and racial hierarchies, and rights-consciousness. It's also probable that no two countries are diverse in precisely the same way. The so-called New World settler societies – Australia, Canada, USA, and so on – have at least three broad ethnic components with some distinct sub-groups. A map for the USA might thus look something like this:

Indigenous Americans ('Amerindians')	
European settlers (since the 16th century)	
'cultural groups that by virtue of race, ethnicity, or religious background differ from the culturally dominant white Europeans' (M.D. Kutzer, 1996. *Writers of Multicultural Fiction for Young Adults*, p. 2)	African Americans Asian Americans Hispanic Americans Jewish Americans

A comparable map for Australia would look like this:

Indigenous Australians	
European settlers (since the 18th century)	
Migrant groups (since the 19th century), but in children's literature mostly imagined as mass migration after 1950 Refugees (political, economic)	European migrants East and South-East Asian migrants South Asian migrants West Asian migrants

On the other hand, a map for the United Kingdom is like this:

'Anglo-Saxons'	
Celtic substate nationalist groups	Scotland Wales Northern Ireland
Migrant groups (characteristically, but not exclusively, from former colonies) Refugees (political, economic)	Caribbean South Asia African countries Etc.

Kymlicka's proposed tripartite structure can be varied in many ways, but a European perspective would wish to include the rather different forms that emerged in various East European countries from the early 1990s and, alongside the masses of principally economic refugees entering Europe, might be seen as components in a global retreat from the multicultural ideologies of the previous two decades. The broad tripartite structures clearly indicate that responses to them in children's literature will be different in different countries, but we need to ask whether in general the practices of representation are ultimately robust enough to respond to the current more sceptical climate. As Clare Bradford (2006: p. 117) remarks, children's literature often produces a weak multiculturalism, and I would argue that this weakness derives not just from naïve optimism but also from weak uses of representational strategies. As has long been recognized, at the inception of multicultural children's literature cultural flows tended to be in one direction, because perspective and focalization were usually located with a principal character from the dominant, or majority, culture. When that deficiency had been addressed by the late 1980s, stronger strategies were enabled, but those processes were not always sufficiently marked by fluidity and processes of dismantling and reformation to stand against the negative public socio-political rhetoric. Young people are still regularly offered versions of weak multiculturalism, as in the following example from Bobbie Kalman, *What is Culture?*, a schematic representation of types of clothing in

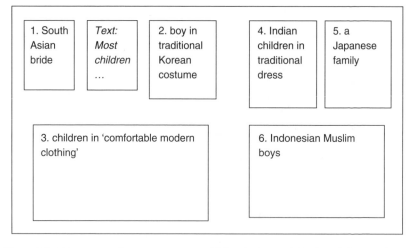

Figure 1.1   Diagrammatic representation of 'The Culture of Clothing', from *What Is Culture?* by Bobbie Kalman

Images: 1. South Asian bride; 2. boy in traditional Korean costume; 3. children in 'comfortable modern clothing'; 4. Indian children in traditional dress; 5. a Japanese family; 6. Indonesian Muslim boys.

an opening from a recent (2009) series (originated in Canada, but published multinationally in four English-speaking countries) (Figure 1.1).

The strategy in this particular volume, as in others in the series, is to stress that all over the world people have different ways of life (p. 5) but a common humanity. How this page is interpreted is determined by its opening statement: 'Most children around the world wear modern clothes, like the clothes you wear' (p. 14). First, the second-person addressee, 'you', locates perspective in an assumed majority culture; second, when the sentence is rephrased as the caption for the group photograph at image 3 it asserts a normative schema: 'Most children wear comfortable modern clothing. Jeans and T-shirts are favourite everyday outfits.' While this may be a consequence of globalized culture, the formulation 'comfortable modern ... everyday' effectively erases otherness, and is the grounding *schema* in terms of which we are to understand the other five images in this opening. The two images immediately above the group photograph (images 1 and 2) are literally marginal, placed on either side of the centrally positioned text, and state or imply a self-conscious dressing up.

This text informs readers that 'Some children wear traditional clothes at special times, such as on holidays, at weddings, or during festivals', and images 1 and 2 depict 'a young South Asian woman' dressed for her wedding and a boy 'in a traditional Korean suit'. The three images on the right-hand page state or imply that they depict archaic practices: children dressed in 'traditional Indian jackets' for a party (4), a Japanese grandmother in a kimono, while 'the rest of the family is dressed in modern clothes' (5), and Indonesian Muslim boys, distinguished by their 'long loose shirts' and 'caps on their heads' (identified as a religious practice). The Japanese family photograph offers the most marked example, as the children are two generations away from traditional culture. In a culturally diverse society no action occurs in isolation, but will to some extent be dependent on actions performed in another part of the system, and what a practice signifies in one place will not necessarily offer the same signification elsewhere. In this example, the grounding schema – clothes that are 'comfortable, modern, everyday' – consigns all 'other' clothing styles to the cultural periphery.

Robust representations of cultural diversity

A more robust strategy for negotiating cultural difference between generations can be seen in *Old Magic* (1996 text, Allan Baillie; illustrations, Di Wu). This is as an important book because of its robustness, on the one hand, and because it was published in the year Australian social policy took a sharp turn to the right. Within five years Australia had passed from what Graham Huggan calls 'multiculturalism fatigue' to 'unofficial dismantling' of multiculturalism through the first decade of the twenty-first century (2007: p. 110). The ideology hammered out in the early 1970s as part of a vision of Australia as a vibrant, culturally diverse country had receded into the background of public discourse as the advocacy of diversity and glocalization that had informed children's literature for twenty years was perforce largely replaced by a literature of resistance against regressive social policies and aggressive border protection.[3]

Old Magic represents a bricolage of cultures: it is the story of an Indonesian grandfather and grandson living in Australia, told by an Australian and illustrated in a Chinese style. The first opening instantiates three schemas. First, the child Omar is an extreme example of the modern global child assumed as the norm in Kalman's 'Culture of Clothing'; second, the *Kakek* (grandfather) embodies traditional cultural practice; third, the setting is a schematic version of an Australian backyard (see Figure 1.2).

The diagonal vector which constructs the scene, running left to right and top to bottom, deploys Omar's almost central placement to emphasize his over-determined display of modern, Western male child icons: reversed cap, back-pack, Walkman, skateboard, basket-ball, Nike trainers. His difference from his grandfather is underlined by repeated colours (each has a garment of red and green), the contrasting head-wear and foot-wear, and the contrast between his grandfather's distinctively Indonesian features and his own less marked features. The scene, then, both depicts cultural fissure and foregrounds Omar's globalized lack of cultural distinctiveness.

Di Wu interprets some iconic features used to represent an Australian backyard – the tree, the style of house, and the clothes-line (known as a 'Hills hoist') – through Chinese painting techniques. The house architecture alludes to a late Victorian cottage design, which is a local icon that frequently appears in Australian picture books, even though examples in Australian suburbs are now becoming rare. The tree, prominent in the foreground, is aesthetically Chinese, and this aesthetic further shapes how viewers look at the house and the Hills hoist, visualized from the elevated near-to perspective of a Chinese painting. The effect is comparable to that seen in 'The Jackpot', in that the sub-schemas that comprise the 'Australian backyard' schema both instantiate that schema and indicate that the historically familiar components can be re-signified if presented in a different representational style. The setting has thus been glocalized by this blending of artefacts and pictorial codes from different cultures. Against this background setting, the grandfather and Omar embody extreme cultural diversity. The verbal text declares a problem in culture – 'Omar was in trouble the moment he stepped into the backyard. The kakek was sweeping the earth before him with a feather.' The nature of this trouble, however, lies not so much in what Omar has done but in his personal embodiment of culture and its opposition to the culture practised by his grandfather. As the story unfolds, Omar enters into a local/global dialogue by setting out to reclaim his heritage. He does this by building an Indonesian dragon kite for his kakek. Once again, however, the kite is depicted from a Chinese perspective,

Omar was in trouble the moment he stepped into the backyard. The kakek was sweeping the earth before him with a feather.

'Hello, Kakek,' said Omar. 'What's happening?' But he knew.

The kakek wound a long braided cord around a painted disc of wood.
'I am remembering, boy.
I am remembering the magic.'

'We don't do that any more,' said Omar.
'Nobody does that any more.'

Figure 1.2   *Old Magic* by Allan Baillie and Di Wu,[4] Opening 1

thus modifying the local by envisaging a kind of global Asian dragon-image. Despite the introduction of this other form of globalization, Baillie and Wu are still able to represent a hybridization of local and global as a glocalization that restores meaning to community, as the final openings of the book depict the kite in flight and assert the healing of the cultural divide.

A further key schema is evoked here with an effect again quite similar to that identified in the Ahlbergs' text. The dragon kite is an idea in the mind, constructed and remembered by traditional cultural practice. But that schema can be instantiated by bringing together surprising, nontraditional variables (such as sheets of plastic and table-tennis balls) so that they form a signifying pattern. When Omar and his kakek fly the kite together, their physical postures are an isomorphic mirroring, and this pattern is repeated in the sky above them where Omar's kite is doubled by a cloud-shape once again painted by means of a specifically Chinese technique. The complex patterns constitute a highly expressive integration of cultural forms.

Multiculturalism, in conjunction with the dominant theme of children's books, that of personal identity development, has been concerned with ways whereby social conjunction and communalism replace conflict and overcome difference to bring about multicultural awareness and agency. In other words, a book such as *Old Magic* conforms to a particular narrative script. Readers may sympathize with Omar, but the script – an action structure consisting of conflict, self-reflection, creative action, and social integration – invokes a cultural and cognitive stereotype about identity that indicates Omar is in the wrong in embracing shallow post-modern culture at the cost of his cultural heritage. Baillie has used a script here that is very common in picture books, and its very stereotypy is quite powerful in affirming an outcome that embraces cultural diversity.

Wherever questions of difference are addressed in picture books, the cognitive instruments employed to model attitudes and possible transformations in attitude are apt to pivot on the representations of scripts and schemas. The process is principally characterized by the unfolding of a schema to a point of full realization, which in turn may take several forms. It may disclose a social good which one or more of the represented participants must recognize and embrace, as in Michael Rosen and Bob Graham's parable *This Is Our House* (1996), or which defines a central participant's state of lack, as in Liz Lofthouse and Robert Ingpen's *Ziba Came on A Boat* (2007); it may express a cultural assumption in such a way that readers will feel obliged to reject it, as in Armin Greder's *The Island* (2007; originally *Die Insel*, 2002); or it can be transformed from a negative to a positive signification, as in Allan Baillie and Caroline Magerl's *Castles* (2005). In all of these variations, schemas develop metonymic functions, and scripts evolve into full-blown parables. The script in each is based on the four-component structure observed in *Old Magic* (*conflict, self-reflection, creative action, and social integration*), although not all four are equally realized in every case, and *creative action* may be distributed variously amongst participants.

Schema and the development of metonymic function

An overt example in which basic cognitive instruments become metonymy and parable is *This Is Our House* (1996), a story about a group of small children struggling to enjoy the use of a large cardboard box they have re-described as a 'house'. At the beginning, one of the children, George, commandeers the house:

> George was in the house.
> 'This house is mine and no one else is coming in,' George said.
> 'It's not your house, George,' said Lindy. 'It belongs to everybody.'
> 'No it doesn't,' said George. 'This house is all for me!'
>
> (Rosen & Graham, 1996: unpaged)

George's schema for belonging and exclusion is framed by a speech act, 'This house isn't for …', which introduces each of the sub-schema categories he identifies as elements of difference that justify exclusion. The text deals with a problem of relations between groups, where those marked as Other are a problem for the protagonist, but not the actual root of the problem, since difference is being imposed upon them. George at no point evokes race as a cause for exclusion, though Graham's illustrations indicate that this is consistently an oblique motive. For example, when Luther (depicted by Graham as of Caribbean descent) enlists Sophie's help, they are rejected because Sophie wears glasses. Graham's illustrations situate the 'house' in an open space surrounded by high-rise residential buildings. Visually, it is like an island, and evokes 1990s discourses in which, as Elaine Vautier succinctly expresses it, 'Britain is figured as a small island with capacity limits and a precarious balance to be maintained against the invasion of foreignness by outsiders who bring their unwanted alien cultures' (2009: p. 131). The most explicit reference to ethnicity occurs when Rasheeda (ethnically South Asian) decides to tunnel into the 'house', with all its hints of illicit entry by would-be migrants, but the text/illustration interaction consistently prompts a metonymic reading of the schema as racialized exclusion. The *conflict* which drives the script is constantly challenged by the *creative action* of the excluded children, who devise inventive and socially constructive reasons for entering the 'house', but finally can only transform the situation when George must leave to go to the toilet. On his return, to find the house crammed with the other children, his practice of arbitrary exclusion is turned against him – ' "This house isn't for people with red hair," said Charlene.' After a futile outburst of frustrated rage, George engages in self-reflection, abandons his obsession with possession and control, and transforms his grounding schema, so that the 'house' is 'for everyone'. The final phase of the underlying script – *social integration* – thus emerges as the book's predominant theme.

This story about a group of children struggling over enjoyment of an imaginatively transformed site succinctly illustrates how a schema develops metonymic function: a cardboard box is also a house, and the house-schema is a metonym for a community, and eventually a country. The signifying process is thus a figurative chain, as the tenor of one figure becomes the vehicle for the next. The figures are metonyms, rather than metaphors, as each tenor maintains its significance as well as acts as a vehicle in a process of further figuration:

> vehicle (*box*) ➜ tenor (*house*)
> vehicle (*house*) ➜ tenor (*community*)
> vehicle (*community*) ➜ tenor (*nation*)

At each stage of meaning transfer the figurative ground linking vehicle and tenor is 'a habitable space shared by a group of people', and hence the transformation of the schema within the script of *conflict, creative action, self-reflection, and social integration* readily enables the interpretative step that enables an understanding of the narrative as a parable about discourses of inclusion and exclusion in England in the 1990s.

Schema and script in the metaphorical relationship of verbal text and illustration

Creative action may be represented as a pivotal narrative element in schema transformation, as demonstrated by Allan Baillie and Caroline Magerl's *Castles* (2005). As with *This Is Our House* (1996), a crucial element of this book is that the script – here a clearly articulated version of the *conflict, creative action, self-reflection, and social integration* script – assumes there is always some form of suspicion of, and hostility towards, otherness in initial encounters with strangers. This suspicion is constituted as a problem that needs to be overcome. In other words, the script naturalizes self-other conflict, and if this is taken to be an everyday life schema – a pre-stored knowledge representation – then self-other relations will always have a fragile basis. In this case, the script is instantiated in a way that conflict is overcome. Like *This Is Our House* (1996), *Castles* (2005) is about a struggle for territory, but in this case between a girl and a boy on an otherwise empty beach.

Castles (2005) follows a picture book convention whereby a metaphorical relationship is established between verbal text and illustration because each of these semiotic codes tells a different story. The strategy is varied here because both codes cross from time to time between a depiction of children playing on a beach and the fantasy world they imagine (readers may immediately recall the great pre-text for such dual narratives, John Burningham's *Come Away from the Water, Shirley* [1977]). *Castles* is grounded in the story opening by the schemas *princess* and *castle*:

> One day a **Princess** came to the beach. She built a **castle.**

The illustration depicts an everyday beach scene, in which a young girl in a swimming costume builds a sand castle. At this point, *Princess* is an indeterminate term, either a general descriptor or the girl's self-image. The second opening introduces a different castle schema, that is, what the girl imagines her castle to be: 'A wondrous castle. Its gleaming towers were so high their bright banners tickled the drifting clouds.' The illustration also shifts to represent this schema, both in castle architecture and the princess's clothes. The ground has now been laid for text and illustration to interact by variously depicting the everyday and the imaginary and hence to interrogate how the princess schema functions to express a sense of self. How this sense of self is depicted in *Castles* (2005) accords remarkably closely with the elements identified in cognitive psychology as central to a self-schema. According to Jean Knox, these are: the central role of physical action in creating agency and identity; the importance of the bodily perspective from which one views the world; the question of peri-personal space; and the impact of other people on our sense of self and our experience of identity and agency (Knox, 2009: p. 308). When the 'Princess' finds her essentially solipsistic fantasy intruded upon by a newcomer – a boy simply labelled as *a Pirate* – each of these elements that ground the self must be modified or activated as the narrative script unfolds by means of some contrasting schemas:

> Then on a dark afternoon a **Pirate** came along the beach.
> 'Watcha doing?' he said.
> 'Something,' said the Princess, trying to ignore him.
> But the Pirate built a **pirate ship with cannons** next to the castle.
> (Baillie & Magerl, 2005: unpaged; my emphases)

Constructing her castle in isolation does not constitute the girl's agency and identity any more than does her Princess-perspective on her real and imagined worlds. While Knox defines peri-personal space as the space within reach of a particular part of the body (such as the hand), she also notes that the use of tools or implements expands the reach of peri-personal space so that 'far' space becomes 'near' space (2009: p. 318). Also pertinent here is Jean Mandler's suggestion (after Lakoff and Johnson) that image schemas – the means whereby 'spatial structure is mapped into conceptual structure' – underlie a person's understanding 'of the metaphorical extensions of objects and events to more abstract realms' (Mandler, 1992: p. 591). *This Is Our House* exemplifies how George's peri-personal space within the carton/'house' readily takes on the meaning of a metaphorical space, and likewise in *Castles* the operations of mind and imagination also function as tools to extend peri-personal space by converting 'far' space into 'near' space. Hence the Pirate's aggressive response to the Princess's act of exclusion (implicitly a gendered act) challenges her peri-personal space in both physical and mental domains, and this becomes an important first step in transforming script into parable.

In a travesty of *creative action* Princess and Pirate project girl-boy rivalry through a script for a fantasy war, which is played by imagining monstrous flying creatures as weapons. The strategy – and hence the rules of the game – is initiated by the Princess, who maintains the upper hand until the Pirate makes a surprise move and disconcerts the Princess by proposing a truce and friendship. Self-schema is then transformed in the sequence depicted in opening 13 (see Figure 1.3): on the left-hand page, the girl asserts control, and hence agency, by a physical gesture that dominates the boy's peri-personal space (an aggression-schema is evoked visually by her out-thrust arm and acute body angle); the boy, in contrast, leans back and holds his arms away, where they are visible and also form an embracing oval shape that visually echoes his verbal proffer of friendship. On the right-hand page, peri-personal space is neutral but expresses potential in a moment of self-reflection, as is evident in the slightly forward-leaning heads and the visible hands. At this point each child is poised to impact upon the other's sense of self and exercise of agency. Social integration follows, as the two join hands, and the final opening depicts the two in everyday beach costume happily chatting as they lie together on the girl's beach towel.

The capability of a picture book to transform the *conflict, creative action, self-reflection, and social integration* script into a parable about human relations in general and the importance of others to individual subjectivity formation are readily evident in *Castles* (2005). The same script can, of course, be varied. The perspective of the Princess dominates *Castles*, if only because she is first to stake a claim to the territory. But the perspective can be inverted if notions of place and ownership are contested.

Schema construction and social context

A common strategy in picture books and narrative fictions for young readers is to instantiate a core schema by accumulating a mix of essential and optional components of the schema across the extent of the text (see Stephens, 1995). This is a powerful strategy for inculcating, questioning, or modifying a schema, and has great potential for thematization of cultural diversity as racial difference. A good example of such schema construction, within a context that renders the framing script variable, can be seen in Armin Greder's

The Princess scowled at the Pirate, but then she sighed and shrugged. 'Oh, all right then.'

The Princess grabbed the shoulder of the Pirate, but stopped. 'Um, what?' She frowned at him.

'Friends,' said the Pirate, and smiled.

Figure 1.3 *Castles* by Allan Baillie and Caroline Magerl, Opening 13

The Island (2007), which demonstrates both an extended schema (*stranger*) and a locally instantiated schema (*wall*). Greder first published the book in German (*Die Insel*, 2002) and an English version was subsequently brought out in 2007 by an Australian publisher (Greder has published in both German and English from time to time). In between these editions, *Die Insel* had been translated into several other languages. The multiple contexts in which *Die Insel/The Island* has appeared have significant implications for the text's schemas, because the very different contexts of reception (re-)create effectively different books. In a review of *Die Insel*, Herbert Huber related the book to xenophobia in Germany and Europe more generally ('*Fremdenfeindlichkeit ist allerorts spürbar (nicht nur in Deutschland)*'),[5] and connected the wall built around the island in the book's penultimate opening with predominantly right-wing demands to wall off Europe from outsiders ('*Europa ist gerade dabei die Mauer um die EU ... weiter zu verstärken*'). The Australian edition of *The Island* (2007) was published without the subtitle that had appeared in the German (and translated) editions – *Eine tägliche Geschichte* ('An Everyday Story') – and without the expansion of this idea that had appeared on the back cover (*Eine tägliche Geschichte/ über den Umgang mit den Fremden und über die Mauern in den Köpfen* 'an everyday story about dealings with strangers and the walls inside the head'). A potential effect of this change is to narrow the application of the book, so that it would be usual to read it specifically as a protest against the then Australian Government's draconian policy on refugees and border control. Instead of a metaphorical wall around the European Union, Australian readers would interpret the wall as literalizing the fortress mentality pursued by government and its cultivation of what Wayne Weiten (2001: p. 561) refers to as 'catastrophic thinking ... which involves unrealistically negative appraisals of stress that exaggerate the magnitude of one's problems'. Thus the treatment of the stranger washed up on the island's shore has strong local resonance: the islanders 'took him to the uninhabited part of the island, to a goat pen that had been empty for a long time ... then they locked the gate and went back to their business'. In 2007, any illegal immigrants who attempted to reach Australia by sea were detained in remote, inhospitable camps or sent to some small neighbouring countries which had been funded to establish detention centres there.

According to this localized reading, *The Island* (2007) exemplifies a post-multicultural mentality that had emerged in the ten years preceding its publication. Australia officially declared itself a multicultural society in 1972, and for the next 25 years Australian children's fiction was constructed either in terms of a narrative which saw Australian culture as moving from a society imagined as grounded in the values of a settler culture with British origins to one embracing cultural diversity; or, alternatively, as a narrative depicting Australia as always already a multicultural society, proclaiming the existence of multicultural tendencies long before modern multicultural policy. Few twenty-first-century texts have reproduced either history, however, and this is probably because between the election campaign of 1996 and the subsequent rhetoric of 'homeland security', which culminated in the shameful handling of illegal immigration in 2001 and beyond, the concept of a multicultural Australian society was 'disremembered',[6] even if the fabric of society was not affected. As the ethnic other became identified politically as would-be migrants from Asia attempting to enter Australia illegally by boat, the multicultural migration narrative in children's literature became replaced by a new, more politically pointed genre, the refugee narrative.

What the cover summary of *Die Insel* (2002) referred to as 'mental barriers' (*die Mauern in den Köpfen*) are evident as a hostile stranger-schema which constrains the narrative script of *conflict, self-reflection, creative action, and social integration* because it precludes both creative action and concluding social integration. *The Island* (2007) is presented from the perspective of the island's inhabitants, who throughout the book accumulate a bundle of components of a xenophobic schema for *outsider, stranger* (the schema is overtly identified as a 'stranger'-schema towards the end of the book when the people decide to take the man, put him on his raft, and push him back out to sea). The following descriptors are thus applied to the stranger:

Not like them
'Wouldn't like it here'
'Would probably work for less pay'
Unhygienic
Unskilled
Unfit for work
Culturally alien
Is a 'savage'
'Eats with his hands'
Is a threat to the community

This schema-building commences with opening 1. In a discussion of system justification theory, Kasumi Yoshimura and Curtis Hardin (2009: p. 298) explain that 'people view group differences and social inequality as legitimate and natural because of epistemic, existential, and relational motivations to justify and rationalise the existing social order', and the full range is exemplified in the stranger-schema in *The Island* (2007). In opening 8 (Figure 1.4), for example, an epistemic community is evoked by the carter and the priest adducing, respectively, existential and relational reasons for excluding the stranger: he cannot carry heavy loads and his voice 'would clash with the rest of the choir'.

The illustrations function in ironical relationship with the text, an irony emphasized by the reciprocal eye contact between the stranger and

The carter said simply, 'Look at him! I need someone who can carry heavy loads.'

And the priest was very sorry, but the stranger's voice would clash with the rest of the choir.

Figure 1.4 The Island by Armin Greder, Opening 8 (right-hand page)

viewers: in the carrying scene, eye-contact from above the kneeling figure stresses that the imaged load is too heavy for anyone to lift, and in the choir scene, where the stranger is explicitly demonized by the attribution of devil's horns, dark skin, and a position behind the other singers (the devil's position), eye-contact past the choristers establishes an appeal against this imposed positioning. Here, and pervasively, the illustrations show that the islanders' shared beliefs and pressure on their fellows to conform – and hence the stranger-schema they construct – are xenophobic and unnecessary. Devoid of both *self-reflection* and *creative action*, the islanders corrupt creativity into phantasmagoric nightmares of otherness. Many children will recognize the citations of iconic images of anxiety from F.W. Murnau's *Nosferatu* (1922) or Edvard Munch's *The Scream* (one of the works of art most frequently cited in picture books), but many will also recognize Fuseli's *The Nightmare* from Anthony Browne's earlier citation of it in *The Big Baby*.

Greder doesn't close the book with the bleak images of the islanders' inhumanitarian action in pushing the stranger out to sea and out of the book, but with a final account of their subsequent isolationism and cultural loss. In this way, it suggests a powerful statement about some consequences of a move away from a society committed to multiculturalism.

Schema and empathic imagination

The function of script and schema as cognitive instruments for portraying cultural difference is illustrated in a contrastive way in another refugee narrative, Liz Lofthouse and Robert Ingpen's *Ziba Came on a Boat* (2007). In contrast to *The Island (2007)*, which elides any possibility of attributing subjectivity to the stranger, *Ziba Came on a Boat* works by narrating the inner thoughts and memories of a child on a refugee boat, a strategy which minimizes the text's status as fiction and privileges instead the activity of empathic imagination. The mixing of high modality and soft focus in Robert Ingpen's illustrations works beautifully with the text to mediate relations between familiarity and otherness, especially in the way the book embeds a major schema within its narrative script:

Schema: normal childhood belonging

laughter of children
peaceful environment
friends
everyday play
shared family life
parents' everyday activities
story-telling

belonging in culture
education and schooling
life without fear
freedom

An important aspect of this schema is its normative content, even though what is visually represented in the illustrations will seem alien or exotic to Western children. The familiar script of *conflict, self-reflection, creative action, and social integration* is deployed here in a way that neatly counterpoints the schema, in that the conflict stems from living in a war zone, but is then deeply experienced as a loss of a *normal childhood* schema. The verbal text presents self-reflection not merely in the form of memories and hopes but in a rhythm of travelling that interlinks the motions of the boat and the motions of Ziba's mind. Her memory of her mother busy weaving is a simple example, but its deft combination of simile and metaphor maintains a figurative and imaginative discourse:

> Up and down went the wool, in and out,
> **like** the boat **weaving** through the murky sea.
> (Lofthouse & Ingpen, 2007: unpaged; my emphasis)

By playing out the script as a story about a journey taken while confined on a small boat travelling through 'an endless sea', and by evoking the *normal childhood* schema as loss and absence, Lofthouse depicts a curtailment of Ziba's self-schema. Her peri-personal space is constrained by the situation, and her opportunity for creative action is limited, except that it occurs as the mind figuratively processes its thoughts and memories and thereby enacts the impact of other people on subjective agency. Because the book doesn't offer an arrival, the self-schema is posed as a future possibility. The third opening before the final one (Figure 1.5) offers what is described as a 'dream' – a reinstatement of the normal-childhood schema in a welcoming, multicultural society, as depicted in the illustration (although not stated as such in the text). This image combines with the penultimate opening to express the hope of *social reintegration* (although this hope is modified by the final opening's reminder that arrival has not taken place). The penultimate opening is structured as an image of hope, with mother and child gazing towards the right-hand page which is empty apart from the five words which express hope for the future: ' "*Azadi*," her mother whispered. "Freedom." ' The empty page emphasizes the left-to-right, top-to-bottom vector running from mother to daughter to doll – a very expressive representation of cultural otherness unfolding symbolically into the schema of everyday childhood.

The ending of *Ziba Came on a Boat* (2007) is very open: the past tense of the title suggests there has been an arrival, but this isn't shown on the

"*Azadi,*" her mother whispered. "Freedom."

Figure 1.5 *Ziba Came on a Boat* by Liz Lofthouse and Robert Ingpen, Opening 14

final page. Adult readers know all too well that at the time of the book's publication what awaited Ziba was not that happy multicultural childhood affirmed by Ingpen, but indefinite detention. That, fortunately, is no longer the case. Again more for adult readers is the context in Australia of the cry *Azadi*, a catchword frequently shouted by Hazara people from Afghanistan during demonstrations in Australia against detention policies (and the title of a notable docudrama on this topic).[7] *Ziba Came on a Boat* espouses a politics of refugee visibility in opposition to the oppressive practices of detention offshore or in a remote region, and it does so through narrative strategies that promote the visibility of other people's cultural values while proposing a restoration of basic human practices. To engage in debate about the status of refugees and the failure of multicultural policy, it makes very effective use of the structure of script and schema.

As vital cognitive instruments, script and schema prove to be widely powerful strategies for investing normative cultural ideas with richness and subtlety. In the case of the representation of cultural diversity, the particular domain I have taken as my focus here, script and schema function as transformative instruments, enhancing understanding of relationships between selfhood and otherness and informing social action designed to foster equity and social justice.

Further Reading

Gavins, J. & Steen, G. (eds) 2003. *Cognitive poetics in practice*. Routledge, London.

> This collection of essays is a useful introduction to cognitive poetics as a field in literary criticism. Contributors show how cognitively oriented theories of language can be used to read literary texts (although there are no direct applications to children's literature). Of particular interest are the essays by Crisp, Burke, and Semino which explore how the body's perceptual interactions within the world structure conceptual representations of that world.

Herman, D. 2002. *Story logic: problems and possibilities of parrative*. University of Nebraska Press, Lincoln. Ch. 3.

> Starting from the distinction between a mere sequence of actions and a narratively organized sequence, in this chapter Herman explores the implications of various uses of the *script* concept, ranging from knowledge representations of actions bound up with everyday life to the plot structures readers use to anticipate story logic.

Stephens, J. 1995. 'Writing *by* children, writing *for* children: schema theory, narrative discourse and ideology.' *Revue Belge de Philologie et d'Histoire*, vol. 73, no. 3: pp. 853–63 (revised and reprinted in Bull, G. & Anstey, M.

(eds). 2002. *Crossing the boundaries*. Prentice Hall, French's Forest, NSW. pp. 237–48).

An approach (through cognitive poetics) to how schemas function within a child's capability for making sense of the world and shaping it as narrative, and how writing for children addresses this capability.

Turner, M. 1996. *The literary mind*. Oxford University Press, New York.

An important work in the emerging field of cognition studies in literary and narrative theory (as well as other disciplines), Turner's study examines the cognitive principles at work in the domains of discourse interpretation and narrative comprehension, and in doing so it includes close discussion of image schemas.

Notes

1 The concept derives originally from cognitive linguistics (especially the work of Lakoff and Johnson (1980) on image-schemas), and more recently from computer technologies. In the last few years it has been taken up in significant ways in areas of narrative theory that are drawing on theory of mind – for example, David Herman's *Story Logic*.

2 In earlier studies (Stephens, 1995 and 2002; Tsukioka and Stephens, 2003) I subsumed *script* within *schema*, distinguishing object or image schemas from story or narrative schemas. Here I follow the practice in neo-narratology of referring to the latter as *scripts*.

3 As Anna Katrina Gutierrez puts it (2009: p. 160), glocalization reconciles globalization and local resistance 'by appropriating the global and localizing it, thus taking the foreign element and giving it a local flavour, returning it to the world with a new significance'.

4 I wish to thank the following for permission to reproduce the illustrations in this chapter: Allan Baillie, for *Old magic*; Penguin Australia, for *Castles* and *Ziba came on a boat*; and Allen & Unwin, for *The island*.

5 The issue was earlier comprehensively summarized by Jacqueline Bhabha (1998: p. 596) in a categorization that implicitly anticipates Kymlicka's tripartite structure: 'Distinctions between [European] Union citizens, third-country nationals, settled integrated residents, more temporary migrants, single and dual nationals, and monocultural and multicultural families generate contestation as to whether the terms intimate consequences of difference. At issue is whether national, ethnic, racial, or religious characteristics affect eligibility for the benefits and protections traditionally associated with citizenship. Many of the divisive political issues that have arisen over the past twenty years within the boundaries of individual member states now arise within a broader European context'.

6 See Jessica Raschke, 'Who's knocking now?' (2005); John Stephens and Robyn McCallum, 'Positioning otherness' (2009); Huggan, Chapter 4.

7 *Azadi* (2005), an Australian short film, written and directed by Anthony Maras, explores the issue of mandatory detention of asylum seekers in Australia.

2
Journeying Subjects: Spatiality and Identity in Children's Texts

Clare Bradford and Raffaella Baccolini

In Maurice Sendak's celebrated picture book *Where the Wild Things Are,* Max's emotional and psychological trajectory is plotted by his movement in and through time and space as he embarks on a journey 'through night and day and in and out of weeks and almost over a year' (1963: unpaged) dreams or imagines a sequence of adventures in the land of the wild things and finally returns to 'the night of his very own room'. The two places which figure in the narrative are set one against the other. Max's home is a site of discipline and authority where his mother sends him to his bedroom without any supper because he engages in disorderly behaviour, but this same room is also associated with reconciliation and appeasement between Max and his mother when, on his return, he discovers that his supper awaits him, 'and it was still hot' (1963: unpaged). The island is a space of freedom where Max participates in the wild rumpus enjoyed by the island's inhabitants. It is also the location where Max achieves dominance over the wild things and is enthroned as their king.

The narrative of Max's journey and return has been interpreted as a 'paradigmatically colonial story' which echoes and disrupts those narratives of exploration and dominance which affirmed the imperial project (Ball, 1997); and it is also interpreted as a carnivalesque text, with Max's sojourn with the wild things understood as 'time out' from his everyday life and especially his relations with his mother (Stephens, 1992: pp. 134–9). These readings, informed respectively by postcolonial and Bakhtinian theoretical frameworks, assume that the places which feature in the narrative – Max's bedroom and the place where the wild things live – embody significances and externalize Max's trajectory from one emotional state to another.

Where the Wild Things Are is a telling example of how representations of spatiality function in children's texts, where they afford more than merely the inert background upon which actions are performed and events occur but are intertwined with processes of identity-formation and the development of interpersonal relationships. To situate our discussion of place and space in children's literature, we draw upon three theoretical frameworks: cultural geography, postcolonial theory, and utopian studies. These domains of theory and criticism share a common interest in the social, cultural, and political meanings of place and the processes whereby places are invested with value and status.

Conceptions and formulations of the significances of place in literary and popular texts developed during the 1960s and 1970s, when new social theories addressed questions of subjectivity, power, and hierarchies of worth. Post-structuralist theories emphasized the interplay between individual human subjects and the spaces where they lived and worked. Thus, Michel Foucault (1967; 1972; 1977) explored the cultural discourses which conferred meanings on places such as the library, the psychiatric hospital, and the prison, and the power of such meanings for those who inhabited these places. Neo-Marxist approaches, exemplified by the work of Henri Lefebvre (1971), focused on how capitalism achieved social reproduction by organizing spaces such as the industrialized city, where everyday life was shaped by the agendas of employers and corporations.

Although the terms 'space' and 'place' are often used interchangeably, it is helpful to distinguish them. Space is generally associated with large and abstract conceptions of spatiality, place, with the local and the bounded. David Harvey, for instance, notes that political action is place-based, because oppositional groups are 'relatively empowered to organize in place but dis-empowered when it comes to organizing over space' (1989: p. 302). Postcolonial theorists have generally distinguished between imperial visions of 'empty' space waiting to be put to use and the intensely local, grounded identities of colonized peoples. In similar and yet different terms, in utopian studies the distinction between space and place is also present, but it has also changed over time. Utopia is traditionally located in a spatial and/or temporal elsewhere. Thus, local and bounded places, even if imaginary, have sometimes been seen – against the authors' intentions – as 'blueprints' of potential utopias (or dystopias). More recently, however, criticism has shown the eventual limits of any utopian project, ultimately shifting importance from the utopian outcome itself to the desire and the process of achieving utopia.

Questions of relationality are crucial to utopian formulations of place; they are crucial as well within the field of cultural geography. Doreen Massey argues that objects in space are 'products of the spatial organization of relations' (1995: p. 317); that is, that we need to consider social and spatial factors together in order to conceptualize identities, places, and socio-spatial formations. Massey emphasizes that 'relations' are not necessarily benign or progressive, but that they embody various kinds of power relation which may be oppressive or unequal. Spatial organization can, for instance, sustain patterns of inequality favouring the rich over the poor, men over women, or adults over children. The 'maps of power' described by Massey are, however, never fixed or absolute, since 'we make, and constantly remake, the spaces and places and identities through which we live our lives' (Massey, 1999: p. 290).

Like Massey, Stuart Hall focuses on the politics of space and place, although from a cultural studies perspective. Hall's influence on theories of place and space is most evident in his approach to diasporic movement and identity formation. Viewing culture as 'a complex combination of con-tinuities and breaks, similarities and differences' (Hall, 1995: p. 208), Hall discusses the conjunctures of culture, identity, and place which enable the production of diasporic subjects whose identity does not reside in a single place but in 'maps of meaning' (Hall, 1995: p. 207) forged from a variety of cultures, languages, and perspectives in a way somewhat similar to Massey's maps of power. There is, however, a degree of tension between Hall's vision of diasporic subjects freed from older affiliations with specific places and the political struggles of Indigenous populations who seek stable ownership of ancestral territories and whose identities are formed from spiritual con-nections with places.

As global forces impact upon commercial and cultural processes, dis-courses of globalization foreground the mobility and open-endedness of cultural flows. According to Arjun Appadurai, we now live in a world which is 'fundamentally characterized by objects in motion. These objects include ideas and ideologies, people and goods, images and messages, technologies and techniques' (2001: p. 5). In response to Appadurai's emphasis on flow, other theorists seek to reclaim the significances of the local. Arturo Escobar notes that 'place has dropped out of sight in the "globalization craze" of recent years' (2001: p. 141), during which Eurocentric forms of globalization have held sway, and argues that 'the reassertion of place thus appears as an important arena for rethinking and reworking eurocentric forms of analy-sis' (2001: p. 141). Indeed, concepts of place have attracted renewed inter-est across the social sciences and humanities and have become central to studies of diasporic, migrant, and refugee experiences and the texts which address these experiences.

As we have noted, concepts of space have always been central to utopian studies. The very word 'utopia' calls for a special attention to the issue of space. The literary utopia takes its name from Thomas More's 1516 work, *Utopia*. More coins the word from the Greek *ou-topos* (no/not place) and *eu-topos* (good place). Thus, utopia is the good place that does not exist, whose primary characteristic is 'its non-existence combined with a *topos* – a location in time and space – to give it verisimilitude' (Sargent, 1994: p. 5). Furthermore, the place must be clearly good or better – or at least would be 'so recognized by a contemporary reader' (Sargent, 1994: p. 5). Therefore, on a semantic level, the word includes both the notion of being 'unreal' and the description of the happiness of the ideal state.

The word 'utopian' was used in just this way during the sixteenth century, but as the genre developed to include the variations of dystopia and science fiction, space in utopia ceased to be associated only with a geographical other – typically a remote island, the peak of a mountain, or an alien planet. Since the publication of Sébastien Mercier's *L'an 2440* (1771), a few years before the French Revolution, the separation of utopia from the present has also been temporal: utopia may not just be geographically distant, it can also be temporally distant, projected into the future. This change in the treatment of 'utopia' eventually allows scholars to move away from mere discussions about utopia's unreachability to the notion of utopia as process. As noted above, utopia does not offer a blueprint, a model, or a goal to be reached; rather it disrupts the present and our common notions about how time is experienced. Space, then, becomes less relevant or significant for what it actually represents: if it is not the actual, bounded place which one must reach, then the emphasis moves to the process of attaining an unreachable place, the state of utopia. More than any scholar, Uruguayan writer Eduardo Galeano summarizes this important shift in his 'Ventana sobre la utopía':

> *Ella está en el horizonte' – dice Fernando Birri – 'Me acerco dos pasos, ella se aleja dos pasos. Camino diez pasos y el horizonte se corre diez pasos más allá. Por mucho que yo camine, nunca la alcanzaré. Para que sirve la utopía? Para eso sirve: para caminar.* (Galeano, 2006)

'It is on the horizon' – says Fernando Birri – 'I advance two steps, it moves two steps backward. I walk ten steps and the horizon moves ten steps forward. No matter how much I walk, I will never reach it. What is the use of utopia? That's its use: for walking' (Baccolini's translation). Utopia, then, does not designate the space to be ultimately reached but, rather, the journey through space that we need to undergo.

Utopian studies scholars have long underlined this element against the common interpretation of utopia as a struggle to reach perfection. As Fredric Jameson has recently stated, the 'desire called Utopia' has been repeatedly defeated in history (2007: p. 84). But what Lyman Tower Sargent calls 'social dreaming' is evoked because we need to choose utopia to create our vision of an alternative to the ills and inequities of the present (1994: p. 3; 2007: p. 306). Such a vision consists of 'the dreams and nightmares that concern the ways in which groups of people arrange their lives and which usually envision a radically different society than the one in which the dreamers live' (Sargent, 1994: p. 3). It involves desire, a wish for a better society, a desire for improvement, both personal and societal. In addition to dreaming and fantasizing, however, there are two other components to utopianism: reason and action. We not only dream, we also 'reason about our dreams' (projects) 'and sometimes we even act on them' (Sargent, 1994: p. 4).

Today, utopian imagination finds its strongest expression in science fiction (sf) and in what critics have called the 'critical dystopia', described by

Raffaella Baccolini and Tom Moylan as a form of dystopia which 'with its disasters and representations of worse realities, retains the potential for change, so that we can discover in our current dark times a scattering of hope and desire that will arise to aid us in the transformation of society' (Baccolini and Moylan, 2003: p. 235). Both sf and critical dystopias can be seen as thought experiments originating in the question 'what if?'. They do not try to foresee the future, but they explore potentialities, possible changes, and possibilities of difference by also warning readers of potentially dangerous trends in societies. Once again space functions in a variety of ways; as Samuel R. Delany (1991) has stated, the setting or background in 'realist' fiction becomes, in sf, the foreground, one of the essential elements of the narrative. But whether utopian or dystopian, the imagined elsewhere also has a pedagogical function which critics such as Tom Moylan (2008) and Phil Wegner (2002) have recently underlined. The presentation of another world or space allows readers 'to perceive the world they occupy in a new way, providing them with some of the skills and dispositions necessary to inhabit an emerging social, political, and cultural environment' (Wegner, 2002: p. 2). Thus, through a 'process of pleasure and pedagogy', the function of utopia reverts from merely that of 'goal and catalyst of change to one of criticism, and the education of desire' (Moylan, 2008: p. 80; Levitas, 2010: p. 226). One of the key functions of utopia, then, is the educative aspect stressed by Ernst Bloch in his *Principle of Hope* (1986), explained by Ruth Levitas as follows:

> The education of desire is part of the process of allowing the abstract elements of utopia to be gradually replaced by the concrete, allowing anticipation to dominate compensation. Utopia does not express desire, but enables people to work towards an understanding of what is necessary for human fulfilment, a broadening, deepening and raising of aspirations in terms quite different from those of their everyday life. (Levitas, 2010: p. 141)

These aspects of utopian and dystopian writing, articulating a geographical and temporal elsewhere (together with the necessary 'journeys' involved), can usefully be applied to discourses of identity formation and development of interpersonal relationships in the literature for children and young adults.

The central concern of children's literature is, in fact, the identity formation of young protagonists and their progress toward enhanced ways of being in the world. Whether located in realist or fantastic settings, narratives of maturation in children's texts are commonly plotted in relation to spatiality. Protagonists may flee dysfunctional and violent societies to seek better lives, like Jonas in Lois Lowry's *The Giver* (1993); or social inequalities may be represented in spatial terms through contrasts between domestic settings, such as the opposition between the homes of the privileged Crosses and the oppressed Noughts in Malorie Blackman's *Noughts & Crosses* (2001). Very often a protagonist's home-coming, like E.T.'s return to his home planet, represents a recuperation of selfhood. Settings, motifs, and tropes of space, place, and travel in children's texts thus offer critical insights into the global and local influences which shape the identities of child protagonists.

Global and local in children's literature

As David Harvey observes, 'the accumulation of capital has always been a profoundly geographical affair' (2000: p. 23). The production of children's texts is inescapably implicated in the capitalist enterprise and is subject to the internationalization of trade and markets, expressed in the global reach of corporations and their products. This global reach imprints itself spatially (as in the spread of the *Harry Potter* books throughout the world) and seems very often to triumph over the local, as global products take market share from locally produced goods. Thus, the marketing strategies deployed to sell, for example, the *Harry Potter* books in many languages and locations are apt to crowd out children's books produced locally. This is especially the case in nations where publishing for children is a relatively new industry, such as Singapore, where imported books flood the market (Miyake, 2006: p. 11), and Indonesia, where publishing for children is dominated by translations of Western books, such as the works of Enid Blyton (Miyake, 2006: p. 11). In India, books in English were central to processes of colonization, and the dominance of English is maintained in the high proportion (50 per cent) among all books published for Indian children, although only 7 per cent of child readers speak English. In comparison, relatively few books are published in Indian languages (Khorana, 2006: pp. 282–5).

Rhetorics of globalization tend to foreground notions of the global village where the world's children are assumed to enjoy uniform access to products and texts. The global village is, however, differentially available to children depending upon their material circumstances. The reassertion of the local in publishing for children is achieved by thousands of independent, often small-scale publishing houses which produce children's texts in local languages. These include Indigenous publishers in countries where European languages were imposed on autochthonous populations.

It would, however, be misleading to imply that the local, the national, and the global inhabit different textual spheres. Rather, children's texts commonly negotiate among local/national tropes and themes, and among the myriad images, references, and intertexts which enter the local through children's consumption of globalized mass media. National literatures distinguish themselves from one another by virtue of the language(s) in which they are produced, but also through the cultural schemas which inform them. Such schemas are based on memories of places, practices, relation-ships, and narratives which are invested with affect and meaning. Thus, children's texts advocate and interrogate cultural values and ideologies without necessarily invoking signifiers of nationhood such as allusions to particular places, native animals, or national festivals.

The DreamWorks animated film *Madagascar* (2005) affords an example of the intermingling of local and global conceptions of place. The film's action is built on a common story 'script' (see Stephens, Chapter 1) in which a protagonist (in this case Marty the zebra) becomes disenchanted with the endless routine of his life and yearns for freedom. Marty's wish as he blows out the candle on his tenth birthday cake is 'I wish I could go to the wild'. Given the privileged life Marty and his companions enjoy as inhabitants of Central Park Zoo in New York, viewers will react sceptically to the idea that these city-bred, effete animals might be transplanted to 'the wild', and will expect them to experience dangers and difficulties. Negotiations between places and identities are central to the plot in which Marty, Alex the lion, Gloria the hippopotamus, and Melman the giraffe are dispatched by boat to the Kenya Wildlife Preserve, only to be shipwrecked on the island of Madagascar when their ship is hijacked by the zoo penguins. The end of the film anticipates another voyage, to be played out in its sequel, *Madagascar: Escape 2 Africa*.

When the film opens, Marty is seen running through lush grass, leap-ing off a cliff, and swinging on vines, Tarzan-like, his action accompanied by the song 'Born Free'. We learn that this sequence is a daydream only when the viewing angle shifts to show the enclosures, trees, and manicured lawns of the zoo, where the four animals entertain the public. Rather than offering the endless horizons of Marty's imagining, the zoo is bounded by the Manhattan skyline, rendered as an idealized cityscape with the warm daylight colours of Fifth Avenue and Times Square modulating into moody night-time scenes where tall city buildings are dotted with lighted win-dows. The picture-postcard appearance of Manhattan in the film constructs New York as the setting of innumerable stories of adventure, glamour, and escape, signalled by intertexts such as the Kander and Ebb song 'New York, New York'. Performed by Alex and Marty against the night-time Manhattan backdrop, this song celebrates an imagined and fictionalized New York, but their performance also undercuts this version of the city as a site of fantasy and insists on the real-world experience of New Yorkers: inhabitants of the nearby buildings switch on their lights and shout abuse from their win-dows: 'We're not all nocturnal, you know!' Nevertheless, even this reference to 'reality' mobilizes a plethora of representations of New Yorkers as loud, brash, and assertive.

Connections between place and identity in *Madagascar* (2005) hinge upon the problematics of authenticity and the effects of nature and nurture on individual subjects. Born and bred in Central Park Zoo, the animals are identified with character-types commonly associated with New York. Thus, the hypochondriac giraffe Melman Mankiewicz evokes Woody Allen's neu-rotic New York characters as he frets about the brown spot he has discovered on his shoulder and delights in undergoing MRIs, CAT scans, injections, and other treatments to address his imaginary maladies. The character of Alex, voiced by Ben Stiller, calls on Stiller's performance in *Zoolander* (2001), where he plays a male model (Derek Zoolander) who is the three-time win-ner of the VH1 title 'Male Model of the Year'.[1] Performing in Central Park Zoo as 'The King of New York', Alex adopts the facial expressions and poses (notably 'Blue Steel') devised by Derek (Stiller) in *Zoolander*. The identities attributed in *Madagascar* to Melman and Alex are thus based upon character schemas which are in turn built upon representations of New Yorkers in popular discourse and across a variety of texts, literary and popular.

Appadurai's discussion of what he terms mediascapes, 'landscapes of images' (1996: p. 35), is pertinent to *Madagascar* (2005) and the web of allu-sions and references which imbues its treatment of New York. According to Appadurai, mediascapes provide consumers with 'large and complex reper-toires of images, narratives and ethnoscapes' where 'the lines between the realistic and the fictional landscapes they see are blurred' (1996: p. 35), and where the more consumers are distant from the actual places represented through the media, the more fantastic and chimerical their imaginings tend to be. Children, too, are consumers of mass media through their access to cartoons, animations, and films, so that even if child viewers are unfamiliar with Woody Allen's films or *Zoolander,* the New York setting in *Madagascar* builds on and contributes to their imaginings of the city.

Like the mobile subjects described by Appadurai, caught up in the global flows whereby local economies export marginalized groups, the four ani-mals are shipped to Kenya, only to chance upon the island of Madagascar, where another field of imagery is introduced: that of 'the wild'. As we learn from the narration in 'Enchanted Island', a component in the DVD's 'Special Features', the film's treatment of the island's landscape is based upon the 'childlike and naïve' (*Madagascar,* 2005) art of the post-impressionist painter Henri Rousseau. This explanation supports the film's aesthetic of a lush and extravagantly verdant landscape, devoid of humans. Nevertheless, the film alludes to the consumer economics surrounding tourism, representing Madagascar as something like an island resort, where the four animals drink saltwater cocktails, eat tropical fruits, and lounge on bamboo furniture.

The island is both enchanted and dangerous, and here the film addresses the tension between Alex's 'authentic' identity as a carnivore and his friend-ship with Marty, the zebra. In the rarified setting of the zoo, Alex has con-sumed steaks which constitute empty signifiers, devoid of references to the dead animals from which they originate. On the island, deprived of his regular supply of steaks, Alex experiences a series of hallucinations in which all animals transmute into steaks on legs, including Marty. It is not until the penguins introduce him to the delights of sushi, in a scene redolent of the Japanese television series *Iron Chef,* that he is converted from a meat eater to a fish-eating vegetarian. Alex's identity, then, has little to do with place but relies upon social norms. At times the film invokes concepts of place-based identities, as when Marty remarks, early in the film, 'Just imagine going back to nature, back to your roots.' But this comment is merely an ironic anticipation of the film's closure, which points to the absence of any originary source of identity.

Indeed, the well-being of all the protagonists in *Madagascar* is contingent upon their attachment to the social group – the four escapees from Central Park Zoo – who provide affirmation and emotional support. Within the logic of the film, place is of second-order importance; articulating the position of the mobile subject, Marty remarks, 'I don't care where we go as long as we're together.' The settings of New York and Madagascar alike function as sites of the film's self-conscious play with imaginings built on a multiplicity of intertexts and allusions.

Although discourses and theories of globalization have become prominent only since the fall of the Berlin Wall in 1989, globalizing impulses are by no means new, since powerful civilizations have always sought to impose their cultural and economic practices on others, notably during the age of European imperialism. In the next section we consider how postcolonial theory and textuality address the transformations of place, space, and time wrought by imperialism and experienced by the inhabitants of colonized territories.

Time, place, space, and postcolonialism

Imperialism, defined by Edward Said as 'the practice, theory, and the attitudes of a dominating metropolitan centre ruling a distant territory' (1993: p. 8), stretches back into ancient times to the Assyrian, Chinese, and Roman empires. The term 'the age of Empire' is, however, generally applied to the European expansion which flourished during the nineteenth century and which reached its end as territories previously colonized gained independence and self-determination. 'Colonialism' refers to the establishment of settlements governed and controlled by a colonizing power. In colonies whose autochthonous inhabitants were of a different race from the colonizers, theories were marshalled to construct a hierarchy of races, with Europeans distinguishing themselves from 'inferior' Indigenous peoples.

The seminal postcolonial text *The Empire Writes Back* (1989) begins with these words: 'More than three-quarters of the people living in the world today have had their lives shaped by the experience of colonialism' (Ashcroft, Griffiths, and Tiffin, 1989: p. 1). Place and displacement are central to this experience; they are central, too, to the field of postcolonial studies, which deals with the effects of colonization on societies and cultures. In many colonial settings Indigenous peoples experienced subjugation and displacement, the results of which persist in contemporary postcolonial societies.

British colonists who travelled to the United States, Canada, Australia, and New Zealand experienced a sense of dislocation: the strange, new places which they encountered, the very flora and fauna, could not readily be described in the language they brought with them (Ashcroft, 2001: pp. 153–56), and the familiar places of the imperial centre were no longer 'home' to them. But these experiences of displacement were insignificant in comparison with the massive, far-reaching changes which affected Indigenous peoples. As Anthony Giddens points out in *The Consequences of Modernity* (1990), all pre-modern cultures developed methods for calculating the passage of time. In everyday life, time and place were intimately linked, as people carried out practices associated with diurnal and seasonal cycles. The invention of the mechanical clock, introduced to Indigenous societies as part of the imperial enterprise, regularized the measurement of time and enabled colonizers to enforce routines which effectively separated time from place. In place of the ancient routines whereby Indigenous people organized their lives around daily activities, seasonal change, and ritual practices, they were obliged to adhere to the regularized, standardized systems of the clock and the calendar. Giddens refers to this change as the 'emptying of time' (1990: p. 18), which resulted in the 'emptying of space' (1990: p. 18) and the separation of space from place. The concept of 'empty space' – that is, space detached from lived and experienced places – was based on the 'discovery' of territories hitherto 'unknown' to Europeans, and on the mapping of such territories, a process which produced a systematic account of spaces ripe for colonization. The transformation of empty space into place was signalled by processes whereby colonizers gave names to the sites where they took up land, instituted businesses, established towns and cities.

Place means different things in different societies. In Australian Aboriginal cultures, for instance, place is intimately bound up with selfhood and with kinship relations. A person is born into a particular kinship group identified not merely with a tract of land but with specific formations such as rivers and mountains. Aboriginal people derive their sense of self from their affiliation with particular places, based on the Dreaming, a time-space when the Ancestors, the spirits who created the land, moved around country establishing relations between humans and the natural world and between different groups of humans.[2] This view of place is utterly at odds with the perspective of British colonizers, who regarded the land, in line with English legal traditions, as property in which one invested labour and capital.

Addressing the contemporary politics of postcolonial nations, Indigenous literatures for children frequently contest the Eurocentric assumptions about space and time which had such a powerful effect upon Indigenous cultures. Elaine Russell's picture book *A is for Aunty* (2000) is set in a space transformed into a colonial place: an Aboriginal mission administered by a manager appointed by the Government. Russell locates the activities of the community in a setting where hierarchies of race are spatialized (Bradford, 2007: pp. 125–36). Aboriginal families live in houses set apart from the larger buildings where the manager lives, and the straight lines and sharp angles of the mission's design symbolize constraints of surveillance and control. However, the book emphasizes the small strategies of resistance whereby the Aboriginal inhabitants of the mission maintain traditional practices. A key example is Russell's account of the humpies (temporary buildings made of tin, bark, or branches) where 'our oldies' live (Russell, 2000: p. 11), the semicircular shape of which is echoed in the cubby house secretly built by the narrator and her friend. The introduction of this semicircular shape into the grids and linear patterns of the mission defines resistance as a reclamation of traditional places (humpies, cubby house) where community members evade surveillance and retain at least limited autonomy.

Whereas Russell's narrative is located within one setting and celebrates the cultural survival of its Aboriginal inhabitants, Sherman Alexie's *The Absolutely True Diary of a Part-Time Indian* (2007) follows the trajectory of a 14-year-old boy, Junior, as he travels between the Spokane Indian Reservation ('the rez') and the white high school in the nearby town of Reardon.[3] The first-person narrative commences with Junior's decision to attend Reardon, and his oscillation between the two settings is symbolized by the names he is known by: Junior in the reservation, Arnold at school. The rez and the school are homologous, respectively, of Indian and white cultures, taking on the varied forms of Junior/Arnold's shifting perceptions and allegiances. At first, the two places seem polar opposites: 'Reardon was the opposite of the rez. It was the opposite of my family. It was the opposite of me. I didn't deserve to be there' (Alexie, 2007: p. 56). The narrative then traces the process whereby Junior/Arnold revises his internalized sense of inferiority and achieves the agency which will enable him to progress beyond the boundaries imposed on him by the cultural expectations of both the rez and the mainstream society of Reardon, enabling him to take up a 'Spokane' identity which is informed by his experiences in both communities.

The places which feature in the narrative are inflected by differences of class, race, worldview, and values, so that, to use Massey's terms, the opposition between the rez and Reardon is built on a mixture of social and spatial factors. By choosing to attend school in Reardon, Junior/Arnold announces to the rez community that he is not satisfied with the inferior, poorly resourced education offered by the rez schools, that he wishes to avail himself of an opportunity to go to college like many of the Reardon students. Junior/Arnold's decision causes a breach with his best friend at the rez, Rowdy, who refuses to associate with him any longer. The distance between the rez and Reardon is thus an emotional and psychological one as well as a geographical one.

Because the narration is mediated by Junior/Arnold's perspective, non-Indigenous readers are positioned as outsiders to the culture of the rez and addressed as an interested but uninformed audience. Having provided an account of his childhood illnesses and their effects (he has poor vision, a speech impediment, and is prone to seizures), Junior/Arnold outlines his experience as 'a retard':

> Do you know what happens to retards on the rez?
> We get beat up.
> At least once a month.
> Yep, I belong to the Black-Eye-of-the-Month Club.

(Alexie, 2007: p. 4)

The novel's narration, at once confiding and entertaining, gradually shifts from such descriptions of the rez's dysfunctional relationships and practices to more nuanced accounts of the circumstances which have contributed to the poverty and hopelessness of its inhabitants.

As Junior/Arnold develops interpersonal relationships with some of the Reardon students and devours the books held in the school library, he gains a degree of critical distance both from rez culture and from the lives of the students at Reardon High School. In particular, the world of the rez gathers texture and complexity as the narrative pulls back from Junior/Arnold's personal experience to consider broader questions relating to its establishment and history. Paul Carter's postcolonial project *The Road to Botany Bay* (1987) is apposite here. Examining the processes whereby 'empty space' was converted into colonial places, Carter comes to the conclusion that textuality was central to these processes. As explorers and settlers endowed 'empty spaces' with names, as they mapped them and relayed stories about them, they brought colonized spaces into being. A powerful metaphor for these places is the palimpsest, which bears the traces of previous inscriptions built up over generations and centuries. Similarly, the history of the rez is gradually revealed through the stories Junior/Arnold tells, stories which superimpose the lives of contemporary Spokane people over the pre-colonial experience of the tribe.

One effect of this palimpsest-like depiction of the rez is that it collapses time and reasserts the connections between time and place disrupted by colonialism. Junior/Arnold's account of the tragic deaths of his beloved grandmother and his father's closest friend Eugene emphasizes the senselessness of these deaths (both were accidentally killed by drunken Indians) and the high proportion of such deaths in the Spokane community. Searching for an answer to the question 'Why?', Junior/Arnold consults the school nerd, Gordy, who suggests that he read Euripides' *Medea*. Here Junior/Arnold comes upon Medea's words, 'What greater grief than the loss of one's native land?', and understands them in relation to the past and the present:

'I read that and thought, "Well, of course, man. We Indians have LOST EVERYTHING. We lost our native land, we lost our languages, we lost our songs and dances. We lost each other"' (Alexie, 2007: p. 173). A pathetic remnant of the vast territories formerly occupied by the Spokane, the rez is inscribed with expressions and experiences of loss stretching back to colonial displacement. Junior/Arnold's recourse to *Medea* intensifies this sense of loss as he reads the text of the rez in the light of an ancient tragedy; at the same time, *Medea* offers him an analogy for the extremity of Indigenous experience.

Following the deaths of his grandmother and Eugene, Junior/Arnold is too depressed to attend school, and when he finally returns he is taken to task by Mrs Jeremy, his social studies teacher, who publicly admonishes him for his poor attendance. His friend Gordy stands and ostentatiously drops his textbook, followed by a similar action by the rest of the class, who then walk out of the room in protest at the teacher's unfeeling behaviour. The high school, formerly a site where Junior/Arnold experienced alienation and loneliness, is now transformed through his friends' actions. This does not imply that the school is now a utopian space, but rather that places are imprinted with the changing dynamics of interpersonal relations. Junior/Arnold's friends have gained a sense of his difference and of the cultural and economic factors which separate him from their middle-class lives. For his part, Junior/Arnold recognizes that while he sometimes experiences the close familial ties of the rez as oppressive, some of his classmates are trapped in dysfunctional family relationships. The closure of the novel foregrounds his realization that although he will inevitably leave the rez, he will be a journeying subject, maintaining ties of affect and affiliation: 'I would always love Rowdy. And I would always miss him, too. Just as I would always love and miss my grandmother, my big sister, and Eugene' (Alexie, 2007: p. 230).

Time, space, and identity in dystopia

Back in 1987, Fredric Jameson was calling for an exploration of the distinctive features of science fiction as a genre which included time and space (Jameson, 2007: p. 313). In a recent contribution on the relationship between utopia and space, Ralph Pordzik has defined utopian writing as a 'locus of literary innovation where writers in the past as well as in the present have experimented with different spatial metaphors in order to explore the experience of power, progress and modernity' (2009: p. 18). Quoting Michel de Certeau, he notes that utopia, 'as a mode of imaginatively shaping the vision of an ideal society or form of life[,] is a "spatial practice"', whereas dystopias 'challenge or even deconstruct the plausibility and feasibility of these ideal spaces' (2009: p. 18). The very notions of space and place evoke the related concepts of location, displacement, community, citizenship, and, of course, identity. Our sense of identity is dependent, among other things, on the place where we were born, grow up, and the spaces we inhabit. In the utopian genre that, as we have seen, is particularly dependent on different spatial metaphors, the well-being of the citizen is very much linked to the quality of the imagined elsewhere. In dystopia, for instance, the identities of its citizens are dependent on the place in which they live. In particular, the 'misfit' protagonist – a convention of the genre – is the quintessential 'displaced' person: the citizen who feels out of place and at odds with the otherwise generally accepted values of the society.

Philip Reeve's *Mortal Engines* (2001) and M. T. Anderson's *Feed* (2002) are two young adult novels set in rather distant and dystopian futures where the articulations of future space and time are very significant for the lives and the developments of their protagonists. Each novel involves a number of characters, but both focus primarily on a boy-girl pair (in *Mortal Engines*, Hester Shaw and Tom Natsworthy; in *Feed*, Violet and Titus). Both novels are set in a distant future with different settings that are not inert, pre-existing spaces, but 'a set of culturally influenced and historically changeable spatial relations' where hierarchies of classes and cultures are spatialized (Hartmann, 2009: p. 275; see Bradford, 2007: pp. 123–46). Both novels present different dystopian settings that the male protagonists do not recognize as such at first; it is their interpersonal relations and the emotional and geographical journeys undertaken with the female characters of the novels that will enable the young men, on different levels, to achieve a mild critical distance from their own societies. Thus, these novels enact an epistemological process whereby readers can come to perceive their own worlds in a new, critical way: far from showing that utopia can be reached, they show the critical process necessary for the education of desire, in accord with the function of critical dystopias.

Set in a very distant future, Reeve's *Mortal Engines* uses space and places as the founding metaphors of his novel. He portrays a post-nuclear society where extreme mobility seems to be the common answer to survival. The story takes place several centuries after the 'Sixty Minute War' that has destroyed Western civilization as we know it (2001: p. 7), and presents a new world order with a 'steampunk' feel where the earth is divided into two main factions: those who follow 'Municipal Darwinism', whose cities are built on tiered platforms powered by huge caterpillar treads; and those who belong to the 'Anti-Traction League', whose villages are firmly grounded on earth. The novel's disorienting opening reveals a displacing, unsettling world order where the strong literally eat the weak:

> It was natural that cities ate towns, just as the towns ate smaller towns, and smaller towns snapped up the miserable static settlements. That was Municipal Darwinism, and it was the way the world had worked for hundreds of years, ever since the great engineer Nikolas Quirke had turned London into the first Traction City. (Reeve, 2001: p. 10)

In this extremely mobile future, however, where survival is dependent on moving, there is very little mobility as regards one's identity. It is a tiered world, where each layer corresponds to one's place in society. Thus, the city of London appears as

> a moving mountain of metal which rose in seven tiers like the layers of a wedding cake, the lower levels wreathed in engine-smoke, the villas of the rich gleaming white on the higher decks, and above it all the cross on top of St Paul's Cathedral glinting gold, two thousand feet above the ruined earth. (Reeve, 2001: pp. 3–4)

Both the philosophy and the spatial organization on which the new world order is fashioned serve to maintain inequalities: on the one hand, the survival of the fittest cities, on the other, a hierarchical division of space according to economic status.

This dystopian setting, however, is not perceived as such by the novel's young protagonist, Tom Natsworthy. Born and bred in the great city of London, and despite his status as a Third Class Apprentice in the Historian's Guild, Tom appears from the very beginning as a naïve young man who is content with what life has in store for him. The other protagonist, a hideously disfigured girl named Hester Shaw, is, in contrast, the dystopian misfit. It is only through the encounter with Hester and the series of extraordinary adventures they share that Tom starts to realize that things are not always as they appear. Shoved out of the city by his hero, Head Historian Thaddeus Valentine, Tom sets out on a quest for survival with Hester; as they repeatedly face death, they come into contact with a variety of characters, including pirates, slavers, and the resistance, that shake Tom's foundations and broaden his horizon, albeit against his own wishes at times. Thus, the seemingly perfect London appears to him as flawed, whereas the despised Anti-Traction League seems to be a more tolerant place than he had expected.

But Tom's and Hester's painful journey through the Out-Country reveals to the reader, if not directly to the characters, yet another feature of this future world: Municipal Darwinism and its 'spatial distribution of hierarchical power relations' account also for an 'active criminalization of urban poverty' (Gupta & Ferguson, 1992: p. 8; MacLeod & Ward, 2002: p. 163). Once out of the seemingly gated communities maintained by Municipal Darwinism, the poor are forced to commit crimes in order to survive. Furthermore, societal economic structure and its spatial organization are responsible for an exclusionary version of citizenship (see Holston & Appadurai, 1996). In Reeve's imagined future, in fact, slavery still exists and Tom and Hester have to defend themselves from the risk of becoming slaves.

At the end of their adventures, Tom and Hester find themselves disillusioned and without a place to go. London is mostly destroyed and Batmunkh Gompa, the vertical city-headquarters of the Anti-Traction League, is still too culturally distant for Tom to accept living there. They choose a non-space, the 'Bird Roads', to go somewhere far away as long as they can go together (Reeve, 2001: p. 293). Far from having reached utopia, the two protagonists have, however, altered their perspectives and modes of existence. The process of education works for the character and even more so for the readers who through the novel's narrative strategies know more than Tom and Hester do. Utopia may have not been reached, but the journey continues and the protagonists are now better equipped for a critical understanding of their respective worlds and of what is necessary to reach human fulfilment.

A similar and yet different journey of education lies at the heart of Anderson's *Feed*. The narrating voice belongs to Titus, a self-conscious young man who thinks of himself as being stupid but is actually the shallow product of a dysfunctional and culturally impoverished society, where writing is obsolete, reading is pointless, and art is absent. Although Titus represents that society's average teenager obsessed with materialism, he is, unlike his friends, capable of thinking about – if not altogether caring for or completely understanding – what is happening. He inhabits a bleak future, where wealthy individuals are hooked up from birth to 'the feed', a kind of computer chip that connects them to a global network through brain implantation. With minimal extrapolation from our current world, Anderson imagines that the feed enables instant wireless messaging and updates users on entertainment possibilities and commercial and social trends, responding to an individual's every thought with targeted advertising. Hence, thoughts and desires are constantly monitored by corporate interests, making this future a grotesque, materialist utopia: the feed 'knows everything you want and hope for, sometimes before you even know what those things are.... It can tell you how to get them, and help you make buying decisions that are hard' (Anderson, 2002: p. 48). It informs teenagers and adults about everything that is fashionable, forcing them to buy just for the sake of buying, with an unprecedented speed. In this future world of instant gratification, trends come and go instantaneously, exemplified by Titus's remark about two of his girl friends who go off to the bathroom during a party 'because hairstyles had changed' (2002: p. 20).

While Titus, despite his self-consciousness, is mostly at ease with his world, Violet clearly represents the dystopian misfit. As she appears to Titus as 'the most beautiful girl [...] ever', she also strikes him as different, an individual amid a society of conformists: 'she was watching our stupidity' (Anderson, 2002: p. 13). Her manners and language set her apart as a critical and independent thinker, so much so that at one point in their troubled relationship Titus tells her that 'it sometimes feels like you're watching us, instead of being us' (2002: p. 168). While the young of this impoverished world go to 'School^{TM}', Violet is home schooled and did not get the feed implanted in her brain until she was seven years old. Her parents' choices are a sign of resistance but also a reminder of their economic status and, hence, of their diminished citizenship. In fact, Violet and her family also represent the disadvantaged segment of humanity, those who cannot afford the feed and live in the poor sectors of this depleted, decadent society despite their uncommon and exceptional education.

The different spaces inhabited by the two protagonists are an example of how power relations are manifested through spatiality (Gupta & Ferguson, 1992: p. 8) and through the hierarchical division in the society. The distance between them is more than geographical; it is also material and cultural. Titus and his friends live in semi-gated communities: suburbs are stacked on top of each other, the poorer ones at the bottom. In the affluent sections of society, each house is its own 'privotopia' (MacKenzie, 1994), built in a 'bubble' under a protective dome, with its sun, artificial wind, and choice of season. Spatial distribution becomes then one more way in which inequalities are maintained and the rich try to compensate for the nearing end of civilization in a world where there are no forests left, the sea is dead, hair falls out in chunks, and strange lesions are starting to appear on people's skin.

Despite their different cultural and material backgrounds, Titus and Violet become friends. Their relationship is aided by the absence of the feed; shortly after they meet on vacation on the moon, they are attacked by a terrorist hacker in a nightclub and, as a result, they are temporarily disconnected from the feed. It is at this point that what looks like a tragic moment in Titus's life – he is left without the feed – becomes instead 'one of the greatest days of [his] life' but also the beginning of a painful education (Anderson, 2002: p. 57). The attack turns out to be much more dangerous for Violet, who slowly starts losing control of her basic functions and is left with a short amount of time to live. So begins a period of education for Titus as Violet shares with him what she knows and what she thinks and her plans to resist the feed. 'They try to figure out who you are, and to make you conform to one of their types for easy marketing,' says an excited Violet to an indifferent Titus. 'What I'm doing, what I've been doing over the feed for the last two days, is trying to create a customer profile that's so screwed, no one can market to it. I'm not going to let them catalog me' (2002: pp. 97–98). Titus's response to Violet's ideas fluctuates: at times he goes along with her just for the fun of it, at other times he seems to understand her intentions.

Titus's educational journey is signalled by his continuous movement between space and places: throughout the book he goes back and forth between his and his friends' privotopias and Violet's suburb, seemingly unaffected by what he sees or the fragments of news he hears from the feed. Titus never seems to close or reduce the distance between the two worlds. One scene in particular seems to encompass this spatial metaphor, where Titus is standing in his room and Violet stands just outside. They remain frozen for a moment and no crossing, no trespassing occurs, until – as usual – it is Violet who takes the first step (Anderson, 2002: p. 257). Thus, Titus's identity does not seem to be particularly affected by what he learns from Violet, and faced with the daunting task of accompanying Violet in her last days, he does not rise to the occasion. As Violet sends him 'hours' worth' of her memories that her malfunctioning feed is erasing, Titus's reaction is to delete all these memories.

It takes Titus two emotional crises to show something other than indifference: the breakup with Violet and a very harsh confrontation with her father who contacts him as requested by Violet who wanted Titus to know '*when it was over*' (Anderson, 2002: p. 282). It is then that Titus's pain and rage seem to find an outlet and partly break the apathy that characterizes him. The book closes with the protagonist still divided by that spatial distance. At home, his only way to react to what is happening to Violet – and to himself – is by indulging in a compulsory shopping spree, whereas at Violet's deathbed he starts talking to her, trying to become Violet's memory and memorial. The novel's ending seems to suggest that Titus, despite being inarticulate, attempts to enact one of Violet's lessons that links memory to identity: '*I'm afraid I'm going to lose my past. Who are we, if we don't have a past? ... I'm going to tell you everything. Some day, I might want you to tell it back to me*' (2002: p. 253, emphasis in original). Together with a series of 'strange facts' that Violet used to research and enjoy, Titus begins to tell her stories and in the act of storytelling he also tries to resist the feed:

> I tried to talk just to her. I tried not to listen to the noise on the feed, the girls in wet shirts offering me shampoo. I told her stories. They were only a sentence long, each one of them. That's all I knew how to find. So I told her broken stories. The little pieces of broken stories I could find. I told her what I could. (2002: p. 296)

But if he can only offer her fragments of stories, he also tries to re-member Violet and to reconstitute her dis-membered body through the act of remembering and storytelling:

> There's one story I'll keep telling you. I'll keep telling it. You're the story. I don't want you to forget. When you wake up, I want you to remember yourself. I'm going to remember. You're still there, as long as I can remember you. As long as someone knows you. ... This is the story.
> And for the first time, I started crying.
> I cried, sitting by her bed, and I told her the story of us. 'It's about the feed,' I said. 'It's about this meg normal guy, who doesn't think about anything until one wacky day, when he meets a dissident with a heart of gold. ... Set against the backdrop of America in its final days, it's the high-spirited story of their love together, it's laugh-out-loud funny, really

heartwarming, and a visual feast. ... Together, the two crazy kids grow, have madcap escapades, and learn an important lesson about love. They learn to resist the feed. Rated PG-13. For language, ... and mild sexual situations'. (2002: pp. 298–99)

Having deleted her memories, this heap of broken recollections, this simplified story is all Titus can offer to honour Violet's memory. But in his storytelling he rewrites Violet's futile resistance and his own failure to break free from the constraints of society. He uses a creative, utopian nostalgia to imagine what could have been, to desire an alternative ending, and, in so doing, his actions are consistent with Walter Benjamin's notion of an empowering, redemptive memory: 'every image of the past that is not recognized by the present as one of its own concerns threatens to disappear irretrievably' (1992: p. 247).[4]

If we think about Titus's overall apathy, it is hard to assess to what extent he has learned throughout this harrowing, emotional journey. The novel provides no information as to whether he has permanently crossed the boundary between his and Violet's world or if, once he returns to his part of society, he will give in to the feed and the pressure to conform and forget the story he has promised to keep telling. Nevertheless, Violet's act of resistance and Titus's storytelling constitute a utopian experiment that disrupts the perception of the present and attempts to offer an alternative set of values. Despite the fact that it may still be a failure for the protagonists, the novel's epistemological process positions readers to adopt a more critical awareness of their own world as well as of the society portrayed in the novel.

The imagination and articulation of a temporal and spatial elsewhere provides the basis for cognitive estrangement,[5] consciousness raising, and the epistemological processes that are distinguishing features of the utopian genre. In particular, in dystopias, the spatial distribution accounts for the maintenance of social inequality, an exclusionary version of citizenship, and the erosion of spatial justice. In Reeve's and Anderson's novels, the female characters represent the misfit citizens: displaced from the very beginning for different reasons, they are more aware and critical than their respective male companions. These young men are educated into displacement and critique of the societies they inhabit through their experiences with the young women, their interpersonal relations with them, and the physical and psychological journeys they undertake. Utopia is neither reached nor accomplished at the end of the novels, but a utopian dimension is maintained for the readers and is fostered through hope and what Levitas has called the education of desire. Thus utopia's function is not just that of promoting change, it becomes one of developing criticism and the education of desire. Such a process entails the achievement of a critical perspective on our own world and an understanding of what is necessary to begin to articulate our desires for a change to the inequities of our societies. The encounter with an imperfect, botched utopian experiment serves to 'create a space in which the reader is both brought to experience an alternative and called to judgement on it' (Levitas, 2007: p. 56).

Conclusion

The texts we have considered in this chapter exemplify some of the ways in which space, place, and journeys function in literature for young people. When protagonists move across and between places, they also traverse cultural differences, value systems, and interpersonal relations. To make sense of the interplay of space, place, and identity we have called upon a range of theories drawn from cultural geography, postcolonial studies, and utopian studies. In doing so we have been concerned not merely to import these concepts into our analysis of textuality but to model how they can be put to work so as to inform readings of children's texts, recognizing that these texts seek to socialize children and induct them into ways of thinking about themselves and their world.

When Max returns to 'the night of his very own room' (Sendak, 1963: unpaged) at the end of *Where the Wild Things Are*, he is both the same as and different from the Max sent to his room without any supper at the opening of the narrative. Whether real or imagined, his journey to another place has subtly altered his subjectivity. Places are never neutral or empty but are infused with histories, memories, and traces of interpersonal relations. Texts for young people pivot on the processes and dynamics whereby humans gain self-knowledge and autonomy in their world; places are crucial to these trajectories, since they constitute a locus for individual and cultural identity, incorporating sensual, aesthetic and emotional dimensions. Sendak's Max is shaped by the places he inhabits and visits as much as he shapes them through his material and symbolic interventions.

Further Readings

Bradford, C. 2007. *Unsettling narratives: postcolonial readings of children's literature*. Wilfrid Laurier University Press: Waterloo, Ontario. Draws upon postcolonial literary theory to inform readings of settler society children's literature from Australia, Canada, New Zealand, and the United States.

Bradford, C., Mallan, K., Stephens, J., & McCallum, R. 2008. 'The struggle to be human in a posthuman world', in *New world orders in contemporary children's literature: utopian transformations*. Palgrave Macmillan: Houndmills.

Hubbard, P., Kitchin, R., & Valentine, G. (eds). 2004. *Key thinkers on space and place*. Sage Publications: London. A useful account of the work of theorists from a variety of disciplinary backgrounds who have contributed to discussions of space and place in culture, society, economics, and politics.

Notes

1   VH1 is a cable network based in New York which hosts popular music videos and music-related programmes.
2   The word 'country' in Aboriginal English refers to land which has traditional significance to a person because of its associations with Dreaming narratives and kinship relationships.
3   Such journeys, from Indigenous to non-Indigenous zones, constitute a common trope in Indigenous fiction, where these journeys commonly model how young protagonists maintain and develop Indigenous subjectivities while engaging with white culture. See Bradford, *Unsettling narratives*, pp. 157–68.
4   On the utopian aspect of nostalgia, see Baccolini, 2007.
5   The term 'cognitive estrangement', coined by Darko Suvin in *Metamorphoses of science fiction* (1979), refers to a key effect of science fiction: that it distances readers from the sf world by foregrounding its difference while simultaneously enabling them to scrutinize their own world from the perspective of an outsider.

3
Local and Global: Cultural Globalization, Consumerism, and Children's Fiction

Elizabeth Bullen and Kerry Mallan

According to Zygmunt Bauman in *Liquid Modernity* (2000), the formerly solid and stable institutions of social life that characterized earlier stages of modernity have become fluid. He sees this as an outcome of the modernist project of progress itself, which in seeking to dismantle oppressive structures failed to reconstruct new roles for society, community, and the individual. The un-tethering of social life from tradition in the latter stages of the twentieth century has produced unprecedented freedoms and unparalleled uncertainties, at least in the West. Although Bauman's elaboration of some of the features and drivers of liquid modernity – increased mobility, rapid communications technologies, individualism – suggests it to be a neologism for globalization, it is arguably also the context which has allowed this phenomenon to flourish. The qualities of fluidity, leakage, and flow that distinguish uncontained liquids also characterize globalization, which encompasses a range of global trends and processes no longer confined to, or controlled by, the 'container' of the nation or state. The concept of liquid modernity helps to explain the conditions under which globalization discourses have found a purchase and, by extension, the world in which contemporary children's literature, media, and culture are produced. Perhaps more significantly, it points to the fluid conceptions of self and other that inform the 'liquid' worldview of the current generation of consumers of texts for children and young adults. This generation is growing up under the phase of globalization we describe in this chapter.

Globalization is a term applied to a complex mix of economic, cultural, political, social, and technological processes that accelerated in the second half of the twentieth century. Its impact transcends national and regional boundaries – although its extent is uneven across the world – leading some to locate globalization within the much longer history of imperialism and colonization. However, the term itself did not come into common usage until after the fall of the Berlin Wall in 1989 (Robertson & White, 2008).

Indeed, it is only since then that the aspects of globalization that have had the strongest influence on contemporary children's and young adult's fictions and their audiences have emerged or crystallized. We use the fall of the Wall to mark a pivotal moment in the globalization process, since it signified not only the end of the Cold War but also the conditions enabling economic globalization.

The metaphorical dismantling of the ideological barrier between communism and capitalism, and the literal freedom to cross the border, heralded a phenomenon that now occurs on a global scale, witnessed in the increased global flows of money, markets, organizations, corporations, individuals, and populations. The fall of the Wall was almost contemporaneous with the election of neoliberal governments in the USA and UK. Neoliberalism alters the role of government and privatizes civil and social well-being for the individual. It also informs globalism, which, according to Steger, 'is a political ideology that endows the concept of globalization with market-oriented norms, values and meanings' (2005: ix). Finally, this historic moment coincided with the technology revolution. Information and communication technologies have been 'instrumental in allowing the implementation of a fundamental process of restructuring of the capitalist system since the 1980s onward', which in turn has shaped the information revolution according to 'the logic and interests of advanced capitalism' (Castells, 1996: p. 13). New technologies are key drivers of the expansion of the global economy and have facilitated the penetration of globalist values into the everyday world of communities and individuals.

While these developments do not exhaust the range of forces under which globalization has escalated, they do help explain how it can be broadly defined as 'the compression of the world into a "single place"' and 'the intensification of consciousness of the world as a whole' (Robertson, 1992: pp. 6, 8). Although geographic distance remains a reality, the time it takes to cross it has been vastly compressed by new modes of transport and communication, including their democratization. Globalization is predicated on new forms of political, economic, and cultural interconnectivity and interdependency, but with contradictory tendencies and tensions between homogenization and heterogeneity, integration and fragmentation, conformity and resistance, global and local. Above all, its impact on countries across the globe is unequal. So, too, is its effect on children and youth, who are variously positioned along axes of agency-exploitation and advantage-disadvantage. In prosperous 'First World' countries, children and youth are the targets of niche marketing, with products and providers jostling for their attention and financial investment. In addition, they are increasingly persuaded to see the importance of consumer products for enacting a meaningful identity in the social world. Meanwhile, in 'sites of cultural diversity and economic inequality' (Stephens & McGillis, 2006: p. 367), young people's access to even basic human rights is often limited by the very forces that produce wealth in so-called advanced economies. Many such young people live in communities seeking both to engage with globalizing pressures for institutional modernization and social change, and to find ways of preserving local identity, customs, and institutions. This is not only an outcome of the interconnectivity of globalization in general, but of cultural globalization in particular, a phenomenon in which the children's literature, media, and culture industries are increasingly implicated. Theories of cultural globalization offer a means of revealing how various globalizing processes are expressed in children's narrative culture: the experiences of protagonists, the identities they construct for themselves, the local, international, and virtual spaces they traverse, and their engagement with the technologies and ideologies of globalization.

This chapter provides a range of theoretical and conceptual strategies that cut through the globalism gloss to reveal some of its key political and social side-effects in the spheres of culture, community, and individual life. Focusing on children's culture, it draws on theories of cultural globalization which are fundamentally concerned with contradictory pressures towards cultural homogenization and heterogeneity to explain some of the ways in which broader globalization processes are translated into narratives. The concepts of McDonaldization, McWorld and Jihad, glocalization, and Arjun Appadurai's notion of the social imaginary and global flows will be used to reveal some of the means by which globalism – but also discourses resistant to it – creates new social formations, interconnections, and ruptures. By attending to the ways a selection of texts attempts to construct youth identity within the context of cultural globalization, readers will be provided with theoretical tools for appreciating the way language constructs textual reality, developing a distrust of totalizing notions such as globalization, neoliberalism, freedom, and equality, and questioning the social, political, and cultural assumptions which underpin the narratives. Before proceeding with a discussion of these narratives, the following provides a brief explanation of the key concepts that underpin our approach.

Globalizing pressures and key concepts

The idea that the world is becoming a 'single place' suggests a process of integration that opens up the possibility of global cooperation; globalist discourses anticipate greater freedom, equality, and prosperity for all. Both of these future projections are belied by the current reality. At issue here is the disjunction between *'globalization from above'* and *'globalization from below'*. Richard Falk defines the former as 'a set of forces and legitimating ideas' – outlined in our introduction – 'that is in many respects located beyond the effective reach of territorial authority and has enlisted most governments as tacit partners' (1999: p. 130). The latter term refers to the disparate material conditions and responses globalization from above produces at the local levels of nation, community, and individual, and the new ethical, humanitarian, and environmental dilemmas it creates. Awareness of these top-down forces is an essential foundation for understanding the theories of cultural globalization we mobilize in this chapter. As Tomlinson (1999: p. 2) explains, it is necessary to understand the 'sources' of globalization in order 'to interpret its implication across the various spheres of human existence', in this instance, children's culture.

'Culture' encompasses the shared beliefs, values, traditions, and practices of social groups, be they institutional, ethnic, or national, as well as the symbolic and material artefacts, texts, and rituals through which shared meanings are mediated. Conventionally, culture has been aligned with nationality and ethnicity, and, in its origins at least, the territory of the nation-state. Under globalization, the economic, political, and cultural life of the state is becoming de-territorialized, blurring local and global, domestic and foreign. Although nation-states still exist as bordered territories, they are being 'denationalized' as a result of being 'criss-crossed and undermined' by a range of transnational processes, actors, and forces (Beck, 2000: p. 11). Theorists of cultural globalization are principally concerned with how these processes, forces, and actors produce shared, divergent, and divided global cultural forms and meanings.

Among the most powerful of the transnational actors are multinational corporations, which are neither bound by the borders of nations and states nor invested in the broader social well-being and sustainability of the countries in which they operate. Rather, their interests 'are directly tied to the outcomes of globalization' (Thomas, 2008: p. 85), in respect both to production and consumption. Under conditions of increased market competition and free trade, much of the manufacturing to supply the First World has been outsourced to the Third World, where transnational corporations can avail themselves of low labour costs and cheap resources, and bypass national systems of labour protection, including those prohibiting child labour. At the same time, multinational corporations continually seek new global markets, not only for goods and services but cultural commodities and consumer experiences that provide resources for identity and lifestyle construction and community building: films, fashion, music, toys, gadgets, games, and foods. Local cultures, including children's culture, are no longer tied to the nation-state; rather, they variously reflect, resist, and accommodate the top-down, homogenizing force of transnational cultural corporatism and the globalization of consumer culture.

The idea that world culture is becoming homogenized is informed by understandings of the cultural hegemony of the First World in general – Westernization – and the United States in particular – Americanization, one aspect of which George Ritzer (1993) calls *McDonaldization*. According to Ritzer, the McDonald's corporation is more than a model for transnational corporate business practices; it is a metaphor for the standardization, technologization, commodification, and rationalization of contemporary life. McDonald's influence is evident in the expanding range of global franchises, not just the fast food industry, but medical, financial, educational, childcare, shopping chains, and television shows with flow-on effects for culture and society. However, if McDonaldization originated in America, its strategies have been adopted internationally. The Hello Kitty franchise is a case in point. Coining a similar term, *McWorld*, Benjamin Barber argues that the pressure towards cultural homogenization and universalization evokes its antithesis, *Jihad*. McWorld refers to 'a commercially homogenous global network', the cultural template of which is American popular culture, 'constructed as image exports creating a common taste around common logos, advertising slogans, stars, songs, brand names, jingles and trademarks' (Barber, 1996: p. 17). Jihad, by contrast, refers to the reactionary and tribal ethno-nationalisms of 'states and, to an ever greater degree, subnational factions in permanent rebellion against uniformity and integration' (2002: pp. 191, 196). Not to be conflated with Islam, Jihad is territorial in origin, 'an emblem of identity [and] an expression of community' (Barber, 2002: p. 197) and a manifestation of the amplified consciousness of cultural difference under globalization. Two further positions exist between these two alarming extremes.

Cultural globalization 'is chaotic rather than orderly – it is integrated and connected so that the meanings of its components are "relativitized" to one another, not unified or centralized' (Waters, 2002: p. 215). Roland Robertson (1995) argues that the homogenizing force of the global, and the heterogenizing effects of the local and specific – facets of globalization from above and from below, respectively – are in fact 'complementary and interpenetrative'. His theory of *'glocalisation'* helps to explain the influence of the global on local cultures and markets, and how the local inflects the working of globalization. In spite of offering a less polarized account of the relation between local and global cultures, glocalization does not act to moderate the march of global capitalism and the expansion of consumer culture. Glocalization facilitates the development of diverse micromarkets, the creation of niche products, and modes of marketing contextualized by, and calculated to appeal to, local and individualized tastes, preferences, and circumstances. In addition, Robertson's theory of glocalization appears to be predicated upon assumptions that local means non-Western and global means Western.

In his influential essay 'Disjuncture and Difference in the Global Cultural Economy' (1990), Arjun Appadurai engages with the debates concerning the nature of heterogenizing or homogenizing effects of global cultural flows, and suggests a terminological shift. He employs the metaphor of *scapes* to explain the complex dialogic construction of social environments through which information, technology, people, money, and ideas move. Like physical landscapes, scapes are 'deeply perspectival constructs, inflected very much by the historical, linguistic and political situatedness of different sorts of actors' (1990: p. 296). Appadurai identifies five scapes to capture the global flows of people (ethnoscape), technology (technoscape), capital (financescape), images (mediascape), and ideologies (ideoscape). He provides a model of the disjunctive scapes through which subjects shift, experiencing and constituting diverse conditions of larger formations, be they members of multinational companies, nation states, diasporic communities, or intimate face-to-face groups.

The remainder of this chapter offers a series of readings of children's and young adult film, novels, and picture books that are informed by theories of cultural globalization and elaborates on them. Organized into two main sections, *Commodities, community and identity*, and *Spatiality, technology and virtual tourism*, it seeks to provide insights into the impact of globalization on the marketization of children's texts and culture, and their engagements with the 'local' and 'global'. More specifically, it examines some of the ways in which globalization and globalism rearticulate the perennial preoccupations of texts for young people, including identity, community, and equality, as well as the ways in which children's texts attempt to account for the altered spatial and technological dimensions of globalization – with the caveat that the texts we analyse have been produced by First World creators, in English, for an implied Western audience.

Commodities, community, and identity

Understood in relation to global economic markets and marketing, cultural globalization is frequently equated with the commodification of culture in general and the expansion of consumer culture in particular. In terms of young people's culture, the history of its alliance with the market is much older than globalization. The precedent for McDonald's Happy Meal toys was set long ago by the sale or promotion of tie-in products with eighteenth-/ nineteenth-century children's books and periodicals. Nonetheless, the surge in market interest in the child- and youth-market segments in the late-1980s and the intensification in the hybridization of advertising and children's books, media, and culture coincide with the acceleration of globalization. Supported by a range of marketing strategies, including character marketing, licensed merchandizing, cross-marketing, and product placement in children's film, TV, and books, advertising and entertainment have become de-differentiated and the pleasures of entertainment and the pleasures of consumption conflated (see Kenway & Bullen, 2001). Children's media culture products function as advertising not only for their own 'brands', they are used by national and transnational corporations to market an array of unrelated goods and services, fast food chains and junk food products not least among them.

In the case of children's films, this is increasingly becoming a global phenomenon, with the worldwide release of major motion pictures coinciding with the promotion of tie-in products by transnational corporations such as Coca Cola, PepsiCo, Nintendo, and Sony. The Dreamworks film, *Over the Hedge* (2006) for instance, functions as an advertisement for the Playstation, Xbox and online games created to capitalize on its success. In addition to licensed merchandise including plush toys, the film's release coincided with promotions by major marketing partners Wal-Mart and Wendy's in the USA. At the time of writing, the film's official web site was promoting Hostess food products, including Twinkies, Ho Hos and Cupcakes. As this suggests, consumer culture increasingly involves a convergence of technology, marketing, entertainment, and consumption. These marketing strategies are reproduced on a global scale because they are successful; they depend on the principle that the desire for one product promotes desire for another in a cycle that is repeated with the release of each new media product. Or, as Beryl Langer observes, because 'Each act of consumption is a beginning rather than an end, the first or next step in an endless series...the moment of possession is the beginning of desire' (2002: p. 70).

Over the hedge and under the radar

The marketing of *Over the Hedge* (2006) would seem nothing out of the ordinary were it not for the fact that the film ostensibly cautions children against consumer excess, a theme apparently reinforced by the avoidance of explicit product placement (although it is difficult not to assume that the stackable Spuddies potato chips are Pringles). In fact, the film's references to toys and technological gadgets, to soft drinks, corn chips, and potato crisps do not need brand names to promote consumption. When transnational corporations buy up companies across the world, they often retain the original branding, as in the case with PepsiCo, which owns Lays Chips (USA), Walker Crisps (UK), Smith Crisps (Australia), and Sabritas (Mexico). In *Over the Hedge*, it is not the brand, but 'the moment of possession [that] is the beginning of desire' for its consumer savvy 'star', the racoon RJ, and for its consumer innocents, a clutch of small woodland animals, to whom he introduces junk food.

The reiterative nature of consumer desire is established in the opening sequence of the film and drives the plot. Unable to extract a packet of Nacho corn chips from a vending machine, RJ sets out to steal junk food from Vincent. Intending to take only what he needs from the hibernating bear's stash, RJ is unable to resist stealing all of it. Indeed, he is unable to resist the can of Spuddies the sleeping bear is holding because, as the advertising slogan for the product indicates, 'One taste is never enough'. This is his undoing: bear is woken, his food destroyed, and RJ is given an ultimatum to replace it (and Vincent's trailer and cooler) within the week or die. Unable to do so single-handedly, the raccoon tricks the woodland creatures into helping him steal the replacement goods. This 'family' – consisting of possums, hedgehogs, a squirrel, a skunk, and headed by a turtle, Verne – is initially resistant to venture 'over the hedge' into the unfamiliar territory of the sub-urban estate built during their 'hibernation'. They are only persuaded to assist RJ when he pops a bag of Nacho corn chips and the cloud of artificial flavours and colours that covers them induces a euphoria that is the begin-ning of their own consumer desire.

The ensuing narrative follows the havoc created by the animals' forays into the suburbs, their betrayal by RJ, and his subsequent redemption. In the process, it cautions against junk food and satirizes the homogenization of suburban life, emphasizing the importance of family and community over consumer desire. The movie also alludes to the environmental impact of modernity. These, at least, are the surface 'messages' of this computer-generated animated film, and Jill Hinkins' (2007) extended analysis of *Over the Hedge* (2006) examines some of the ways in which the film undermines its own anti-consumerist theme. We therefore ask: what does a cultural glo-balization perspective add to a reading of the film? In the following, we draw on the concepts of McDonaldization and McWorld to examine the links between consumption and community the film constructs.

There are no Golden Arches in El Rancho Camelot, but the estate evokes the principles that characterize McDonaldization. The indistinguishable McMansions have clearly been efficiently assembled if the timeline in *Over the Hedge* (2006) is any indication. These houses are super-sized, standard-ized, and advertised, which is what RJ also does when he describes the hedge separating wilderness and suburbia as 'The gateway to the good life'. The effect of standardization is conveyed by the aerial views of the housetops, uniformly manicured gardens, and spacious streets. Even the animation of the human characters creates a quality of simulacra or airbrushed same-ness, despite the momentary appearance of an African American family. The Disneyfied quality of simulation is further evoked when Dwayne, the 'Verminator' brought in to exterminate the marauding forest creatures, tar-gets animal garden statues by mistake. However, the critique of the homog-enizing forces of McDonaldization and its excesses is not as clear-cut as it may initially seem.

The film's warning against the excesses of consumer culture and the McDonaldization of social life is almost exclusively conveyed through the one character, Gladys, autocratic president of the Residents' Association and the nemesis of the animal characters. What distinguishes her from both groups is the fact that she does not have a family. As a single woman, her supersized McMansion, her SUV, massive plasma TV, and gleaming stain-less steel double fridge are clearly excessive to one person's needs. In this respect, *Over the Hedge* (2006) considerably weakens its satire of suburban consumer excess by confining its critique to the one 'evil' character. This narrative strategy also mutes the film's probably unintentional commentary on global flows of peoples, and the clash of cultures between the West and the rest, between the ideologies of McWorld and what Barber calls Jihad, directed at a very young audience.

At the same time as globalization creates a movement towards a homogenous McWorld, it produces an opposing retreat to tradition and nation, magnifying awareness of global diversity, difference, and the inequalities created by uneven economic development. De-territorialization creates a world in which borders and boundaries have become permeable, a characteristic evoked by the hedge in the movie. Cultural traditions, practices, and identity are subject to the influences not only of the global media but the increased mobility of individuals and populations. In the McWorld of *Over the Hedge* (2006), such mobility leads to chaos in the suburbs and disharmony within the tribe of forest animals. It alters the animals' traditional way of life: only a week is needed to amass junk food to last the winter, not 274 days of foraging. Their simpler, less technological way of life is undermined by the instant gratification of McWorld, as is Verne's role as patriarch of the group. Viewers are clearly positioned to identify with the animal characters, enjoy their slapstick raids on the riches of El Rancho Camelot, and to condemn Gladys for bringing in the Verminator, Dwayne, who uses various high-tech weapons of 'mass extermination' against the creatures 'terrorising' the suburbs. However, in situating the clash of cultures between (anthropomorphized) animals and humans, the narrative offers no alternative to Verne and his tribe, now including RJ, other than to retreat to their natural 'state' (territory) and a traditional way of life in the forest. This not only excludes them from the plenty of McWorld, but also denies the implied viewer a position from which to enact a comparable resistance to consumer excess.

The marketization of resistant identities

The drive to expand the global market economy has propelled 'multinational capital into every facet of daily life and phase of the life cycle, turning things once done by families, friends, and neighbours into commodified services, and reconstituting "life stages" as market categories' (Langer, 2002: p. 69). The child and youth demographics constitute among the most lucrative of these age-segmented markets, with their own entertainment, magazines, fashion, toys, and celebrities. As child and youth cultures of consumption have grown, they have become increasingly subject to rapid 'cycles of fashion and obsolescence'. Their cultural commodities have become what Langer (2002: p. 70) calls 'commoditoys', products 'characterised by their capacity to stimulate rather than satisfy longing [and a] short but intense "shelf life" as objects of desire'. To the extent that 'satiation is endlessly postponed', commoditoys undermine young people's 'sense of sufficiency' and intensify the 'nexus between identity and consumption' (Langer, 2002: pp. 69, 70).

McWorld contributes to this phenomenon, but when it comes to the nexus between identity and the marketing of brands to young adults, it is clear that another process is in play. On the surface at least, youth culture eschews the standardization and predictability of 'McDonaldized' products and services in favour of the novel and new in order to construct a sense of self and peer belonging that is itself often tribal in its assertion of cultural differentiation. In reality, contemporary young people lack sovereignty over the formation of their culture. According to Naomi Klein, this is a generation for whom

> identity has largely been a pre-packaged good and for whom the search for self has always been shaped by marketing hype, whether or not they believed it or defined themselves against it. This is a side effect of brand expansion that is far more difficult to track and quantify than the branding of culture ... ; it is the colonization not of physical space but of mental space. (Klein, 2000: p. 66)

The effects of youth 'brand expansion' are difficult to track precisely because the principles of McDonaldization do not apply, at least not overtly. Taking a leaf from Klein's book, *No Logo*, Scott Westerfeld's *So Yesterday* (2004) explores the operations of transnational corporations, marketing, and advertising in an urban youth mystery story. It aims to expose the subterfuges of 'cool hunting' and 'culture jamming', which promote and subvert consumer cultural globalization, and provide examples of globalization from above and below, respectively.

Seventeen-year-old Hunter is a cool hunter employed by an advertising and marketing agency which has a transnational sporting goods corporation, thinly disguised as Nike, as a major client. Employed by market research consultancies, cool hunters infiltrate the youth 'in-crowd' in search of innovative style and cutting-edge cool. This information is used by brands to style and advertise their products as the next new trend. According to Hunter, however, it is not just the brands that need cool hunters, so does the consumer: 'you need us. Someone has to guide you, to mold you, to make sure today turns into yesterday on schedule. ... It's not like you can start making your own decisions, after all' (Westerfeld, 2004: p. 1). His later description of the consumer style pyramid links youth consumption, identity, and the pursuit of cool: the innovator who thinks up the styling on top, followed by the trendsetter who makes the manufactured product cool, the early adopter, the consumer, and the laggard. Consumers are 'The people who have to see a product on TV, placed in two movies, fifteen magazine ads, and on a giant rack in the mall before saying "Hey, that's pretty cool." At which point it's not' (p. 20). By then, the next trend is already making its way down the pyramid, and a new cycle of fashion of obsolescence has begun.

Although youth commodity culture also hybridizes entertainment and consumption, it distinguishes itself from child consumer culture in micromarketing to an array of youth identity categories based on lifestyle activities such as basketball, surfing and inline skating. *So Yesterday* foregrounds the corporate appropriation of American street culture, in particular the skate park, as prime cool hunting territory. It also points to the seduction of young people who, in accepting sponsorship and gifts of logo-emblazoned clothing, skates, and related paraphernalia, become walking advertisements for brand name products. From a globalization perspective, this suggests that innovation begins at the level of the local – it is co-protagonist Jen's innovation with shoelaces that attracts Hunter's attention and leads to their friendship – and it is the role of corporations, marketers, and the viral marketing performed by trendsetters to co-opt local youth cultures and exploit them globally.

Culture jamming is the term used to describe attempts to subvert the commodification of culture and cultural space, not least through parody of the advertisements and logos that have proliferated in public space. In *So Yesterday*, the jammers are referred to as the anti-Client and, in the process of tracking them down, Hunter and Jen uncover their various strategies of subversion, including a hoax product launch, a fake issue of a magazine, and the creation of a training shoe with the Nike swoosh logo cut through with the bar sinister, the symbol of prohibition, which in this case signifies no logo. These strategies are designed to destabilize consumer culture as a resource for identity construction. However, Westerfeld's novel is by no means a no logo zone, nor are the commodities of cool only American. *So Yesterday* avoids brand names, but not their identifiers: Hunter trials a new Nokia phone (Finnish), Tina Catalina has a fetish for Hello Kitty (Japanese), and Jen rides in a 'single-advertiser' train carriage advertising Swatch watches (Swiss).

As Emma Wortley notes, part of the ambiguity of *So Yesterday*'s activism is created by the linguistic play involved in the encoding and decoding of global brands in which Hunter and the implied reader engage. This playfulness may 'valoris[e] media and consumer culture' (Wortley, 2009: p. 284); it may also be part of a larger narrative strategy which, like culture jamming and its appropriation of the tools of marketing, is used for the purposes of subversion. Coolness, the elusive object of youthful desire in general, and of Hunter in particular, is also a quality of the culture jamming anti-Client. However, in seeking to avoid spoiling the pleasures young people take in consumer culture with overt didacticism, it evades the uncool reality behind the globalization of consumer culture. With the exception of a passing reference to the controversies about Third World sweatshops and child labour in which Nike was implicated in the 1990s, its focus on the market manipulation of the First World young consumer is designed to appeal to the reader's sense of individual autonomy, not an ethical or political awareness of the global community.

Glocalizing consumer culture

In deploying cool to sell its activist message to young adults, the rhetoric of *So Yesterday* arguably parallels 'the broader promotional rhetoric of the children's culture industry', which in 'deploying the "magic", "innocence" and "enchantment" of childhood to sell things, ... reinforces the belief that children should be "protected" from the market' (Langer, 2002: p. 75). By market, Langer means the sphere of production, or what Lee calls 'the night-time of the commodity: the mysterious economic dark side of social exploitation which is so effectively concealed in the dazzling glare of the market-place' (1993: p. 15). At stake here are not only the interconnections between consumption and production, but between pleasure and plenty and suffering and deprivation, which have evolved alongside economic and cultural globalization. Elizabeth Laird's novel, *The Garbage King* (2003), seeks to show some of these interconnections.

The Garbage King describes the experiences of two adolescent boys who briefly live together on the streets of Addis Ababa. Impoverished orphan Mamo has been sold into slavery and recently escaped his brutal master. He meets Dani, a sheltered boy from a private school who has run away from his strict father, when they both seek refuge in a cemetery. Through the strategies of alternating narrative events and shifting focalization, *The Garbage King* contrasts their lives and their experiences as members of a gang of street children. Underscoring the disparities between wealth and poverty across the binaries of urban and rural life, tradition and modernity, individual and community, it links the implications for children with the aftermath of civil war and famine in the nation-state. Interpreted through the lens of cultural glocalization, however, the narrative uncritically accedes to the broader forces of globalizing modernization and, moreover, betrays an undercurrent of globalist neoliberalism that becomes explicit in the closure of the novel.

The narrative begins shortly after the death of Mamo's mother. While his sister, Tiggist, is out at work in a shop, an opportunistic trader of child slaves lures the boy away with promises of a job, and then sells him to a farmer. Mamo's trauma, however, is not so much a result of the separation from his family, but dislocation. He is a city boy, unaccustomed to traditional rural life and afraid of lions and hyenas. He trades stories of modern urban life – TV and buses – for the other herd boys' local knowledge: how to tend cattle and to tell when the prickly pears are ripe. For Mamo, the countryside might as well be a foreign country and, from his point of view, it is a 'dump' where 'Everyone's always hungry' (p. 54). His perspective, reinforced by the wonder of the herd boys, Hailu and Yohannes, at the technologies of the metropolis, suggests modernization and westernization to be superior to the local and traditional. This is in spite of the novel's attempts to avert a cause and effect relationship between traditional life in Ethiopia and Mamo's exploitation and abuse.

When Mamo attempts suicide after a beating from his master, Yohannes's family nurses him back to health. Their kindness functions as a counterpoint to the cruelty of Mamo's master's family. Yohannes's father provides context for his neighbour's purchase of the boy – the death by drowning of his elder son, the inhumane treatment he metes out, and crop losses due to the impact of drought, fire, and flood. These explanations link the stresses of traditional rural life in Ethiopia with the vicissitudes of nature and its risks. Insofar as the narrative connects human trade to larger forces, it is as an outcome of the recent history of the nation-state. Significant as this may be, it ignores how the larger forces of globalization are localized, producing conditions that might make it difficult for small-scale agriculture, and potentially creating a market for child slaves. In other words, the narrative depicts but does not interrogate the effects of economic globalization as it is experienced from below.

The majority of the novel is set in Addis Ababa, where the contradictory tendencies of cultural globalization are overt. Its glocalized inflections signify the uneven processes of modernization, cosmopolitanism, and westernization that produce extremes of wealth and poverty. The lifestyles of the street children point to the heterogenizing impact of cultural globalization on the local: the gang functions as a local subculture split off from society. Dani's access to Western cultural and consumer commodities reflects the homogenizing tendencies of cultural globalization. However, with the exception of household servants, the signifiers of his privilege seem modest by Western standards: owning a pair of trainers, a baseball cap, or having money for a Coke. Insofar as they would be taken for granted by implied readers, the novel offers the reader a subject-position from which to interrogate Dani's privilege, but also his revulsion at the degradations of street life. In doing so, however, the novel emphasizes the suffering of poverty rather than its structural relationship to wealth, depoliticizing the links between Dani's westernized lifestyle and the garbage, waste, and excess of consumer culture on which the street children survive.

Globalization allows a freer circulation of 'things', but a more controlled circulation of people, as *Over the Hedge* (2006) also implies. This is reflected not only by the fact that the street boys occupy a world of gutters and garbage dumps, but through their awareness of not being able to gain entry to shops and businesses, a recurring motif in *The Garbage King* (2003). They experience cultural glocalization from the 'outside', their status brought into relief by the fact that Dani's first meal away from home is as an 'insider'. Hungry and lost, but well-dressed and with money in his pocket, he finds himself in the city centre. He recalls his mother's words as he passes the Ethiopia Hotel: 'The old Ethiopia? But it's so *dowdy*. No one goes there any more, not since the new Sheraton opened' (p. 96, emphasis in original). Ironically, Dani feels more at home in an international hotel chain eating club sandwiches, French Fries, and Coke than in the street bar serving *injera*, a traditional pancake eaten in place of bread. Mamo, by contrast, almost misses out on the ubiquitous truck-stop breakfast of fried eggs to which his truck driver rescuer treats him. The waitress warns the boy to move away from the door, telling him, 'They don't let beggars in here. Hop it' (2003: p. 107).

A more potent and poignant allusion to cultural glocalization occurs through the repeated allusion to the Bob Marley and the Wailers song, 'Survival'. This is Mamo's favourite song, he sings lines from it at various points in the narrative, but it is only when Dani translates the English lyrics into Amharic that he understands the words: 'We're the survivors! Yes! / The black survivors!' One of the gang, Getachew, misunderstands the cultural cue as American, prancing about and exclaiming, 'Look at me! I'm like a Black American! Hey, Rasta! Give me five!' (2003: p. 198). In fact, Marley was Jamaican and the term Rastafari derives from the Amharic title of the last Emperor of Ethiopia, Haile Selassie. The fact that none of the characters appears to be aware of this signals the way in which cultural globalization detaches goods from their original cultural context, commodifies them, and sells them back to the source culture. The added irony is that Rasta promotes an Afrocentric ideology, which, as the lyrics of 'Survival' suggest, rejects westernization. In spite of this, *The Garbage King* finally promotes a Western liberal humanist – indeed globalist – solution to the problems of glocalization it realizes.

This solution is in spite of the unsympathetic portrayal of Dani's father. Ato Paulos has transformed himself from the boy who didn't wear his first pair of shoes until he was twelve – a biographical detail that links him with the street children – to a cosmopolitan businessman who travels the world. However, as he tries to tell his wife, 'The modern world's not like the old days, when your father got your brother a job in a government department because of who he was. You're nothing now without qualifications. It's a skill-based economy. If Dani doesn't make something of himself, no one else can do it for him' (2003: pp. 47–8). While it is a return to family that brings about a change in Mamo's fortunes, the ethos of neoliberal individualism that informs Ato's viewpoint is evident in Mamo's growing disenchantment with the street gang's code of ethics – 'What belongs to one belongs to all' (2003: p. 193) – and in the closure of the novel. When Tiggist marries, she and her husband are able to take in the boy and give him a job in an electrical appliance shop where he can learn skills that will make him more employable. Mamo finds a way out of poverty by contributing to the global consumer economy.

Spatiality, technology, and virtual tourism

A paradox of cultural globalization is that, on the one hand, it brings together diverse cultures, enhancing appreciation of regional differences and diversities, and, on the other, it displaces 'culture', eventually stripping it of its local components. The agents of cultural globalization, particularly telecommunications and tourism, contribute to this dual process, which results in the 'standardisation, homogenisation, and routinisation of contemporary world spaces' (Holmes, 2001: p. 3). As Holmes notes, the screen (computer, television), shopping mall, tourist precinct, theme park, and the modern city are among the most common and familiar expressions and outcomes of this effect of cultural globalization. These world spaces are both virtual and physical, eliding what Bauman refers to as 'natural borders' (1998: p. 77). They also support a global flow of people, objects, ideas, exotica, and imagination. But as Shome notes, the naïve notion of internationalization that 'we are the world' fails to take account of the 'asymmetrical and uneven relations between geographies and spaces' (2006: p. 256). In speaking of 'we' there is an implied Western audience; a similar assumption informs the examples of world spaces.

It is this perspective of occupying 'geographically privileged spaces in globalization' (Shome, 2006: p. 257) that is carried through many popular fictions for children and young adults. In such fictions, the protagonists are caught up in the ubiquity of media technologies and are often ignorant of a different kind of life. While some fictions similarly offer limited subject positions without space for reflexive assessment or different points of view, others engage with the possibilities and limitations of global technologies. The motif of travel or tourism is also employed in varying ways in texts to explore the implications of characters' mobility in physical, social, and virtual spaces with respect to observing and participating in new spatial experiences.

Tourism and media consumption tend to follow a shared logic whereby both are part of individuals' lifestyles but are nevertheless experienced differently depending on classes of mobility. Bauman describes two polarized worlds – one that is 'globally mobile', the other that is 'locally tied' (1998: p. 88). However, he contends that despite the limits of locality and mobility, television provides a means for '*virtual* accessibility of distances that stay stubbornly unreachable in non-virtual reality' (1998: p. 88). In the past decade or more, since Bauman offered this view, there has been considerable development of satellite television, the Internet, online social networking (Facebook, MySpace), and mobile technology in 'developing'/non-Western countries, with indicators that there will be an exponential increase in these areas over the next few years.[1] This development brings to the fore how the digital divide needs to be re-examined in ways that do not simply see low income or non-Western status as precluding participation by individuals and nations in the consumption practices offered by capitalist consumerism and global technologies.

In this section, we consider the interplay between neoliberal consumerist signs and how they can be read in terms of the broader contradictions and tensions that emerge through the processes of cultural globalization such as technology and tourism. To assist us in our theorizing we draw on Appadurai's notion of 'scapes' as a means for understanding 'the complexity of the global cultural economy' (1990: p. 296). Appadurai uses scapes as a way to frame and analyse the dynamics of the complex relationships between local and global forces and environments. Scapes also offer a way of conceptualizing real and virtual places and spaces that children vicariously encounter as travellers through television programs, films, magazines, fictions, advertisements, and postcards (see also Augé, 1995; Urry, 1995).

(E)scaping

An example of how scapes interrelate can be found in Tohby Riddle's picture book *The Great Escape from City Zoo* (1997). The story concerns the exploits of a group of animals – an anteater, an elephant, a turtle, and a flamingo – that escape from the city zoo, where they have been transported from their homelands and held involuntarily. In this sense they are a diasporic community who have had to undergo forced 'migration' (capture and transportation) to a new place. As a controlled space that exists within a city, the zoo entertains visitors through the simulation of space, place, and experience. The opening page shows visitors moving around the various enclosures that contain the animals. The space between the visitors and the animals is controlled and safe, and, indeed the concreted, sanitized zoo means that potentially dangerous situations that could arise between humans and wild animals are reduced and the activity of 'looking' can be undertaken without fear of its consequences. Thus, the simulated space of wild animals on show ensures a virtual experience whereby visitors can stroll, observe, and act like tourists in an exotic place. However, Riddle's book is not about humans as tourists, but the animals as tourists.

When the four animals escape they find themselves interacting in what could be regarded as Appadurai's scapes, and to avoid recapture their identities move from fixed (as zoo objects of the gaze) to fluid as they adopt disguises so that 'no one would notice them' (Riddle, 1997: unpaged). Their disguises transform them from zoo animals into ordinary 'people' who move through the city, blending and interacting in the different sites. In dressing as a sailor, a chef, a postman, and a businessman, they recode their bodies as cultural citizens who appear to belong to a cosmopolitan world. While readers are drawn to the incongruity of the disguises, the other characters in the text fail to notice anything out of the ordinary.

In adopting disguises and devising strategies for living undetected, the animals are like the ordinary people Appadurai refers to who must employ their imagination in the practice of their everyday lives. As he explains, 'mass migration and electronic mediation make the world of the present, not as technically new forces but as ones that seem to impel (and sometimes compel) the work of the imagination' (1996: p. 33). We can read the animals as a metonym for persons who are able to subvert (even if temporarily) the 'imagined world' of the entrepreneurial mentality that shaped it. In escaping, they too take on an entrepreneurial mentality in order to participate in another kind of imagined world, even if it is only a brief respite before they are captured and returned to the zoo.

In Appadurai's terms, we can understand *The Great Escape from City Zoo* as creating 'irregularities', whereby neither the images nor the readers are bound by local, national, or regional spaces (1996: p. 4). Rather, the depicted city is a global space, which is interpenetrated by the mediascape and the ethnoscape. Images from old movies, famous artworks, famous people from the past (Sigmund Freud), popular cultural artefacts, and a postcard of the Loch Ness Monster are incorporated into the text. This mediascape forms part of the 'reality' of the animals' world and offers the scripts that enable the fantasies of their life on the run; each of the animals is also depicted in a scene from a movie as part of their individual adventures. The ethnoscape of the text resembles a global reality in that the animals and other characters constitute a shifting world of tourists, immigrants, workers, and other moving groups and individuals as the story traverses North American urban and rural spaces. Just as Appadurai regards 'scapes' as 'deeply perspectival constructs' that could be viewed differently from every angle of vision, *The Great Escape from City Zoo* also works as a perspectival construct inviting readers as well as the characters to view the world depicted in the text in terms of different angles of perception and according to the situatedness of its characters.

'PLZHLPme. Im gng under'

As indicated earlier, in many countries around the globe there is a flourishing cyberculture and network society supported by government- and private-sector-sponsored computing and telecommunication infrastructures, applications, and devices. Various online environments enable young people to communicate and interact across spaces that are simultaneously 'real' and 'virtual'. Online environments and digital products provide markers for youth identity in globally networked societies. In many countries, young people are among the highest users of a diverse range of digital technologies and actively participate daily in online communities through network gaming, social network sites, mobile phone, email, and instant messaging. The ubiquity of these technologies brings immediacy and connectivity, as well as demands and challenges, as young people negotiate the diverse intersubjective situations that arise from these interactions across glocal contexts.

The young adult novel, *I Lost My Mobile at the Mall: Teenager on the Edge of Technological Breakdown* (Harmer, 2009), evokes the immediacy and seamless

flow of Appadurai's *technoscape* whereby communication and information move fluidly and swiftly across various kinds of boundaries that were
once impervious. As the title foregrounds, the challenge of doing without
a mobile phone seems initially overwhelming for Elly Pickering, the first-
person narrator of this story. When her family's home is burgled and three
computers are stolen it seems that she is indeed on the edge of technological
breakdown.

The story attempts to provide a window into the contemporary (Western)
world of middle-class teenagers immersed in media technologies. It also
attempts a dialogic engagement between past and present, with constant
references from Elly's parents to 'Days Before Mobile Phones Were Invented'
(p. 52) and her Nan's stories of the love letter correspondence with her fiancé
when she was a young woman. The nostalgia for the past intersects with the
present to demonstrate the benefits of 'past-present' as a desirable mode of
living. However, despite the somewhat romanticized closure of convergence
between old and new, past and present, modern technology interpenetrates
and reconfigures social space away from and beyond previously delineated
physical and human limits that were imposed upon social interaction. This
is most effectively realized in the grandmother's purchase of two computers
(one for herself, the other for Elly) so that they can communicate through
a social network site. In this sense, by venturing into the technoscape, the
grandmother, as a metonym for an older, technologically-naïve generation,
is seduced by the lure of the technoscape, and in doing so moves forward or
beyond her previous geo-physical space into a global-mediatized space.

The 'time-space compression' that Harvey speaks of with respect to
increasing capitalist expansion (what others term 'globalization') has
resulted in the 'speed-up and acceleration in the pace of economic processes
and, hence, social life' (1990: p. 230). In this process of increasing rapidity,
time annihilates the barriers of space. Three hours after discovering that she
lost her mobile at the shopping mall, Elly experiences the phantom-limb
sensation: 'My phone's been amputated. I can feel it vibrating in my pocket,
beep-beeping with a message or ringing in my ears, and I turn and reach for
it, but it's gone' (p. 9). Without her mobile, time passes slowly. Time is dou-
bly encoded through Elly's constant references to the slowness of time passing and the temporal distance from when the mobile first became lost. The
chapters' titles also serve to remind readers of how time is now measured –
for example: 'Sunday. 3pm. Three hours PM (post mobile)' (p. 6). The titles
also underline how time now features as a heavy reminder of Elly's feelings
of growing isolation and disconnectedness from the world. Elly and her generation live in *time,* a perpetual present, in which being connected to others through texting, phoning, or online social networking is a way of life.
Even when friends are present, they are often communicating at the same
time with someone on their mobile. Elly complains that her best friend (BF)
Bianca texts her latest boyfriend (Jai) nonstop – 'I have only had her full

attention for random three-minute intervals' (p. 15). When her computer is stolen, she misses the instantaneous time of virtual spaces forcing her to experience time as a constraint.

When the 'anything-anywhere-anytime' of cyberspace and the autonomy of mobile telecommunications are withdrawn, Elly experiences herself as occupying a liminal space that is in between new technologies and old technologies. While this liminality supports a renewed subjectivity for Elly, it also demands that she negotiate the complex relational connections that impact on being 'in-between'. These intersubjective relations are imbricated in issues of connectivity and immediacy, which shift from the inconvenience of not being 'connected' to the politics of representation that arise with the circulation of images through mobile technologies and social network sites. In today's media-saturated world, the uploading of embarrassing photos on social network sites is becoming a regular occurrence and engenders wide interest, especially when the subject is a celebrity. Therefore, when Jai uploads unflattering photographs of Elly from Bianca's mobile on to FacePlace, she is affronted and embarks on a course of revenge that ends badly.

Shome considers a further aspect of representation, namely, the mediated space of the transnational female body, which functions 'as a sign of a cosmopolitan imagery through which neoliberal consumerist logics are circulating' (2006: p. 259). She claims that through popular cultural products and marketing – fashion, style, beauty, music, and entertainment – a cosmopolitan imagery is harnessed in different national contexts to shore up a consumerist logic of cultural citizenship (2006: p. 259). A global aesthetic that encodes Western or exotic signs tantalizes consumers who are drawn to the imaginative possibilities of what being 'other' could offer. Hence, whitening products, jeans, corporate dress, henna, mehndi, nose rings, and saris circulate and construct the global subject who performs cross-cultural identity work on the body. With Elly's *real* BF, Carmelita Consuela Martinez, daughter of Spanish immigrants, the girls in the novel experiment with the self as a transnational female subject when they pretend to be in a Bollywood musical, dancing their way down the escalators in the mall, and re-enacting wet sari scenes wading through the fountain in the town square (p. 56).

The girls' cross-cultural play opens up a temporary imaginative world, which can be understood as an interrelated scape that corresponds with the global cultural flows of ethnoscapes, mediascape, and ideoscapes. As Appaduari explains, 'scapes' are the building blocks of 'imagined worlds' (1996: p. 33). Rather than dismiss the imagination as ephemeral, Appadurai argues that the notion of imagination needs to be theorized differently in the new global, cultural economy (p. 31). Ideas, images, and sounds flowing rapidly across the globe are not passively consumed in local places. This point is borne out in the text when Elly and Carmelita actively engage in the appropriation and indigenization of these cultural signs and images. A similar situation was noted in *The Great Escape from City Zoo* (1997).

The closing scene of the novel – Nan's 70th birthday party – offers an imagined community in that diverse individuals who form a spontaneous transnational community of harmony and hope constitute its configuration as a utopian, heterogeneous space. Here the technoscape, ethnoscape, and mediascape merge: Elly's friends Tenzin and Carmelita, along with her family, mix and mingle with all BFs from Elly's FacePlace. 'All the possible human configurations' (p. 314) are photographed with digital cameras and mobile phones, which are then downloaded and projected as slide shows on a big screen on the restaurant wall. Chinese lanterns decorate the (presumably Italian) restaurant and music from Beyoncé to the Beatles is played. To add to this global flow, Elly recalls the words of Buddha that Tenzin passed on to her: 'With our thoughts we make the world' (p. 316). However, within this utopian scene of harmonious cultural globalization there is a final overlapping disjunctive order.

The British Royal Family is a recurring motif in the novel: the Pickerings live in Buckingham Street, in the City of Britannia, where all the streets and facilities carry a regal nomenclature. While this is a fictitious place, it evokes Australia's status as a former colony of the British Empire. The family refers to itself as the 'Royal family' as each shares a first name with a member of British Royalty (past and present), and even the dog and cat are named Harry and Camilla. After Nan makes a short speech, the final words of the text resonate with the traces of British rule:

> The entire Royal Family of Buckingham Street raise their glasses and toast Good Queen Nan.
> Hip, pip, hooray!
> And long may we all live!
>
> (p. 319)

The collective is now a 'family' and the cultural imperialism of a former world has been transformed with a much more subtle form of ideological articulation and benign globalism – 'we are the world'.

Conclusion

The production, marketing, and circulation of children's cultural products (fiction, film, games, television programs, toys) are part of an integrated system of global capital flows and transnational networks of consumption and culture. At the same time, narrative cultural commodities typically fictionalize local worlds where the dimensions of globalization from below are materialized and experienced. In those fictions that thematize globalization, consumerism, and marketing, contradictory tales of caution and delight are offered to young people. As this chapter has demonstrated, the extent that such fictions are produced and consumed in countries that are the chief beneficiaries of globalization tend to reflect and – more rarely, contest – its ideological foundation, globalism. Its discourses promise freedom and equality; in reality, globalism subordinates politics, culture, and society to the primacy of the world market (Beck, 2000). Children's cultural products provide sites where the assumptions of globalism and aspects of globalization are reproduced, reshaped, and sometimes resisted.

Children's literature and film also bring to the fore the paradox of globalization that is played out between the local and the global. On the one hand, many texts produced and marketed in the West, such as the examples we have discussed in this chapter, appear to support the view that globalization produces cultural uniformity or homogeneity. On the other, they also demonstrate the significance of the local and the nostalgia it evokes. Rather than seeing the local and global as incompatible, the children's texts in this chapter express their interconnectivity, with place and belonging becoming fluid concepts as new allegiances and spaces replace or extend old ones. These interconnections become evident in the subthemes that many of the texts share, which attempt a subtle syncretism between contrasting positions: community and individualism; private and public; poverty and wealth; belonging and homelessness; freedom and escape; old and new technologies. These attempts to reconcile the local–global relationship are achieved by closure, which inevitably reinforces a glocal perspective. Nostalgia, too, emerges to express a desire or longing for a time when life was less complicated, slower paced, and where family and community were important sites of identity formation. The interplay among these thematic concerns, especially for family and community, is central to children's literature and opens up a dialogical space in which we can examine the tensions and clashes, along with the points of shared communality.

Further Reading

Bradford, C., Mallan, K., Stephens, J., & McCallum, R. 2008. 'Masters, slaves, and entrepreneurs: globalized utopias and new word order(ings)'. In *New world orders in contemporary children's literature: utopian transformations*. Palgrave, Houndmills, pp. 35–58.

Kenway, J. & Bullen, E. 2001. *Consuming children: education, entertainment, advertising*. Open University Press, Buckingham. See Chapter 2: 'Inventing the young consumer', pp. 35 –62 and Chapter 3: 'Polarizing pleasures: the allure of the grotesque', pp. 63–89. These chapters provide background on the historical forces that have produced the child consumer and children as a market segment, and elaboration on the various modes through which advertising and entertainment, market and culture, have become hybridized.

Note

1. According to the United Nations Conference on Trade and Development (UNCTAD) 'Information Economy' Report (2009), mobile penetration in Africa is such that mobile connections exceed fixed connections ten to one. Similarly, in South America, 80 per cent of the population have a mobile phone compared to just 25 per cent with regular fixed Internet access. http://colibria.com/media/press-releases/2818 Accessed 4 December 2009.

4
Monstrous Women: Gothic Misogyny in *Monster House*
Maria Takolander

Computer-generated feature films for children, which emerged with *Toy Story* in 1995, have come to dominate children's animated cinema in the Western world. Indeed, in 2006 Walt Disney Studios, the dominant force in children's culture since 1923, bought Pixar, the production company behind *Toy Story* (1995) and five other hugely successful computer-animated children's films (*A Bug's Life*, 1998; *Toy Story 2*, 1999; *Monsters Inc.*, 2001; *Finding Nemo*, 2003; and *The Incredibles*, 2004). John Lasseter, one of the founders of Pixar, was installed as the Chief Creative Officer of Walt Disney Studios, a move indicating that Disney planned to privilege investment in computer animation in future production, a suggestion endorsed by Lasseter himself at the time (Maddox, 2006). Other production companies, such as DreamWorks Animations, Twentieth Century Fox (NewsCorp), Sony, Warner Brothers (Time Warner), and Paramount (Viacom) have also moved into the burgeoning market of computer-animated children's films.

Acknowledging that the socializing function of children's literature is one of its defining characteristics (Stephens, 1992: p. 8) and that 'children's literature emerges from, and impinges upon, a nexus of social, political, and economic relations wherein adult desires are played out with "children" as a constantly and conveniently constructed category' (Gupta, 2005: p. 299), theorists of children's literature have increasingly turned their attention to the kinds of lessons present in children's texts. Bob Dixon's *Catching Them Young: Sex, Race and Class in Children's Fiction* (1977) was an early and influential study of sexism, racism, and classism in children's literature. Since the 1980s, traditional Disney animated films have been a prominent target of critics concerned with interrogating what Elizabeth Bell et al., in *From Mouse to Mermaid: The Politics of Film, Gender and Culture*, describe as 'the "trademark" of ... innocence that masks the personal, historical and material relationship between Disney film and politics' (1995: p. 5). The ways in which children's culture 'en-genders' subjectivities has remained a prominent area of concern.

Little research, though, has been done on the emergent area of computer-animated movies for children. In existing commentary, mostly in the form of popular reviews, CG films (as they are called) are commonly promoted as a new, exciting alternative to old-style Disney animation, with overriding attention being paid to their technological innovations. However, as David McCooey and I have argued (Takolander & McCooey, 2005), discussing the enormously popular CG children's feature *Shrek* (2001), the novelty of the animation cannot disguise old-fashioned politics.[1] *Shrek*, which overtly presents itself as a revisionist fairy tale and in opposition to the saccharine tradition of Disney interpretations, remains profoundly rooted, like the Disney fairy tale it allegedly mocks, in patriarchal ideologies.[2]

Monster House, a CG children's feature released by Sony and Columbia in 2006 and the focus of this essay, has been, like most CG films, appraised in terms of its innovative computer animation. In an essay published in *Computer Graphics World*, Martin McEachern (2006) focuses solely on the feature's technological originality. He commends the film for its use of clay hand-modelling to inform the computer animation process and concludes: 'In a summer flooded with CG features, each competing for technical supremacy, *Monster House* also steps out of the beaten digital path to assert, not hide, the authorship of the human hands behind it' (2006: p. 48). However, while this film looks new – even apparently as a CG picture – its thematic interests and politics, particularly with regard to gender, are decidedly old.

The old-fashioned gender politics are suggested by the gothic modality of *Monster House*, in which an entire neighbourhood – its children, young adults, and even police force – are terrorized by a grotesquely obese dead woman named Constance who haunts the house built for her by her uxorious, downtrodden husband, Nebercracker. The gothic genre has long been associated with misogynistic politics. The genre emerged in the eighteenth century but underwent a significant resurgence in Victorian England, when the 'New Woman' emerged to contest her patriarchal subjugation and was portrayed by Bram Stoker as akin to a vampire. The gothic also has a long association with children's literature, as Dale Townshend outlines in 'The Haunted Nursery: 1764–1830' (2008), and continues to be a conspicuous force in children's culture, as the popularity of the *Harry Potter*, *Lemony Snicket*, and *Spiderwick Chronicles* series suggests. Indeed, Karen Coats contends that 'children's Gothic has become prevalent enough as a phenomenon to represent what can be considered a cultural symptom – an indicator that points to an underlying trauma' (2008: p. 77). For Coats, the necessary rejection of the Oedipal mother is a possible source of the psychic disturbance therapeutically resolved by the gothic, which typically enacts the defeat of what Barbara Creed, in a landmark study, has called the 'monstrous-feminine' (2003 [1993]).

Whether we accept this thesis or prefer, like Adrienne Harris, to see culture as misogynistically 'underwriting' rather than helpfully facilitating maternal denial (2003: p. 259), the gothic certainly did not invent misogyny. The longevity of misogyny is also evidenced in *Monster House* (2006), which evokes older traditions of woman-hating, such as those embodied in the Genesis story of the Fall and in historical tracts portraying women as physically repellent or subhuman. Indeed, in its dramatization of the defeat of the archetypal figure that Julia Kristeva has described as the abjected, powerful, primordial mother (1982), *Monster House* is reminiscent of fifth-century-BCE Greek tragedy, which often re-enacts the conquest of the archaic mother to allegorize the founding of patriarchy.

Henry Giroux writes: 'Under the rubric of fun, entertainment, and escape, massive public spheres are being produced through representations and social practices that appear too "innocent" to be worthy of political analyses' (1995: p. 45). CG films, which emphasize spectacle and comedy, much like other contemporary children's texts, as David Buckingham argues, are certainly 'demanding – imploring, begging even – *not* to be taken seriously' (1995: p. 58), and their innovative technology, as I have suggested, provides an additional distraction from their political work. However, CG films for children, with their sensational popularity both in cinemas and as DVDs available for repeated viewing, are increasingly implicated in our public sphere and consequently require our concern. Certainly, *Monster House*, despite its fantastical plot and revisionary look, manifests profoundly misogynistic sentiments. This chapter, employing feminist and psychoanalytic perspectives and looking closely at the gothic genre that informs *Monster House*, urges reflection on the traditions of woman-hating that continue with disturbing potency in our culture today.

The gothic and the 'monstrous feminine'

While some literary critics have suggested that men occupy the central place in gothic narratives, the majority of gothic theorists envision the genre in terms of its preoccupation with the female. For example, Claire Kahane argues: 'What I see repeatedly locked into the forbidden center of the Gothic which draws me inward is the spectral presence of a dead-undead mother, archaic and all-encompassing, a ghost signifying the problematics of female identity' (2004: p. 279). Creed similarly argues that, in the gothic and horror genres, 'when woman is represented as monstrous it is almost always in relation to her mothering and reproductive functions' (2003: p. 7), while Carol Clover suggests that the 'occult genre in general is...remarkably interested in female insides' (1992: p. 105). The latter is suggested by both the invasion and mutilation of female bodies and the gothic iconography of enclosed spaces in which women are repeatedly located and which are often seen as contiguous with not only 'the womb from whose darkness the ego first emerged' but also 'the tomb to which it knows it must return' (Fiedler, 1982: p. 132). Indeed, if critics such as Fred Botting contend that the 'key figure' in gothic fiction is 'the father' (2002: p. 282), who assumes 'a variety of guises: tyrants, murders, rapacious villains, ghostly revenants' (p. 283), it is only, as Dale Townshend (2007: p. 102) concedes in the context of his similar argument, because the gothic plays out 'the trope of maternal elision: maternity recedes into the depths of the crypt, the dungeon, the grave, or the abyss in order to clear the stage'. In other words, while male 'monsters' may often inhabit the foreground in classic gothic texts such as Matthew Lewis's *The Monk* (1796), Bram Stoker's *Dracula* (1897), and Alfred Hitchcock's *Psycho* (1960), it is against a disturbing and enigmatic background, at times brought into dramatic focus, of abject maternity or feminine sexuality.

For example, *The Monk* ostensibly concentrates on the crimes of the monk Ambrosio, but the novel offers various encrypted and abject spectacles involving what Kahane calls the 'dead-undead mother'. The most striking example is the character of Agnes who, while sequestered in a convent, becomes pregnant by her lover. Agnes' lover, Don Alphonso, comes to be haunted by a spectre called the 'Bleeding Nun', a murderous and murdered woman who clearly functions as a *doppelgänger* for Agnes, representing her treacherous fertility. Meanwhile, Agnes is entombed alive with the rotting corpse of her infant in a sepulchral space of horrifying darkness that is inhabited by worms and toads. *Dracula* proves similarly interested in encrypted and terrifying visions of maternity and sexualized femininity. While the bloodsucking activities of Dracula, as Bram Dijkstra puts it, happen 'virtually all offstage' (1986: p. 345), what we do see is the newly married Mina drinking from a bleeding slit in the effeminate Dracula's breast – an image that confuses menstruation and breast feeding – before denouncing herself as 'unclean' (Stoker, 1997: p. 259). We also witness Lucy Westenra, with her 'bloodstained, voluptuous mouth – which it made one shudder to see' (p. 190), when she returns to her tomb after preying on children. Both Mina and Lucy, who are affianced at the beginning of the novel, with Lucy fantasizing about marrying all three of her suitors, become aligned with the category of the abject sexual female through their vampirism. In *Psycho* the preserved corpse of Norman Bates's mother compels her son to kill the women he finds sexually desirable, with the links between the horrors of female sexuality and maternity made strikingly clear.[3]

Monster House (2006), like its gothic predecessors, initially positions a man in the role of the ostensible villain before its prototypal 'conflict with the all-powerful devouring mother' (Fleenor, 1983: p. 16) is made manifest. At the beginning of the movie, Eliza, a girl, rides her tricycle along the footpath outside the haunted house and gets a wheel stuck in the lawn. The frail and elderly Nebercracker rushes out to the child and menacingly asks: 'Do you want to be eaten alive?' The film, which is largely focalized through another child protagonist called DJ, who lives across the road from

Nebercracker, initially encourages us to believe that the old man is the sole occupant of the house and is independently responsible for terrorizing the neighbourhood children. However, when Nebercracker is taken to hospital after he suffers a heart attack chasing DJ and his friend Chowder from his lawn, and when the house begins to behave in a more outrageous fashion, the true source of the house's terror is revealed. Nebercracker's obese, long-deceased wife Constance lies in a concrete tomb in the cellar of the house and preys on the neighbourhood children after luring them with their own stolen toys. Nebercracker, in policing the boundaries of his property, has in fact been trying to protect the neighbourhood's children from his abominable wife.

Constance is, then, another manifestation of Kahane's 'dead/undead mother'. Constance not only dislikes children but is also childless, the film thus eliding the reproductive essence of maternity (in favour of a destructive vision of maternity) in a manoeuvre common in gothic texts. However, various elements suggest the monster's association with motherhood. To begin with, Constance is obese, her body constituting a grotesque parody of pregnancy. In fact, her size – and, by implication, her procreative power – is explicitly marked as unnatural and dangerous by virtue of Nebercracker's flashbacks, which reveal that Constance, when he met her, was the 'fat lady', a freak in a circus show. On stage we see her pelted with rotten tomatoes, signifying her abject status, while off stage we witness her enclosure in a cage, suggesting the animal-like, dangerous nature of her body. Indeed, Constance is all body, which leads to my second point: Constance (notably voiced by Kathleen Turner, an actress recently in the tabloids for her obesity, alcoholism, and rambunctious behaviour) barely speaks. Rather, she groans, yells, and pants like someone barely human, recalling pathological and atavistic conceptualizations of the feminine from Aristotle's in the fourth century BCE – 'The female is as it were a deformed male' (quoted in Huet, 1993: p. 3) – to the criminologist Cesare Lombroso's in the nineteenth century – 'woman is a male of arrested development' (2004 [1893]: p. 37). As Kelly Hurley writes in *The Gothic Body: Sexuality, Materialism and Degeneration in the fin de siècle,* woman is rendered 'a Thing: a body that is at best imperfectly animated by a "human mind" and a "human spirit"' (1996: p. 120) in the scientific discourses of Victorian England – and, indeed, well before – in ways that clearly infected the gothic. However, Constance's noises are also reminiscent of those of a woman in labour. In fact, the house, which Nebercracker builds for Constance and in which she becomes entombed, comes to embody her corporeality in ways that clearly suggest the primeval maw of the archaic mother or what Creed describes as the 'mother-as-abyss … the cannibalizing black hole from which all life comes and to which all life returns' (2003: p. 25).

We learn from Nebercracker's flashback sequence that Constance becomes interred in the cellar of the house when, prevented by her husband from

attacking trick-or-treating children with an axe, she falls into the concrete pouring into the basement of the new structure. From the time that
Nebercracker is taken to hospital, leaving Constance's ghost unsupervised,
the house and grounds are increasingly anthropomorphized. While the
door of the house is ostensibly the mouth, with the hallway rug serving as
a long, funnelling tongue, the house and its grounds are also represented in
ways that evoke images of the female genitalia and reproductive system. The
lawn serves as a pubic mound, and the front door provides the entrance to
the red-carpeted hallway, which represents the vaginal canal. This narrow
space, at dramatic moments in the film, gives way to a terrifying tooth-filled
gateway – clearly representative of the *vagina dentata* or toothed vagina.[4]
There is also a toy-filled uterine space in the cellar in which Constance
herself lies buried.

The reproductive nature of the domestic space and the conjunction
between mouth and vagina are explicitly acknowledged in various flip-
pant ways in the film. DJ, Chowder, and Jenny Bennett, a precocious older
schoolgirl, seeking to defeat the monstrous house in Nebercracker's absence,
are advised by a male adolescent gaming 'legend' to kill the monster thus:
'You've got to strike at the source of life'. After a pause, this is clarified as 'the
heart' and ends up being the furnace. When the children find themselves
inside the house armed with phallic water pistols, Jenny identifies a light-
fitting as a uvula, to which Chowder responds, confusing uvula with vulva:
'Oh, so it's a girl house'. Jenny later saves them from being devoured in the
saw-tooth-filled abyss – the *vagina dentata* – that opens up in the hallway (or
vaginal) floor by swinging on the uvula and causing a gag reflex. The children are washed out onto the lawn, and the birthing nature of this scene is
underscored when Jenny says to the boys, 'you're acting like babies'. 'We are
babies', replies DJ.

The confusion of mouth and vagina through the motif of the *vagina dentata* is further supported in the film by the fact that DJ's father is a dentist.
In a strange scene, DJ's father carries various larger-than-life-sized models of
teeth as he and his wife pack their car for a dentistry conference (thus leaving the children alone to fight the beast in a convention typical of children's
culture). As they pack the car, DJ's father asks his wife, 'Will you help me
bring out the incisor?', and as they drive away, he resists his wife's appeals
to tell DJ that he loves him and to blow kisses to him. The conjunction
seems to suggest something about DJ's mother's own monstrous, devouring
instincts, which are barely contained by DJ's father.[5]

The *vagina dentata*: desire and danger

In *The Monstrous-Feminine: Film, Feminism, Psychoanalysis* (2003), Creed lists
a number of cultural examples of the motif of the *vagina dentata*, which
appears in mythical traditions around the world as well as in contemporary

Western horror. In regard to the latter, Creed refers to *Dracula*, a novel preoccupied with descriptions of the fanged, voluptuous mouths of its lascivious female vampires, who flirt with notions of the 'New Woman', accused in fin de siècle Victorian England, as Ann Ardis writes, 'of instigating the second fall of man' (1990: p. 1). The more contemporary *Alien* films (1979–1997), Creed argues, combine a similar interest in a powerful female protagonist (with her potency marked by androgyny and phallic weaponry) and the dripping, toothy mouth of a monster.

Creed also considers a number of psychoanalytic explanations for the prevalence of the *vagina dentata*. She argues that we can interpret it in terms of a residual fear 'of the oral sadistic mother' (2003: p. 109), who might wish to feed on others just as children feed on her, or 'of the dyadic mother; the all-encompassing maternal figure of the pre-Oedipal period who threatens symbolically to engulf the infant, thus posing a threat of psychic obliteration' (2003: p. 108). In a persuasive revision of the Oedipal complex, in which Sigmund Freud presents the mother as horrific because she is castrated and the father as powerful because he threatens castration, Creed contends that the *vagina dentata* can be read as an expression of man's fears about a *woman's* 'powers of castration' (2003: p. 87). The *vagina dentata*, Creed argues, is an expression of 'male fears and phantasies about the female genitals as a ... black hole which threatens to swallow them up and cut them into pieces' (2003: p. 106) in punishment for their aberrant desire.

In *Misogyny: The Male Malady*, David Gilmore similarly notes the 'universal' nature of myths involving the *vagina dentata* (2001: p. 148) and reflects on the psychic importance of childhood experiences of the maternal figure in such gynophobic and misogynistic traditions. Gilmore considers the Oedipal child's 'unacceptable impulses' (2001: p. 142), identifying the castration threat, like Creed, with the dominant mother and arguing that maternal rejection threatens 'the vulnerable male body and ego' (2001: p. 154). However, Gilmore argues that the pre-Oedipal stage, when 'Mother looms larger than all other objects in the world' (2001: p. 157), is more important. He contends that 'the boy develops powerfully ambivalent feelings towards this fantastically omnipotent figure' (2001: p. 157) in response to his narcissistic wounds of helplessness.

Both Creed and Gilmore, like Freud, ultimately reveal that *male* experience is the source of their interest. This is understandable in the case of Creed and Gilmore, whose area of concern is a misogyny diagnosed as a 'male malady' (although it is certainly one that women learn within the patriarchal symbolic orders of world cultures). What Creed and Gilmore also ultimately uncover, regardless of their different emphases, is that women seem to be experienced as threatening by men because women are invested with an archaic power that exceeds men's. This power, as Kristeva argues, is clearly tied up with the maternal function (1982: p. 77), which is, as Creed suggests, a potent threat to men and to patriarchy because of its denial of patrilineage and its emphasis on the originary bonds between mothers and children (2004: p. 270). As Donna Heiland argues, quoting Robin Lydenberg's counter-Freudian thesis that the Oedipal dilemma serves as an effective distraction from the mother as the 'envied source of plenitude and procreation' (1997 quoted in 2004: p. 81), 'patriarchy inevitably celebrates a male creative power that demands the suppression – and sometimes the outright sacrifice – of women' (pp. 10–11) and their generative potential.

However, the threat encapsulated by women does seem, as Creed's and Gilmore's readings suggest, profoundly related to desire (which is, in any case, an intimate companion of envy) for the maternal figure. The condition of desire, as Gilmore unselfconsciously reveals in his characterization of the narcissistic wounds suffered by male children, is essentially one of disempowerment.

The intimate interplay of desirability and danger in regard to the maternal and the feminine is represented by the ambiguous motif of the *vagina dentata*, which typically, as Creed puts it, 'points to the duplicitous nature of woman, who promises paradise in order to ensnare her victims' (2003: p. 106). While the gothic certainly cannot claim to have invented this conceptualization of the feminine – in the second century Tertullian represented woman as a 'devil's gateway' strategically disguised by tempting ornament (quoted in Bloch, 1991: p. 40) – the representation of the *vagina dentata* in gothic texts is characteristically associated not only with horror but also longing. In *Dracula*, for instance, the men find the vampiric women both irresistible and atrocious. In *The Monk*, Don Alphonso is mesmerized as much as terrified by the 'fallen', murderous Bleeding Nun: 'Her eyes…seemed endowed with the property of the rattle-snake's, for I strove in vain to look off her' (1973: p. 160).

In another rendering of the *vagina dentata* and its double dynamic of desire and fear, gothic texts, like early Christian documents with their interest in 'copresent images of the "Devil's gateway" and the "Bride of Christ"' (Bloch, 1991: p. 164), also often pair innocently attractive women with monstrous *doppelgängers*. There is Agnes and the Bleeding Nun in *The monk*, and there is the twinning of Ripley and the alien, most apparent in *Aliens*, in which Ripley, her biological child dead and with a pseudo-adoptive substitute, defeats a breeding female monster. Even Mina in Stoker's novel, who is praised by Van Helsing as 'one of God's women' (Stoker, 1997: p. 169), proves susceptible to the beast, requiring Van Helsing to keep an eye on the development of her incisors (p. 291). In these doublings, as David Punter and Glennis Byron write, the safely desirable, 'good' woman constantly threatens to turn into the lethal fiend – with Agnes on the verge of joining the Bleeding Nun in death, Ripley's body vulnerable to alien invasion, and Mina's will and mind infected by Dracula – revealing all women as potentially treacherous (2004: p. 40).

In *Monster House* (2006), the *vagina dentata* is similarly associated with both desire and danger, and all of the female characters in the film are implicated in the duplicity encapsulated by that motif. In one scene, DJ and Chowder are shown keeping an overnight vigil on the untrustworthy house from DJ's bedroom. Various elements are suggestive of the boys' desire, such as the erectile telescope through which they watch the house and, significantly, their love interest, Jenny, when she appears on DJ's street the following morning selling candy for a school fund-raiser. During their overnight vigil, the boys urinate into empty soft-drink bottles, an activity resonant of ejaculation. Chowder also confides to Jenny, after they rescue her from the clutches of the house and return to their post at the telescope: 'Fascinating, isn't it? It just sits there waiting, mocking us with its... houseness.' Indeed, DJ and Chowder come across as nothing less than Oedipal pubescent voyeurs, something made explicit when DJ's father, before leaving for the dentistry conference, reminisces about using a telescope when he was younger to watch the 'lovely Jensen twins'.

The joke, with its reference to twins, also alludes to the film's strategy of doubling and its emphasis on double-dealing when it comes to the female characters in general. Jenny, whom the boys first see against the backdrop of the monstrous house, is explicitly associated with that graphic representation of the *vagina dentata* as well as with deceitfulness. When the viewer first meets her at DJ's door, she is wearing a Halloween mask, having adopted the guise of a trick-or-treater as a sales tactic in order to persuade DJ's babysitter to buy candy from her. She tells DJ's babysitter: 'You've just witnessed a simulation of what you'll see this evening'. The warning is ambiguous, referring to both the imminent Halloween tradition of mask-wearing and trick-or-treating and the house's impending revelation of its full, climactic monstrousness. In fact, 'trick-or-treat' epitomizes the ambivalence of the *vagina dentata* and its representation of pleasure and danger. Jenny's façade of innocence in her role as a fund-raising candy seller is further belied as she makes a deal with the babysitter to share the profits of the candy sale. The babysitter, as this transaction suggests, is similarly dishonest. We see striking evidence of this when, in her guise as the ingenuous Elizabeth, she arrives at DJ's house listening to Olivia Newton-John's 'Little more love'. As soon as DJ's parents leave, Elizabeth is transformed into the scheming 'Z', throwing off her wig and revealing a t-shirt decorated with a skull and bones, the logo of her boyfriend's heavy-metal group, whose music quickly replaces Newton-John's. Indeed, even the innocence of the girl on the tricycle, Eliza (whose name is a shorter version of Elizabeth), is compromised. The opening scene of the movie emphasizes the autumnal season (the Fall) by its close-up of a drifting leaf and showing the girl carelessly naming objects in the world – 'hello fence, hello bees, hello sky, la la la la' – before she gets stuck in the lawn of the monstrous house policed by Nebercracker. This evocation of the Genesis myth of the Fall provides an immediate reminder of the temptation and treachery associated with women since at least early Christianity.

Monster House (2006), in its use of the *vagina dentata* motif, asserts the importance of vigilance when it comes to women as the source of both desire and profound danger. The film also starkly and disturbingly demonstrates, like other gothic literature, Kristeva's process of abjection involved in overcoming what Jerrold Hogle refers to as 'the pull of the masculine back toward an overpowering femininity' (2002: p. 11).

Abjection and overcoming desire

Following Kristeva, Creed argues that 'Woman's abjectification is crucial to the functioning of the patriarchal order' (2003: p. 166), enabling resistance to the dangerous lure of the mother and participation in the symbolic order of the father, which is marked by its ascendency and mastery over the desirable and annihilating feminine. Creed also contends, like Kristeva, that the gothic or horror genre itself provides one of the rituals through which patriarchy 'stages and re-stages a constant repudiation of the maternal figure... in order to secure and protect the social order' (2004: p. 270). That is, the gothic genre, through its representation of feminine abjection, serves to cure men of the disempowering experience of desire in relation to the maternal figure.

Indeed, in the gothic genre, the process of feminine abjection, achieved through ancient motifs such as the *vagina dentata*, is arguably as stark as the millennia-old 'menstrual cure', documented from pre-Christian to medieval times, which involved displaying a woman's stained menstrual cloths to her lover in order to turn his unmanning desire into an empowering revulsion (Dawson, 2005). In *Dracula*, for instance, all three of the men who love Lucy (her fiancé Arthur Holmwood, Dr Seward, and Quincy Morris) learn to see Lucy, under Van Helsing's tuition, as a 'foul Thing' (Stoker, 1997: p. 190). When Arthur stakes the vampiric Lucy in her coffin, when she returns from feeding upon children, we read in Seward's diary:

> The Thing in the coffin writhed; and a hideous, blood-curdling screech came from the opened red lips. The body shook and quivered and twisted in wild contortions; the sharp white teeth champed together till the lips were cut; and the mouth was smeared with a crimson foam. But Arthur never faltered. He looked like a figure of Thor as his untrembling arm rose and fell, driving deeper and deeper the mercy-bearing stake, whilst the blood from the pierced heart welled and spurted up around it. (p. 192)

As this example suggests, the abjection of the maternal figure in gothic texts is often complemented by the violent reassertion of patriarchal power. The scene, as Dijkstra argues, resembles nothing less than a 'therapeutic rape' (1996: p. 120) with the men 'rightfully reasserting their control over the offending body of the sexual female' (p. 122).

Monster House reveals a similar pattern involving the abjection and overthrow of the monstrous woman. The bottled urine of the boys, referred to earlier, is a striking demonstration of the abjection that should appropriately accompany desire. In fact, the uxorious and unmanned Nebercracker, who is carried over the threshold by Constance after they marry, is himself depicted as an abject figure (something suggested by his feminized appearance in an open-backed hospital gown for the latter half of the film) before he resolves 'to make things right' by abjecting his wife. To overcome his enthrallment to Constance and restore patriarchy, Nebercracker provides the boys with the dynamite they use to destroy the house in a scene that recalls the 'therapeutic rape' of Lucy in Stoker's novel. DJ and Chowder battle the monstrous house, which has broken free of its foundations to become mobile, with diggers and cranes in an abyss-like construction site, where a lake has been drained. It is a vista that pits the modern instruments of men against the primordial power of the *vagina dentata*, with the house's maternal nature invoked by Chowder fearfully calling out 'mummy' as the house attacks. During the battle, he yells, 'You ain't nothing. You're a shack. You're an outhouse', recalling age-old expressions of disgust for the feminine genitalia, such as Jean Palfyn's 1708 description of a woman's organs as 'the most contemptible place of the body … the main sewer for all elements' (quoted in Huet, 1993: p. 59). Constance is defeated when DJ, swinging on a crane, throws the dynamite into the house's chimney to strike at 'the source of life'.

The film, though, does not end there, and the closing scenes offer a resounding vision of the defeat and abjection of the feminine. In the last frames, we see a dog urinating at the former location of the monstrous house, now also a pit, extinguishing a small flame that persists inside a pumpkin lantern. This occurs just after Bones, Z's ex-boyfriend, who had been lured into and swallowed by the house, crawls out of the hole. Z, making out on the bonnet of a car with her new boyfriend, says to Bones: 'Skull's not like you. He gives me the respect I deserve and makes time for me'. Bones responds with 'Whatever' and walks away.

Kristeva identifies a cultural pattern, which occurs beyond the gothic and horror genres, in which 'it is always to be noticed that the attempt to establish a male, phallic power is rigorously threatened by the no less virulent power of the other sex, which … becomes synonymous with a radical evil that is to be suppressed' (1982: p. 70). This pattern is identifiable not only in *Monster House* but also in texts as old as Aeschylus's fifth-century BCE Greek play, *The Oresteia*, which has been read by Johann Bachofen in *Das Mutterrecht* (1861) as evidence of the historical overthrow of matriarchy by patriarchy, seen as necessary for progress. In the third play of the tragedy,

The Eumenides, the reproductive power of women is not only depicted in abject ways but also explicitly denied when an Athenian court rules, on a god's testimony, that women are vessels rather than active participants in the reproductive process. The verdict justifies Orestes's murder of his mother, Clytemnestra.

As Lynne Zeavin writes, in such misogynistic texts, 'frightening experiences of maternal power are replaced by fantasies of masculine dominance and superiority.' She continues: 'No longer feared, femininity is reviled. The sexuality that once was a site of the most profound desire, envy, and longing, is now a socially structured site of possession' (2003: p. 237). At the close of *The Eumenides*, not only is patrilineage asserted over maternity but also the Furies, who had sought vengeance on Orestes for his matricide, are transformed into the Eumenides (or The Kindly Ones) of the play's title and installed outside the city's limits. By the end of *Dracula*, Mina, who had once entertained the feminist notions of the 'New Woman' and who had once threatened the male characters with her possible metamorphosis, is the tamed receptacle for a child that is claimed by all of the male characters. Similarly, in *Monster House*, after Constance is destroyed, the two male police officers who were overpowered and engulfed in an earlier scene crawl out of the hole left by her destruction in a symbolic restoration of patriarchy. DJ, Chowder, and Nebercracker take over the pit and, working happily together, return the stolen toys of the neighbourhood children.

Conclusion

Gothic texts, as noted at the beginning of this discussion, in their encryption and abjection of the maternal, ultimately tend to focus on men. Indeed, Heiland argues that 'gothic novels are all about patriarchies, about how they function, what threatens them, what keeps them going' (2004: pp. 10–11). What seems to keep patriarchies going, as Kristeva suggests, is the production of subjects within a patriarchal symbolic system which works to abject and destroy the matrilineal power that threatens it (1982: p. 70). The gothic genre, as Kristeva argues, plays a ritualistic role in supporting patriarchy. Judith Halberstam, in *Skin Shows: Gothic Horror and the Technology of Monsters*, similarly contends that gothic fiction is a technology of subjectivity, which produces, through the vehicle of the monster, the 'perfect figure for negative identity' (1995: p. 22). While Halberstam argues that 'the monster works as a kind of trash heap for the discarded scraps of abject humanity' (p. 143) and can 'represent gender, race, nationality, class, and sexuality in one body' (pp. 21–2), she also concedes that 'part of the power of horror within a contemporary context lies in the reception of horror as always very literally about the destruction of a woman' (p. 127).

However, if misogyny is, as Gilmore writes, 'a sexual prejudice that is symbolically exchanged (shared) among men, attaining praxis' (2001: p. 9), it is not only the gothic that plays a role in promoting this 'public value system' (p. 14). Indeed, Bloch identifies misogyny as a 'cultural constant' (1991: p. 7), and the various references to older gynophobic traditions within both the gothic and *Monster House* are a testament to the enduring presence of misogyny in Western culture.

The source of misogyny is certainly of interest. While Gilmore and Creed, as we have seen, posit psychoanalytic explanations that focus on the powerful maternal figure of early dyadic life, Bloch contends that such accounts serve only to naturalize misogyny (1991: p. 79). Intervening in the debate, Harris argues:

> I see no value in sanitizing or diminishing the power of early dyadic life and consequently the power of the maternal object as an object of desire and of fear. I think it is one of the poignancies of contemporary culture that maternal power is so unusable, so unmetabolizable. The human processes of attachment and individuation that I am describing leave inevitable sequelae of anxiety and excitement. (2003: p. 264)

However, the problem of misogyny, she writes, is ultimately 'not the primary process effects that surround our experience of early mothering but the fragility and absence of secondary process that could be deployed to modulate the archaic form both inside us and in the culture' (pp. 259–260). In other words, traditions of woman-hating are formed by 'patriarchal structures that draw out and capitalize on these deeply emotional feelings that women in various incarnations evoke' (p. 264), demonizing rather than celebrating maternal potency.

Monster House, which is aimed at a child audience and which pits children against the archaic mother, is certainly a film that resonates in the context of Harris's argument. Largely through its utilization of the age-old motif of the *vagina dentata*, powerfully conflated with the domestic space traditionally attributed to the feminine, the film evokes the original gravitas of the maternal figure for the child and promotes a violent response of abjection and rejection. While the media spectacle offered by CG children's films such as *Monster House* hardly encourages serious analysis, as Susan Miller and Greg Rode argue, children's culture forms a significant 'site of persuasion' (1995: p. 88), constituting an 'entirely permeating extracurricular identity-schooling' (p. 102). In addition, studies such as Susan Auty and Charlie Lewis's have shown that children are more vulnerable to media messages than adults (2004: p. 118). As Dijkstra puts it, 'an image can kill. It can eat into reality and force our world to take on the shapes and colors of our fears' (1996: p. 311), something attested to, I would suggest, by the enduring power of misogynistic conceptions of women. All of this makes children's culture, perhaps even more so than adult culture, a necessary site for interrogation as well as for innovation, less in terms of animation technology than content.

Further Reading

James, K. 2009. 'Verisimilitude: representing death "in the real"'. In *Death, gender and sexuality in contemporary adolescent literature*. Routledge, New York.

Mallan, K. 2000. 'Witches, bitches and femmes fatales: viewing the female grotesque in children's film'. *Papers: Explorations into Children's Literature*, vol. 10, no. 1, pp. 26–35.

Notes

1   In fact, Jack Zipes argues that in traditional Disney animation attention was similarly drawn to 'innovative camera work, improved colour, greater synchronisation, livelier music and lyrics, and unique drawings of exotic characters' (1995: p. 111), while ideology and plot remained relatively unchanged over decades.

2   According to the Executive Producer Jeffrey Katzenberg, the message of the film, which stars a green ogre as its hero, a princess/ogress as his love interest, and a donkey as his trusty mate, is that '[w]hether you're a princess, a donkey, or even a big, green, stinky ogre, you can find love and happiness' (cited in Hopkins, 2004: p. 33). However, *Shrek*, with its heroic male and Jekyll-and-Hyde female, is in fact another version of humanism-as-masculinism and the male as normative (even as it presents men as victims and outcasts). While masculinity has been exposed as 'the dominant ideology of patriarchy' (Hanke, 1992: p. 190), *Shrek*, with its carnivalesque emphasis on scatological humour and violent adventure, suggests that it is, rather, about being natural and having innocent fun.

3   A distinction is sometimes made between the male gothic and the female gothic on various and legitimate grounds. Kari Winter, for example, argues that male-authored gothic texts locate 'evil in the "other" – woman, Catholics, Jews, and ultimately the devil', while female-authored gothic novels reveal 'the terror of the familiar: the routine brutality and injustice of the patriarchal family, convention, religion, and classist social structures' (1992: p. 91). However, Juliann Fleenor persuasively argues that the 'dread of female physiology and female sexuality is a constant' in both male-authored and female-authored gothic texts, where 'this fear of sexuality … is linked to attempts to destroy the mother' (1983: p. 14). As an example, Fleenor refers to Mary Shelley's *Frankenstein, or the modern prometheus* (1818), in which birth and death are grotesquely mixed in a womb-tomb-like laboratory but in which the disturbing phenomenon of maternity is occluded by the focus on paternity. Fleenor also cites Ellen Moers's well-known reading of the novel as an expression of a female writer's horror of motherhood (1977). Karen Stein agrees with Fleenor's reading. However, unlike Fleenor and Moers, who consider female gothic gynophobia as an expression of a 'natural' horror of an uncontrollable generative force and of female bodily transmogrification, Stein also contextualizes female gothic misogyny in terms of a cultural discourse about women that has been historically determined by men: 'it is precisely this male disgust with woman's sexuality, the male hatred and fear of women's awful procreative power and her "otherness", which is at the root of the Female Gothic' as much as the male gothic (1983: p. 124). I will return to the patriarchal context for gothic gynophobia and misogyny, upon which *Monster house*, as I have suggested, provokes reflection.

4 Indeed, this is so clear that it was noted in a popular review (Brown, 2006), not normally a forum for psychoanalytic or feminist readings.
5 Significantly, Chowder's father is a pharmacist. While we never meet Chowder's mother – or father – the ways in which the patriarchs of the film are associated with medical practice would seem to underscore the main spectacle of feminine pathology and the necessity of male intervention.

5
Splitting the Difference: Pleasure, Desire, and Intersubjectivity in Children's Literature and Film

Christine Wilkie-Stibbs

The terms 'splitting', 'difference', 'pleasure', 'desire', and 'intersubjectivity' are recognized aspects of fields of enquiry in their own right; but in their combination here, they locate this work predictably in the space of psycho-analytic gender criticism. 'Gender', however, is noticeably absent from my title and thereby hangs a complex set of questions, interrogations, and, let's face it, trouble. The trouble with gender – to distort and borrow from Judith Butler's seminal work (Butler, 1999) that unquestionably opened up the field of possibilities for the reconceptualization of gender in ways that no other work had previously managed to achieve – is that there appears to be little confidence or mutuality in its shared meaning. In this postfeminist, post-structuralist, post-millennial, post-individualist, post-guru period of the discipline's discursive history (and with no small debt to the gurus them-selves), one may wonder what is left to be said that is new or different about gender in children's literature. Has the subject not already been discussed, analysed, interrogated, argued over, and critiqued to the limits? Are the debates not already exhausted in the welter of excellent works from eminent scholars in and out of the field: about the subject itself, about the subject position within the subject, about who *is* the subject *of* the subject and their relations to each other, and, indeed, what is understood, and by whom, about the subject we call gender? (See, for example, 'infield' works from Butler, 2008; Mallan, 2009; Flanagan, 2008; Rabinowitz, 2004; Stephens, 2002; Lehr, 2001; Norton, 1999; Kidd, 1998; and Trites, 1997).

It may come as no surprise, and at the same time it is every bit surprising, that a genre featuring children and young adults as its protagonists and target audience has, on one hand, exercised regulation and constraint in relation to such matters as the body of the child and, on the other hand, has leapt fearlessly and unflinchingly into this space of identity politics. The journey from the 1970s world of Judy Blume's forays into the sexual activi-ties of young adults, through Aidan Chambers' 1980s narratives of young male homosexuality, to the millennial, lesbian, gay, bisexual, and trans-sexual (LGBT), and often homo-erotic, worlds of Julie Anne Peters and her contemporary LGBT company of writers has been painfully slow (or, should I say, painful and slow?). But in the last decade or so, children's literature has emerged as something of a trailblazer in the range and complexity of its LGBT narratives, of which the selection in this chapter is but a representative sliver. The clutch of children's literature and film narratives I address has dared to venture into this tendentious space. I focus mainly on Julie Anne Peters' *Luna* (2004), Shyam Selvadurai's *Funny Boy* (1995), and Alain Berliner's film *Ma vie en rose* (1997). I also include Joe Babcock's *The Boys and the Bees* (2006). Each portrays the experience of a young child protagonist whose assigned bodily inscriptions are at odds with their felt and preferred identities, and whose ideas of self are more complex and more diverse than the standardized discourses of the child would have otherwise admitted.

By shifting the ground of gender away from its binary inscription in the male/ female divide of regulatory practices in social life, Butler raised the necessary questions about the relationship between the 'materiality of the body to the performativity of gender' and 'how the category of "sex" figures within such relationships' (Butler, 1993: p. 1). She criticized the discursive tendency to collapse 'sex' into 'sexuality' and to essentialize both: 'As a result, the analysis of sexuality is collapsed into the analysis of "sex", and any inquiry into the historical production of the category of "sex" itself precluded by the inverted and falsified causality' (Butler, 1999: p. 121). By identifying what she called this 'exclusionary matrix' as the premise upon which the normative gendered subject is rendered visible, she thus simultaneously exposed a domain of 'uninhabitability' in social life occupied by what she identified as the 'not yet subjects' whose identities lay outside the defining limits of the binary (Butler, 1993: p. 3).

Butler's work problematized the too simple waters of stable gender definitions by subjecting their fundamentalist assumptions to this repositioning of material bodies in social spaces as multiple and differently sexed, any permutation of which is figured as an unstable indicator or determiner of individual identity and performance. The implication of this particular economy of equivalence (which may be, even yet, aspirational and utopian) is that social, physiological, and psychoanalytical discourses are in conversation with each other: hierarchies of difference are dissolved; the term 'gender' as normatively understood is subsumed into sexuality and neither gender nor sex is fixed, either in relation to the other or to sexual identity; 'male' and 'female', 'masculine' and 'feminine', are not reducible to normative categories that are positioned as naturalized at the extremes of the binary but are instead inscribed with equal status on the spectrum of multiple representations and identities. This is the space that has been so effectively occupied by queer discourse,[1] summarized by Eve Kosofsky Sedgwick as the drive to 'Scramble and repudiate the definitional sex/gender boundaries…The open mesh of possibilities, gaps, overlaps, dissonances, and resonances' (Sedgwick, 1993: p. 8.). The queer thesis does not, however, seek to scramble difference into a homogenous soup, but, rather, to enter the space occupied by difference and hold differences in equivalence while sustaining, maintaining, and recognizing the discreteness of each. In its bid for the dissolution of the kinds of dualism that inaugurated and sustain an oppositional logic, it promotes a fully worked ethics of difference that is interpersonally, intrapersonally, intrapsychically, and intersubjectively negotiated. The ascendancy of the queer discourse has not only dismantled the imperialism of binarism but has also by default rendered normative gender definition discursively untenable as a vehicle for the complex territory of identity and behaviour that the field itself has laid bare. Gender, then, has effectively become an absent presence in the disciplinary field as it is an absent presence in my title, and in this work. This begs the question about the need for a different and new set of signifiers to locate differently nuanced identity categories. Nevertheless, 'gender' continues to be the signifier of choice in the discourses of this contested triad: of bodies, identities, and performativity. This is the ground on which the narratives in focus here are played out, and they do so, I believe, with a disarming capacity to mobilize in opposition to prevailing hierarchies by their beguiling frankness and unfettered ability to say it the way it is.

Not playing the game

The child subjects (of whatever orientation) of children's literature, whose fluid and transitional lived bodies and identities fall all too easily into this domain of 'uninhabitability', have emerged as an unsurprisingly rich site on which to focus and sharpen these debates. Nowhere are the debates more contentiously conducted, however, than over the bodies of *young* children; and it is the literature featuring especially young child protagonists that I have decided to focus upon here. *Luna* (2004) is narrated from the viewpoint of Liam's younger sister, Regan, in a series of shifting time frames that move between present-day realities and their earliest childhoods told as (italicized) flashbacks. They reveal the transformation of Liam's daytime identity as 'Liam' into his nighttime identity as 'Luna', 'A girl who can only be seen by moonlight' (Peters, 2004: p. 2). *Funny Boy* (1995) is set in 1970s Sri Lanka and is also narrated in the first person, and retrospectively by the now adult protagonist, Arjie, who recounts the 'remembered innocence of childhood' (Selvadurai, 1995: p. 5) and tells the story of his 'transfiguration' into 'another, more brilliant, more beautiful self' (Selvadurai, 1995: p. 4) through his playing with his girl cousins their childhood game of 'bride-bride': 'the culmination of this game, and my ultimate moment of joy was when I put on the clothes of the bride' (Selvadurai, 1995: p. 4). The French film *Ma vie en rose* focuses on seven-year-old Ludovic whose first appearance is as a reflection in a mirror through subjective camera focusing on the range of fetishized objects with which Ludovic is adorning himself with elegant hands: bejewelled earrings; necklace; lipstick-painted full, red lips. The action then cuts to a pair of slim feet wearing (his mother's) too big red shoes, tripping downstairs to present himself (late) to the assembled guests at his parents' garden party. Ludovic emerges in the form of an idealized Greek goddess, clad in a pink silky dress (his sister's princess dress), and is viewed by the party guests (and by us, the viewers implicated in the male gaze[2]) as a freak, a comic turn, 'The joker of the family', his father announces.

These narratives break rank with the heterosexual imaginary that works to produce, uphold, and perpetuate an ideology of the child as gendered and normatively heterosexual but necessarily asexual; it is one of the most taboo, least discussed, most regulated, and least researched areas of child development (see Sedgwick, 1998; Kincaid, 2004). It is arguable that each of these child protagonists hovers on the cusp of an ambiguity over the question of child sexuality in the transgender identities portrayed. In every case, the process of the children's redressing is unambiguously and subjectively sensual as they make their transition to their 'other' self that is unequivocally experienced as a source of bodily pleasure. Thus, Luna 'shimmied in front of the mirror. The layered fringe on the dress she was wearing swayed in waves. ... Examining the length of herself, she hooked her long hair over her ears and wiggled her hips again' (Peters, 2004: p. 1). Arjie recounts the moment of becoming dressed as the bride, 'and then, by the transfiguration I saw taking place in Janaki's cracked full-length mirror – by the sari being wrapped around my body, the veil being pinned to my head, the rouge put on my cheeks, lipstick on my lips, kohl around my eyes – I was able to leave the constraints of myself' (Selvadurai, 1995: p. 4). He also recalls his experience of opening his grandmother's jewellery box, 'with a joy akin to ecstasy' (Selvadurai, 1995: p. 15). The reflected image through the mirror of Ludovic's slow process of adorning the erotogenic bodily zones – ears, lips, hands, feet – signals his unmistakable experience of *jouissance* at the point of his transition to his female self. For these children, dressing in this exaggeratedly stereotypical girly garb is not simply the experience of erotic frisson that is implied. Their particular choice of clothing and adornment is also an indisputable marker, a statement of their requirement and desire for social affirmation of a female self that would be otherwise erased, elided, or euphemized in and by any safe unisex clothing choices they might otherwise have made; it is both the sign of their desire for total immersion in the codes of femininity and their unwitting rejection of the politics of assimilation.

The debates provoked by the unspoken question of child sexuality oscillate in these narratives with the tensions, fears, and pathological anxieties between, on the one hand, individual child agency, and, on the other, a cast of adults and other child characters which embodies the institutional drive for the child to achieve what developmental psychology describes as 'I-identity' (coherence understood as normative). 'I-identity', as the drive to achieve a coherent sense of self, works in tandem with 's-identity' (also understood as normative) and is constitutive of the child's acquisition of community/intersubjective relations and sense of identity with others (Gallese, 2003). This 'I-'/'s-'identity dichotomy is just one site of the Self/Other split in the specular field, shifting between the points of observer and observed in which the child protagonists are caused to perform by turn within these familiar polarities as subject and object of the viewpoint. The very concept of intersubjectivity implies the inevitability of some level of relationship with the other – even if only insofar as the subject of intersubjectivity is able to conjecture that the other is a being outside the self – and is, therefore, inevitably structured between polarities of difference. Jessica Benjamin points to a third intersubjective position, however, that is arguably a less sophisticated version of the queer discourse but is distinctive in being located within the intersubjective space: one that is able, as she describes it, 'to break up the reversible complementarities and hold in tension the polarities that underly them' (Benjamin, 1998: p. xii). This particular stance informs her idea of a triadic relation in which self and other find a point of mediation in a third dimension that is the transcendent space. Judith Butler refers to this space as 'the Other of the Other' (Butler, 2004: p. 135). Benjamin refers in this context to the inevitable paradox of dyadic intersubjective relations: that if the other is also to be regarded as a desiring subject aspiring to a full subject position (like the self), it then follows that the other 'will share our wish to affect, have impact on, transform others' (Benjamin, 1998: p. xix). This is what she refers to as the 'reciprocity of dialogue... the risk of being transformed... the common burden of subjectivity':

> The possibility of mutual recognition that survives negation. ... Symmetry is necessary in which both self and other own the burden of subjectivity, the tendency to assimilate or deny the difference of the other. (Benjamin, 1998: p. xix)

Intersubjectivity, in other words, in its unreconstituted dyadic state is rooted in difference, and it brings with it not only threat but also responsibilities and resistance. In its drive to achieve its own subjectivity, the other threatens to destabilize the supremacy of the gazing subject, provoking the need to sustain and protect the self in a reciprocal process.

But the intersubjective position is negotiated not only in relation to self and other but also between 'self' and 'not self', where the 'not self' relates to the splitting of the subject. In every case in these narratives, the children record their clear sense of experiencing another and quite different self that is only fully realized through and within their acts of cross-dressing. Their mirrored reflections behave as a metaphor for this experience of the split between 'self' and 'not-self' that is a normative experience of developing subject identity rendered more complex by transgender and transsexual subjectivities. Cross-dressing is not necessarily synonymous with transgender or transsexual identities – as a number of contemporary, cross-dressing subjects bear witness (the English artist Grayson Perry, for example). The act of cross-dressing itself is eroticized and is the *raison d'être* in such examples. Jonathan Goldberg has pointed out that 'there is no such thing as the singular cross-dressed body; nor does it carry with it a univocal meaning' (Goldberg, 1993: p. 11). Luna is unequivocal about the subject identity category distinctions for which Regan speaks on Luna's behalf:

> 'He's a ... cross-dresser?'
> 'No! God. Don't call him that'... 'It's not the same. Liam's dressing because he wants you to see what he is on the inside. His true identity. Hers, I mean. Luna's'.
>
> (Peters, 2004: p. 192)
>
> 'He's not gay,' I said. 'He's trans. He's not what he appears. He'll show you. He's going to change into her girl role. Except, it's not really a role. It's who he really is, Luna. Who she is'.
>
> (Peters, 2004: p. 191)

Luna has developed a marker of this disjuncture between the self who is Luna by holding conversations – often angry – with her 'not-self', who is Liam, whom Luna repudiates and actively wishes to annihilate: 'He's talking to himself again. Conducting a conversation with an invisible being – someone other than me. He's such a head case' his sister, Regan, observes (Peters, 2004: p. 93). The name change is significantly and profoundly tied up with identity: Luna's shift to Liam releases her from the tyrannies that structure and fix her identity as male and from the 'baggage' conferred by his maleness as Liam. Arjie has already spoken about his ascent into 'another more brilliant, more beautiful self' in the game of bride-bride (Selvadurai, 1995: p. 4), and associates his separate selves with being located in two separate worlds: the everyday world of family and his playing world in the 'girls' territory', for which he mourns after his family banishes him from the girls' space and forbids him to play with them:

> I glanced at the sari lying on the rock where I had thrown it and I knew that I would never enter the girls' world again. Never stand in front of Janki's mirror, watching a transformation take place before my eyes. No more would I step out of that room and make my way down the porch steps to the altar, a creature beautiful and adorned, the personification of all that was good and perfect in the world. (Selvadurai, 1995: p. 39)

In *Ma vie en rose* 1997, Ludovic's ideal female Self is projected through a series of fantasy sequences onto a Barbie-like doll figure, 'Pam'. Ludovic aspires to *become* Pam (not just to be like her), and he requires her as both the sublimated embodiment of, and his desire for, the absolute freedom and pleasure of instinct-satisfaction in the female self that is socially effaced by his little boy self. The intercut scenes depicting Ludovic with Pam are brightly etched in fairyland colours and feature Ludovic's out-of-body female Self flying through the sky with Pam. There is no doubt in Ludovic's seven-year-old understanding that he *is* a girl, and that his body will grow into full girlhood.

In these scenarios the clothing and the objects with which the child protagonists adorn their bodies function as 'transitional phenomena' in the Winnicottian sense, meaning that they are the pleasure objects that fixate the child's projected desires. And the spaces of their individual transformation are inscribed as 'the potential spaces'. Donald Winnicott designated the potential space as 'intermediate zone' situated between the 'individual and the environment' that is also synonymous with the scene of playing (Winnicott, 1971: pp. 135, 144). In the examples of Luna and Ludovic, the topographical markers of these liminal zones are the occluded spaces of, respectively, their sister's and mother's bedrooms. For Arjie it is both his grandmother's bedroom and the 'girls' territory' at the back of their grandparents' house where he and his girl cousins are left alone to play all day away from the adults' gaze. Ludovic's potential space, as well as being the bedroom, is also located in the fantasy world of 'Pam', where he engages in what Winnicott has described as 'fantazying': a 'dissociated' state experienced, he says, by many 'who do not feel that they exist in their own right' (Winnicott, 1971: p. 39). Playing is also the location of inner and outer realities in which the child learns to identify the 'me' and 'not-me' phenomena. Winnicott points out that 'It is in playing and only in playing that the individual child is able to be creative ... and it is only in being creative that the individual discovers the self' (Winnicott, 1971: pp. 72–3). In these undisclosed and creative locations of the potential space, these children rehearse the self they believe themselves to be, with the significant twist that the preferred role they assume in 'play' is not coincidental with their ascribed role in a wider social reality. The domain of the potential space raises questions in this context about which, if any, of these 'worlds' is more 'real' or are as clearly demarcated as these binary role inscriptions suggest, or can be explained by the psychic split between self and not-self. Regan, again, speaks on behalf of Luna:

'It's horrible because you want to be this person you are in here,' ... 'But you can't because you don't look the way you should. You look like a guy. And that's what people expect you to be. Every day you have to put on this act, play a role, and the only time you can ever be free is when you're alone, when nobody's watching and you can let yourself go. In your world, your private world you can present yourself the way you want the world to see you and treat you'. (Peters, 2004: pp. 191–2)

Arjie realizes his female Self through game-playing. In *Ma vie en rose* (1997) there is a ludic element in the party context in which Ludovic first appears wearing a dress and make-up. His appearance could be easily interpreted as fancy dress, and it explains, or conveniently excuses, his ambivalent reception by the party guests whose facial and bodily gestures of unease suggest that they are not at all sure whether Ludovic is playing or is serious about his dressing in a dress.

We see this dialectic of self versus other being played out in the narratives between the transgender children and the power figures struggling to uphold and protect their own inscription in heterosexual hegemony that is the source of so much misery for these protagonists. In this process, the three transgender children are subjected by turn to taunts and ridicule, are dismissed as a joke, or are excused for behaving as they do because 'it's all in good fun' (Selvadurai, 1995: p. 50). Their immersion in the intersubjective space is, however, also the concomitant moment of exclusion from the regimes of heteronormativity and of their repudiation. Ludovic is negated in the gaze of his parents and their friends; Arjie is denounced as 'a pansy', 'a faggot', and 'a sissy' (Selvadurai, 1995: p. 11) by a girl cousin newly arrived to participate in the game of bride-bride. Luna's moment of exclusion happens at his ninth birthday party, which he shares with his little girl friend, Alyson. His father questions Liam's mother about why there are no boys at the party:

'Doesn't Liam have any of his own friends?'
'He has lots of friends . They just happen to be girls.'
'A boy his age. I found his birthday wish list. A Prom Barbie? A bra?'
'He was kidding, Jack...It was a joke'.

(Peters, 2004: p. 13, italics in original)

After his own and Alyson's birthday presents have been unwrapped and none of Liam's birthday wish list has materialized, he is distraught:

'Come on. Where are they?'...
'That's not what I asked for. Where's my bra?'...
Liam whirls at Mom. 'You asked me what I wanted and I told you'.

(Peters, 2004: pp. 16–7)

His father then drags off Liam back to the house. Regan, from whose memory the scene is narrated, recalls:

I see Liam's face turn red. Dad's spine goes rigid...
Whatever Dad said in the house that day had caused a rift in Liam's universe.

(Peters, 2004: p. 17)

These are three distinct moments of 'knowing' in which the transgender subjects return the heteronormative gaze upon themselves and recognize themselves in difference.

Bending the rules

One of the recurring narrative themes in these and other LGBT texts is the corrosive impact of this gaze upon the transgender subject, and the manner in which the exclusionary power relations in the intersubjective space operate to 'authorize' or 'deauthorize' not only the individual child subject's power to act but also their power *to be* and to properly inhabit the identity conferred by their being so named (see Butler, 1993: pp. 226–7). There is an element of intention and more than a metafictional import here in my borrowing the words 'authorize' and 'deauthorize' from Butler, because the child characters in these and other LGBT texts *are* authored, and often by writers who themselves openly subscribe to LGBT identity.[3] So, writing from within the discursive space, so to speak, offers these texts an important note of authenticity.

There is much to be said, too, about naming identity, not only as lesbian, gay, bisexual, transexual, and any other variation or permutation of the queer identity that must also (in this particular reading of the theory) include the so-called heteronormative naming of female and male. This is because the celebrated moment of subscribing to the subject position in the speech-act of *naming* oneself 'gay', 'straight', 'trans', and so on[4] is not only an epiphany but also a moment of circumscription when the subject assumes, is subsumed in, and becomes an effect of the identity category that is already understood – historically and socially. Typically, in these texts, it is the moment when each protagonist makes such a declaration: when Luna names herself 'I'm a Trans girl. A T-girl. The way you're a genetic girl, a G-girl' (Peters, 2004: p. 190); and when Ludovic announces his irrefutable belief that he will grow to be a girl and will marry Jérôme; and when Arjie meaningfully and openly admits to his brother, Diggy, his liking his school friend Shehan 'very much', following his first ever homo-erotic kiss (Selvadurai, 1995: p. 255). In the normative economy of identity categories, there is no return from this position, no half-measure identity between this and/or any other categories, because, as Butler points out, the identity is fixed in the name by 'the history of the usages that one never controlled, but that constrain the usage that now emblematizes autonomy' (Butler, 1993: p. 228). Hereafter, the democratized child subjects must negotiate their identity within the constraints of the identity category definition in which they are inscribed and within the intersubjective space that comprises a cast of others outside themselves who bring their already coded understandings to bear in a dialectic of 'me' and 'not me' suppositions. The trouble with such inscriptions of self as hermetically located in 'boy' and 'girl' identity categories to which Liam/Luna, Ludovic, and Arjie subscribe (who, after all, have only the already existing identity models to work within) is that they can be entirely and accurately described in old binary, pre-Butler terms and, furthermore, raise questions not only about the limitations imposed on the categories by the linguistic signifiers but also by how far the categories themselves can be identified as unitary and coherent *within* the signifiers. Such clearly marked girl and boy identities, articulated as oppositional, would seem misleadingly to suggest that a fully coherent, unified and univocal self is both possible and achievable, and further reinforces the binary paradigm. In fact, the individual manifestations and experiences of these transgender identities are much more complex, nuanced and different, between each child than it is possible to articulate within a simple boy/girl duality.

These questions return us once again to the queer discourse and to Sedgwick's bid for 'an open mesh of possibilities', and they suggest that a more fluid, more versatile field of concepts and indices be mapped on to the paradigm to articulate not only the *spectrum* of sexual identity differences but also the multiple identity *planes* and their correspondences across various axes.

The intersubjective relations that emerge in these and so many other LGBT narratives can only be described as rampantly homophobic.[5] Sedgwick has identified our society as 'brutally homophobic' in a way that is not 'arbitrary or gratuitous, but tightly knit into the texture of family, gender, age, class and race relations' (Sedgwick, 1992: pp. 3–4). The agents of homophobia in the three texts already discussed are the parents – especially the fathers – and other adults who, with only a few notable exceptions, exercise unfettered power to criticize, undermine, and marginalize their transgender children. Interestingly, in the context of Oedipal supremacy, the fathers who are in every case most vocal and censoriously opposed to their boy children's behaviour are also unwittingly most instrumental in confirming their child's identity predilection for the children themselves.[6] Arjie's father, for example, packs him off to an all-boys boarding school, 'The Academy will force you to become a man' (Selvadurai, 1995: p. 210); Ludovic's father, backed up by his mother, presses for Ludovic to attend psychotherapy sessions with a view to correcting his behaviour.

At this point I want to bring in Joe Babcock's *The Boys and the Bees* (2006), a text that focuses on the homosexual identity of its boy protagonist, sixth grader Andy Bobsees, and narrates, among other things, the homophobic behaviour of his peer group community in a Catholic coeducational day school. This text is exceptional in articulating the social psychology of difference in the minutiae of homophobic violence rampaging across the everyday lives of its homosexual children: the petty cruelties of peer group and parents, the exploitations, jealousies, deceptions, duplicities, ostracism, and acts of victimization. As an 11-year-old closet homosexual, Andy wants desperately to be seen and accepted as 'one of the guys', in which process he becomes wilfully complicit in the homophobic tyrannies of the 'guys' against their fall guy, James. James is regarded as a loser and a wimp; the paradigmatic 'sissy boy' who cries a great deal and whose every gesture and lisped utterance provoke a homophobic response. James is also Andy's longest-standing best friend and the shared source of homoerotic 'games' played since early childhood, hotly pursued under cover (and under the bed covers) during their sleepovers. When the homophobic gaze begins to focus on James, Andy senses that he too is implicated by association. He rejects and publicly disowns James, telling him, 'We seriously can't be friends anymore...You're too much of a girl' (Babcock, 2006: p. 62), while continuing to privately desire and invite James to sleepover with him. Thus begins a deeply psychological drama of desire and repulsion as each boy attempts to negotiate his homosexual identity across this homophobic minefield and which is focused on the body and emotions of James. Andy records: 'I hated James. He was such a sissy' (Babcock, 2006: p. 19). The polarization of Andy's feelings of love and hate, attachment and rejection projected onto James, and his unwillingness to publicly associate with the hapless and (to him, now) transparently homosexual James is not only the sign of Andy's denial of his own homosexuality but is also a characteristically primitive archetype of psychic splitting and a powerfully unconscious source of protection. Andy and James are also effectively two sides of the Oedipal triangle as Andy repudiates his primary and homoerotic attachment with the feminine (his mother) in James and makes his bid for identification with the Oedipal father who emerges in the shape of Mark Saddler. Mark is the archetypal masculine boy hero: a natural leader, natural sportsman, blonde, and good looking (Andy describes him as 'the most beautiful boy ever' [Babcock, 2006: p. 12]). He is adored by the girls and respected by the boys, is boyfriend of the most popular and attractive girl of the class, Anna, and is basketball supremo and captain of the team. Andy sets his sights on Mark and effectively courts him in his bid for acceptance into the community of boys who nevertheless continue to exclude him from their social circles and regard him as a 'faggot', like James. Here, as in *Funny Boy*, 'faggot' is the favourite and most often used term of homophobic abuse, even though these two stories are set thirty years apart:

> 'I'm not a faggot.'
> 'Yes you are,' Brett said.
> 'No, I'm not.'
> 'Yes you are. I can tell.'
> I was staring Brett in the eyes, trying not to back down, wondering frantically how he could tell. What did he see? Did everyone see it? Did I look like a faggot right now?
>
> (Babcock, 2006: p. 22)

The site of the Oedipal struggle is the male-coded narrative space of the local football field known (interestingly enough in this context) as 'the triangle', and it is the place at which all the boys, attended by the girls, congregate after school. Andy is hopeless at sport but – with James watching from the sidelines – he joins the basketball team to be close to Mark, who begins to give him private coaching to improve his game. Mark is the veritable Adonis of the boys' world: tough, fair, and lithe of body. Andy's transition, endorsement by, and bid for inclusion in the world of Mark could be his passport into the patriarchal (Symbolic) order and his confirmation in the codes of masculinity that mark him out as 'normal'. But Mark, like Andy, is playing a double game of identity. He too is eventually exposed as 'a faggot' through his growing association with Andy, and he is relegated both by the guys and his former girlfriend, Anna, to the margins, suffering homophobic abuse along with Andy and James. Neither Andy nor Mark has openly admitted to being gay, either to themselves or to each other, and so their conversations around the topic are coded in innuendo and inference. Mark's father reacts to the suggestion that his son may have been identified as gay by promptly removing him (with echoes of the fate of Selvadurai's Arjie) from the coeducational 'St Marks' to 'Trinity', a strictly regulated all-boys Catholic day school that Mark describes as 'The dumbest move given the circumstances' (Babcock, 2006: p.126). In a final twist, Andy discovers Mark in bed with James:

> I pushed the door open slowly and there they were. Mark and James, in James's bed dressed only in underwear. All I could see was Marks's white briefs as he straddled James…I knew what I had seen, because I had played that game with James dozens of times. I wanted to kill James. (Babcock, 2006: p. 134)

The narrative focus thus moves away from Andy and on to James, investing the formerly passive, wimpish James with agency and self-determination and as legitimate and visible within his homosexual identity. What follows is an even more remarkable turn of events that is also the moment Andy both reconciles and recognizes his identity within the homosexual community: instead of turning away from Mark and James, as was his first and instinctive reaction, he goes back to embrace them:

> Mark and James were like me, and something about seeing them together on the front porch made me feel left out. So I decided to join them…
> 'Are you two, like, boyfriends together?'
> 'We're just friends,' Mark said. 'Like me and you. Like you and James'. (Babcock, 2006: p. 135)

A number of points arise from these events that mark a paradigm shift and something of a watershed in LGBT children's literature by returning the narrative to the queer discourse. By blurring the sexual identity categories of Mark, the narrative exposes the instability of dominant identity fantasies that pathologize difference by exposing the fact that difference – as articulated through heterosexual norms – is a fluid and shifting ground. Andy's pursuit of Mark effectively usurps the phallic paradigm of Oedipal desire when Mark is shown to be ambivalently situated in relation to the male and female aspects of the primary matrix. Ultimately, however, the queer discourse is materialized in the triumphant triangular relationship that emerges between Andy, James, and Mark because it serves to break down the heteronormative paradigm of relationships as romantically situated in the male and female dyad which serves only to sustain the myth of dualism. Here, instead, the vision is plural in a newly articulated sexual economy of equivalence-in-difference.

The sense of the endings?

In every case, it is the question of relations within the intersubjective space that is at issue in these narratives and the possibilities they raise for greater resistance to normalization and harmonization within the paradigm of queer discourse. Sadly, however, the endings of *Luna, Funny Boy,* and *Ma vie en rose* are not as optimistic or paradigmatically progressive as the concluding scenes of *The Boys and the Bees* and bring neither closure nor resolution. Neither do they bring any real sense of reconciliation with, nor recognition of, these transgender subjects in terms of Benjamin's third area. The narrative endings are, rather, a perpetuation of the status quo that sadly rings true. As a young adult, Luna – who remains unacknowledged *as* Luna by all but his sister, who has acted throughout as confidant – is unable to exist in Liam's body. He eventually finds it necessary to leave home for a new life of anonymity in a different State, and what we are left to assume is that it will involve surgical reassignment. Arjie is sent off to a life of misery and victimization in an English, all-boys boarding school and assumes an uneasy homosexual identity. There is an unanswered question about how far the familial denial of Arjie's childhood penchant for being with the girls, self adornment and wearing of saris, has been instrumental in an enforced disavowal of transgender identity and, equally, – if also ironically – how far it has driven him in later life to take up relationships with the 'opposite' sex. Butler might say of this particular inscription of subjectivity that Arjie's homosexuality could only be understood on the basis that 'heterosexual desire is presumed' and that 'opposites attract'. Butler also makes the point that 'There are various ways of crossing that cannot be understood as stable achievements. ... It is difficult to say whether the sexuality of the transgendered person is homosexual or heterosexual' (Butler, 2004: pp. 79, 142). In *Ma vie en rose* (1997), Ludovic's family is presented as being reconciled to his transgender identity and the film ends with a family 'love-in' carrying the unspoken message that 'We love you *even though* you're transgender'. The scene of their reconciliation is the fancy dress birthday party of Ludovic's new-found friend 'Chris' (Christine), at which the classical hero turns hero-ine, and, conversely, when Ludovic and Christine swap clothes: his cavalier suit for her princess dress. Both sets of parents are seen to acquiesce in an unwritten rule of equivalence and fairness by which Ludovic's determi-nation to wear dresses gives way to the more naturalized, more tolerated, and less pathologized paradigm of the 'Tomboy' and an implied assump-tion that Ludovic will either grow, or be trained, out of 'it' (see Halberstam, 2004). This scene of reconciliation does not provide the counter-hegemonic moment that producers may have hoped or viewers may have anticipated; instead it returns viewers to the carnivalesque context of the party in which Ludovic first launched his transgender identity, and ultimately resituates the transgender identity of the young child in ambiguity and ambivalence as a safer and more comfortable haven.

Further Reading

Benjamin, J. 1995. *Like subjects, love objects: essays on recognition and sex-ual difference.* Yale University Press, New Haven. Benjamin introduces the notion of 'gender heterodoxy' to examine the nature of gender and intersubjectivity.

De Lauretis, T. 2000. *Alice doesn't: feminism, semiotics, cinema.* Indiana University Press, Bloomington. This collection of essays focuses on sexual difference. De Lauretis brings a feminist perspective and psychoanalytic and semiotic approach to the study of cinema.

Halberstam, J. 2005. *In queer time and place: transgender bodies, subcultural lives.* New York University Press, New York. Halberstam proposes a queer time that is an alternative to herteronormative time or one that is based around marriage and child rearing.

Stacey, J. 1994. *Star gazing: Hollywood cinema and female spectatorship.* Routledge, London. See Chapter 2: From 'Male gaze to female spectator'.

Notes

1 Butler (1993) comments on the 'reterritorialization' of the term 'queer' as a former term of homophobic abuse: 'For an occupation or reterritorialization of a term that has been used to abject a population can become the site of resist-ance, the possibility of an enabling social and political resignification. And this has happened to a certain extent with the notion of "queer"', p. 231. See also, T. de Lauretis (1991) 'Queer Theory: Lesbian and Gay Sexualities'; E.K. Sedgwick *Epistemology of the closet.* Katherine Gantz (2000) comments on the changing use of the term within academia: 'As the political construction of "queer" became increasingly disciplinized in academia, the emerging body of "queer theory" lost its specifically homosexual connotation and was replaced by a diffuse set of

diverse sexual identities. Like the path of feminism, the concept of queerness had been largely stripped of its political roots and transformed into a methodological approach accessible to manipulation by the world of predominantly heterosexual, white, middle-class intellectuals. It is possible that this chapter falls into this kind of reading of "queer"', pp. 164–90; p. 165.

2 See L. Mulvey (1975) for her analysis of how multiple modes of 'looking' in narrative cinema are created through the 'male gaze' as voyeur and fetish.

3 Julie Anne Peters, for example, identifies her orientation as 'Lesbian' on her 'My Space' Biography. Shyam Selvadurai's *Funny boy* is an acknowledged fictional autobiography.

4 The words themselves evoke and connote the supremacy of heteronormativity in Western discourse. See, for example, S. Seidman (2004). 'Gay identity constructions reinforce the dominant hetero/homo sexual code with its heteronormativity'. If homosexuality and heterosexuality are a coupling in which each presupposes the other, each being present in the invocation of the other, and in which this coupling assumes hierarchical forms, then the epistemic and political project of identifying a gay subject reinforces and reproduces this hierarchical figure. pp. 105–41; p. 131.

5 There is a tendency in LGBT children's literature narratives to concentrate on LGBT identities as problematic. However, there are a number of exceptions in which the LGBT identity is fully integrated within the characters and the social context. For example, David Levithan's *Boy meets boy* (2003) is the story of unrequited same sex desire of high school sophomore student Paul for Noah in the pattern of any young adult romance novel, and for which the backdrop and social milieu is a web of complex relations across a fully integrated, fully realized, fully acknowledged, fully tolerant community of queer identities – from drag-queens to transexuals and straights – that is undoubtedly utopian in its vision but in the power politics that privileges the discourses of homophobia, there is interestingly no name. Doug MacLeod *Tumble turn* (2003) is a gently articulated novel in the mode of 'Adrian Mole', told through a series of email exchanges between 11-year-old Dom and his uncle Peri. Through these exchanges Dom conjectures the possibility that he may be gay and reveals that his family is in turmoil; his father's infidelity, and the impending breakup of his parents' marriage laced with their homophobic conversations. Dom's parents are the greatest source of denial of Dom's potential homosexuality and so they take him for therapy, while his uncle Peri (a Buddhist, like Dom) is quietly supportive. It is Dom's matter-of-fact tone that marks out this novel as exceptional in this context of LGBT children's literature.

6 I am using 'Oedipal supremacy' in the Freudian/Lacanian understanding that inscribes the child's developmental severing of its primary identification with the Mother and pull towards the dominant order of the Father in patriarchal discourse.

6
Children As Ecocitizens: Ecocriticism and Environmental Texts

Geraldine Massey and Clare Bradford

Children's environmental texts – that is, texts which thematize contemporary ecological issues – reflect shifting global agendas and predict future possibilities. One of their primary functions is to socialize young people into becoming the responsible and empathetic adults of tomorrow by positioning readers as ecocitizens, dedicated both to sustainable development in the local sphere and also to global responsibility. This chapter focuses on the intersections between environmental discourses and the ways environmental texts seek to position children. We draw on the field of ecocriticism to develop a transdisciplinary framework for investigating a selection of contemporary texts. Our overview demonstrates the paradigmatic shifts which have characterized the development of ecocriticism.

Since the middle of the twentieth century, theorists have sought to make sense of interactions between humans and the environment (Mühlhäusler & Peace, 2006). Indeed, Rom Harré, Jens Brockmeier, and Peter Mühlhäusler conclude that 'the [environmental] "crisis of our time" is at root a discursive phenomenon' (1999: p. 3). Within the context of a contemporary socio-political framework based on Western cultures and textuality, John Dryzek (2005) analyses popular texts and environmental reports to identify the environmental discourses which inform discussions of ecological issues. According to Dryzek's analysis, each discourse includes motivated agents: 'enlightened elites, rational consumers, ignorant and shortsighted populations, virtuous ordinary citizens ...' (Dryzek, 2005: p. 18; see Bradford, 2003).

Many contemporary Western environmental discourses are built on the assumption that individuals are aware of the dangers facing human and environmental survival and are willing to moderate their engagement with the environment; that is, that such citizens have access to environmental discourses and actively construct themselves as ecological subjects. Certain characteristics can be identified in accounts of ecocitizenship. First, the use of the 'eco' prefix suggests an understanding which coincides with the first of the 'Four Laws of Ecology' articulated by Barry Commoner (1971): that everything is connected to everything else; what affects one, affects all. Second, the term 'ecological' opens up more conceptual possibilities than 'environmental', since it implies an awareness of relationships of interconnectivity and interdependence and includes the possibility of ecocentric perspectives which reject the idea that the natural environment exists in order to serve the needs and interests of humans. Third, 'ecocitizen' signals an attempt to avoid the anthropocentric connotations of the word 'environmentalist', which presupposes action initiated and controlled by humans.

It is undeniably the case that ecosystems are threatened by global warming, environmental degradation, and the destruction of wild habitats, and that future generations will experience their negative effects. Strategies for addressing them are complex, unstable, and often contradictory. A socio-cultural assumption which pervades Western thought is that human survival depends on dynamic, self-motivated people whose awareness of environmental concerns allows them to reflect on their relationships with the environment and to take responsibility for their actions. This culturally privileged form of behaviour is actively endorsed by international organizations such as the United Nations Environmental Program (UNEP) and the International Panel on Climate Control (IPPC), as well as nongovernmental organizations such as Green Peace and the World Wildlife Fund (WWF). Expectations of ecocitizenship are also set out in educational agendas. For example, in Australia, the *Melbourne declaration on educational goals for young Australians*, produced by the Ministerial Council on Education, Training and Youth Affairs, states that all young Australians should 'act with moral and ethical integrity... work for the common good, in particular sustaining and improving natural and social environments... [and be] responsible global and local citizens' (2008: p. 9).

Literature does not merely reflect what happens in local and global settings, but persuasively constructs settings and environmental events in order to socialize children into ways of being and behaving. The values presented to children are contingent upon the views and values of the adults who produce environmental texts. If readers adopt the subject positions offered by environmental texts, they may potentially assume the worldview that such texts propose; that is, readers' understandings of ecocitizenship may be constructed as they engage with texts. In this way children's literature responds to environmental issues and attempts to enlist readers in taking action, encouraging them to reflect on the world as it is, and to imagine future scenarios if environmental degradation proceeds unabated.

Ecocriticism

The field of ecocriticism focuses on literary and artistic expressions of the relations between humans and the natural world. Its premise is that 'human culture is connected to the physical world, affecting it and affected by it' (Glotfelty, 1996: p. xix). Scholars have advocated various approaches to ecocritical research. Michael P. Branch et al. (1998) suggest that biocentric worldviews are an essential element in an ecocritical approach which encompasses 'an extension of ethics, a broadening of humans' conception of global community to include nonhuman life forms and the physical environment' (Glotfelty, 1996: p. xiii). Similarly, Lawrence Buell has emphasized the role of literature in enabling reflection on the ethical dimensions of environmentalism and in impelling readers to take up 'a stronger ethic of care for the nonhuman environment', so making the world 'a better place, for humans as well as for nonhumans' (2001: p. 6). Glen A. Love (2003) bases his approach to ecocriticism on evolutionary biology, thus aligning literary understanding with research findings from earth and life sciences.

Ecocriticism is neither a harmonious nor a unified field. However, its various strands share a fundamental commitment to the physical world (Estok, 2001; Glotfelty, 1996; Kerridge & Sammells, 1998). As a scholarly movement, ecocriticism was a response by literary scholars to the escalating environmental crises of the 1960s. At about the same time that socially conscious movements with regard to race, class, and gender were developing in literary and cultural theory, ecocriticism gave a voice to literary theorists who espoused environmental consciousness. Cheryll Glotfelty (1996: pp. xxiii–xxiv) identifies three stages in the course of ecocriticism: (i) scrutinizing images of nature to raise awareness of stereotypes; (ii) investigating writing that manifests ecological awareness; (iii) developing critical, theoretical frameworks for literary analysis.

Whereas Glotfelty classifies the evolution of ecocriticism in terms of stages, Buell (2005) regards the following developments as the 'first wave': early tendencies to focus on the pastoral/wilderness canon; biographical studies of nature writers; regional studies; genre studies, for example, poetry from a particular time such as the Romantic period. As well, during this first wave of ecocriticism, scholars collected and edited anthologies of nature writing or revisited literary works to reinterpret them from a perspective of environmental awareness. In the 'second wave', the ecocritical lens was expanded to include urban as well as rural environments, ecofeminism, environmental justice, and the profound impact of humanity on the environment as depicted in contemporary texts (Buell, 2005: pp. 22–23).

Common to these two accounts of the historical development of ecocriticism is an awareness of a move from formalist approaches, with their emphasis on studying the text in isolation, to the development of a more critical approach, conscious of the cultural forces that shape, and to some extent are influenced by, the text. More recently, scholars have conducted critical appraisals of the field and its various strands (Buell, 2005; Cohen, 2004; Easterlin, 2004; Levin, 2002; Phillips, 2003). Of these, some of the most strident criticisms have been levelled by Dana Phillips (2003), who accuses ecocritics of the following: wishing to escape from academic constraints;

fixating on the pastoral; rehabilitating the concept of texts as mimetic representations of reality; espousing interdisciplinarity to strengthen literary criticism but in effect weakening it; and espousing overly ambitious aims for the role of literature in contributing to environmental protection and restoration.

However, Phillips' criticism regarding the deleterious effects of interdisciplinary approaches is overstated. Ecofeminism, for instance, applies feminist theories to the interpretation of human interactions with the environment and emphasizes the examination, disruption, and replacement of patriarchal worldviews. Some ecofeminist approaches claim that androcentric practices have contributed to the environmental crisis (Warren, 1998), envisaging new ways of living with the environment which do not involve patriarchal oppression. However, ecofeminism should not be regarded as a homogeneous cluster any more than ecocriticism, since its proponents base their analysis on different versions of feminism (Warren, 1995: p. 106).

The use of gendered (female) metaphors and metonyms associated with the environment – as mother, damsel in distress, virgin, and sexual object – has provided a productive field of study for some ecofeminists, whose viewpoints connect environmental degradation with the patriarchal domination and oppression of women (Kolodny, 1996; Soper, 2000). Ecocritical studies of British and American historical and contemporary children's literature similarly examine representations of the environment through gendered metaphors: a damsel in distress in need of rescue (Apol, 2003); an efficient housekeeper dutifully caring for her charges (Wood, 1995); and a harsh, cold mother (Wood, 2004). These critics discuss the historical and cultural significances of these representations, which encode contradictory concepts of the feminine.

The examination of gendered representations of nature carried out by ecofeminists corresponds to the broader function of ecocriticism, which examines 'how metaphors of nature and land are used and abused' (Howarth, 1996: p. 81). It is beyond the scope of this chapter to argue in favour of one of the plurality of positions proposed by ecofeminist scholars such as Jim Cheney (1989), Annette Kolodny (1996), Val Plumwood (1993), and Karen J. Warren (1998). It is more profitable to note certain implications of ecofeminist approaches that could be useful in the analysis of environmental literature for children. For example, ecofeminist approaches to texts, like feminist readings, problematize dualisms based on hierarchies of worth, from male/ female binaries to other binaries associated with human interactions with the environment, such as living/nonliving and human/animal. Peter Hay suggests that in place of dichotomous concepts favoured by science such as subject/object, knower/known, ecofeminists favour ideas of union, engagement, and empathy. We would argue that such ideas are more in keeping with ecological awareness than concepts based on the intrinsic superiority or inferiority of species, habitats, and behaviours.

In a related way, postcolonial criticism enables different approaches to textual analysis by taking into account the marginalization of voices and perspectives of those who do not conform to Eurocentric or Western norms and practices. As Edward Said (1978) argued, a Eurocentric universalism takes for granted that European epistemologies are normative, enabling Europeans not merely to influence other cultures but also to produce them as objects of knowledge. Postcolonial readings examine texts with regard to how binaries are constructed, particularly those on which colonialism was built: colonial (civilized) in opposition to colonized (primitive, barbaric) (Bradford, 2001). Graham Huggan points out that 'ecocriticism, at present, is a predominantly white movement' (2004: p. 703), and this is true also of children's texts, which in the main are informed by Western thinking about a moral subject whose whiteness is central to formulations of relations between humans and the nonhuman world.

As this overview suggests, ecocriticism affords multiple perspectives from which to analyse children's environmental literature. Representations of ecocitizenship in contemporary environmental texts for children and young adult readers exist at the intersection of environmental and narrative discourses, opening up opportunities to consider how such texts position readers through narrative strategies such as focalization and point of view. An ecocritical approach can be strengthened and enriched by the incorporation of ecofeminist and postcolonial perspectives which examine the extent to which environmental texts are informed by patriarchal, colonial, and/or postcolonial ideologies.

Ecocriticism and children's literature

Across popular political and cultural domains, the dominant environmental discourse is that of sustainability. The United Nations report *Our Common Future* (1987) calls for economic measures (such as compensatory financing and targeted assistance) to ensure that developing countries are supported in raising standards of living while improving the health of ecosystems. Children's books have been slow to address this aspect of environmental sustainability, focusing rather on individual human subjects and their relationships with the natural world, issues surrounding the sustainable development of industries and urbanization, and the desirability of community action to sustain local ecologies and the well-being of individuals and groups.

However, other environmental discourses also inform children's environmental texts. Deep ecologists view humanity as only one of many interrelated components that together contribute to the survival of the biosphere. Individual humans count only in their contribution to the whole, not as isolated individual beings (Naess, 1989). Yet the possibility of texts presenting an ecocentric position is problematic. The environment has no ability to speak for itself, although it could be argued that the environment speaks for itself in terms of global and local responses such as climate change, fires, floods, or drought. All environmental discourses are constituted by humans who speak on behalf of the environment, which means humans always have the potential to adopt a patronizing, custodial approach.

Tohby Riddle's picture book *The Singing Hat* (2000) foregrounds the ethical choices facing an individual and the consequences of these choices. The protagonist, Colin Jenkins, is a somewhat unlikely subject for a picture book: a businessman who works in a city office block. Colin has ecological citizenship thrust upon him when, as he takes a lunch-time nap under a tree in the park, a bird builds a nest on his head. The narrative outlines the complexities of Colin's decision to leave the nest, complete with bird and, later, egg, on his head.

The Singing Hat, like other picture books by Riddle, derives its effect in part from the interplay between a deadpan, understated narrative and illustrations which nudge against absurdism. Colin's variety of ecocitizenship is not an established fact at the beginning of the book, but is constructed through vignettes during which he encounters various people, including his young daughter. As he goes home on the train, unaware of the bird and nest on his head, the visual perspectives over the two pages of the train journey position readers to shift between Colin's and the passengers' point of view. From Colin's point of view readers see the passengers' faces as they 'looked at him in ways that he had never been looked at before' (Riddle, 2000: unpaged), evincing surprise, wonder, amusement. When the viewpoint changes, showing the passengers' perspective, Colin's oblivion to the presence of the bird and its nest, expressed in his calm, matter-of-fact expression, prepares readers for the moment when, viewing his reflection in a mirror, he sees the bird and must consciously determine how to approach his dilemma.

Colin's decision to leave the nest in place on his head tests his friends and casual acquaintances, who divide into two groups: 'those who didn't seem to mind what he had on his head, and those who did' (Riddle, 2000: unpaged). The bird's increasing vociferousness proves disruptive at meetings and eventually Colin is dismissed from his job. The dismissal scene shows Colin and his boss confronting each other. The bird's 'Squawk Squawk Squawk' is countered by a speech bubble from his boss's mouth, containing meaningless columns of figures. This contrast between the two represents Colin's ecocitizenship as a rejection of a corporate and mercantile world in which the bird's survival is judged in relation to a balance sheet. Ecological values are thus seen to be at odds with commercial interests, and Colin's departure from the world of balance sheets is in effect an escape from a barren, instrumentalist view of the world.

His predicament is resolved when he returns to the tree from which the bird originally flew to his head. He encounters a man 'who might have been an ornithologist' (Riddle, 2000: unpaged), and who reassures Colin that the bird on his head is rare and endangered. At this moment the bird takes off and disappears into the sky. Colin's transformation from anonymous office worker to ecologist is tracked through his clothes: from the dull grey of his business suits at the beginning of the narrative, to the corduroy trousers and open-neck shirt he wears at the end. In addition, the illustrations, formerly featuring human figures against featureless office blocks, now incorporate intertextual references to a world of popular entertainment. Film posters advertise 1936 films: *My Man Godfrey, Down to the Sea, The Texas Rangers,* adding temporal specificity to scenes previously empty of cultural references. Depicted next to these posters, Colin stands out from the crowd, his figure rendered in colour against the black and white outlines of men and women walking to and from the city. Ecological awareness, then, seems to invite colour into Colin's life. However, the contrast between Colin and the city environment enforces a sharp distinction between the city and the natural world, and between the mass of people working in the city and Colin the ecocitizen. This distinction plays into the sense that commerce and business exist outside ecological systems and are antagonistic to the natural environment.

Colin takes the empty nest home and places it on a table by the window, where it becomes 'a pretty ornament that delighted everyone' (Riddle, 2000: unpaged). The nest, metonymically associated with new life, is now merely decorative. Nevertheless, 'from time to time [Colin] would find the most beautiful and improbable things' in the nest beside the window (Riddle, 2000: unpaged). The indeterminacy of the narrative's closure in itself constitutes an invitation to readers to 'fill the space' by imagining future ecological scenarios.

Graeme Base's picture book *Uno's Garden* (Base, 2006) is far more overtly didactic than *The Singing Hat* and traces the ecological history of a site as it is transformed from pristine forest to city and back to a forest environment with minimal human habitation. The eponymous Uno is the first human to settle in the forest, whose ecological history is plotted against a generational timeline from Uno to his grandchildren.

The illustrations in *Uno's Garden* show the initial pristine environment as fantastically exotic, with brightly coloured plants and imaginatively named animals such as 'Moopaloops', 'Lumpybums', and 'Frinklepods'. The playfulness of these names accords with the movement of the narrative, which deploys Base's strategy of a counting game in which readers are asked to find certain numbers of creatures, such as '7 Puddlebuts, 49 Plants, 4 Buildings and 1 Snortlepig' (Base, 2006: unpaged). The game is then deployed to involve readers in following the book's representation of unrestrained anthropocentrism and species loss. As animals decrease in number and buildings increase, the numbers game highlights the extinction of a single species, the 'completely ordinary Snortlepig'. The Snortlepig is less spectacular than the other animals and its dull colours and timid habits (in most illustrations it is half hidden from view) draw attention to the complexities of species extinction, since its ordinariness and lack of obvious usefulness for the characters suggest that this creature is easily overlooked in comparison with more showy or appealing creatures. The disappearance of the Snortlepig, which appears to be permanent by the end of the narrative, foregrounds the ignorance and lack of care demonstrated by Uno and his descendants, who neither reflect on the Snortlepig's disappearance nor seek to prevent its extinction. The book's final page shows Uno's descendants, gathering around a fire and surrounded by an abundance of plant and animal life, listening to a story about the Snortlepig:

> Stories were told of the days when an extraordinary creature had lived in Uno's Garden. The children listened with wide eyes. And they never stopped believing that one day they would see a real, live Snortlepig for themselves. (Base, 2006: unpaged)

The Snortlepig has become extraordinary because it is extinct and is now the object of stories. This outcome invites comparison with other fabled and extinct creatures (the Tasmanian tiger, the great auk, the dodo) and invests the Snortlepig with a similar kind of pathos.

The symbolic space of Uno's garden is laden with edenic associations sustained by images of fruitfulness and plenty. However, Uno himself appears in the opening illustration dressed in what resembles a khaki uniform and carrying a hiking stick. His appearance is suggestive of a young colonizer discovering 'new' territory, and the alarm and concern on the faces of the ten Moopaloops he encounters presage what is to occur. On every page opening following Uno's domestication of the forest into a garden, levels of anthropogenic impact are represented. One brightly coloured illustration depicts the carefree holiday enjoyment of tourists, who dominate the frame as they trample all over the shrinking forest. Visually the forest diminishes further, as a steam train, metonymic of industrialization, moves across the double page, and, comparable with the transformations wrought by the industrial revolution, the village in *Uno's Garden* becomes a town, and the town a city. Thus the spatial inversion visually encodes the effects of uncontrolled anthropocentrism and its contribution to environmental crisis.

The turning point of the narrative occurs when the inhabitants of the city recognize that their environment is no longer aesthetically pleasing: 'One gray morning, the people of the city woke up, looked out over the endless buildings and were sad. "Why do we live in a place like this?" they asked themselves. "There are no trees." So they left' (Base, 2006: unpaged). Having invested no care in protecting their natural environment, the city-dwellers evince no compunction or concern for intergenerational justice but merely move on, presumably to destroy the next location to which they move. While the counting game of the narrative draws attention to the steady degradation of the environment, it seems, then, that Uno is the only human to value the natural world, since he alone has preserved a collection of plants in his garden. The implication is that it is 'normal' for humans to despoil and exploit the natural world, and that the ecocitizen is an exceptional human, having little in common with the bulk of humanity.

After Uno's death his children care for his collection of trees and plants, 'and slowly the forest returned' (Base, 2006: unpaged), accompanied by the creatures who originally occupied the forest habitat. The city buildings and railway line fade from view until, in the final fold-out spread, only the village buildings remain, integrated into the forest setting. The text accompanying this spread says: 'And on a beautiful day at the very beginning of spring... the forest and the city found themselves in perfect balance' (Base, 2006: unpaged). This transformation occurs despite the fact that Uno's descendants take no action other than to care for his plants; nature does the rest, restoring balance to the garden. Like James Lovelock's early articulations of his Gaia hypothesis in the 1970s,[1] *Uno's Garden* appears to be posited on the supposition that nature is capable of regenerating despite all the negative consequences of humanity's destructive and exploitative behaviour. This edenic outcome undermines the text's potential to offer readers positions as ecocitizens willing to assume responsibility to ensure environmental balance.

While *The Singing Hat* follows the progress of an individual ecocitizen, *Uno's Garden* examines the environmental consequences of greed and lack of care on a particular geographical setting and its inhabitants. George Miller's animated feature *Happy Feet* (2006) addresses the environmental effects of oil spills, global warming, and overfishing in the Antarctic region. The narrative is built on a humanist trope common in children's texts: the predicament of the outsider rejected by his community, who eventually earns respect by being true to himself. The film's protagonist, Mumble, is an outsider to his nation of emperor penguins because he alone cannot sing and thus find the 'heart song' which would have endowed him with selfhood, a life partner (Gloria), and a place in the community. However, Mumble is a gifted dancer, and when researchers film the community tap-dancing they broadcast this footage on television, so drawing attention to the parlous situation of Emperor penguins. Consequently, representatives of global powers pass a resolution banning all nations from fishing in Antarctic waters.

The penguins of *Happy Feet* are attributed with human emotions and motivations, relying on viewers' familiarity with the actors who voice the protagonists – Hugh Jackman, Nicole Kidman, Robin Williams, and Elijah Wood. Audiences are invited to align themselves with Mumble, and to accept the implication that the survival of one species (penguins) takes precedence over others, such as the leopard seals and skuas cast as predators of Mumble and his companions. Subjectivity is accorded to Mumble through cinematic strategies such as point of view shots. Late in the film, when Mumble is trapped in an oceanarium, Marine World, he attempts to explain the penguins' predicament to the 'aliens' (humans) who run the facility. In a shot showing him back-on, we are positioned to align with Mumble as he attempts to speak to the families who watch him: 'Excuse me, why are you taking our fish?' The shot then changes to the perspective of the humans, watching Mumble through glass, seeing his bill open and close but hearing only indistinguishable sounds. Scenes like this build a sense of Mumble's subjectivity, encouraging a sympathetic response from audiences. The film makes its appeal particularly to children and families, representing children as instinctively responsive to Mumble's message: in the Marine World scene, a small girl taps on the glass to attract Mumble's attention and he begins to dance for her. Entranced by this sight, she brings her mother to watch, and soon a crowd of onlookers gathers, leading to the film's climax in which Mumble is returned to the Antarctic, endowed with a tracking device leading scientists to his tap-dancing nation. The fish which are tossed into the air to be caught by the Marine World penguins for viewers' entertainment are, however, accorded no such subjectivity but are cast simply as food. The implication of such representations is that the Antarctic ecosystem is seen to revolve around one species rather than comprising a highly complex system, each part of which is essential to the health of the whole.

The film's tendency to fall back on a version of anthropocentrism where humans take account only of those species on which they can project human-like emotions and desires is somewhat offset by its emphasis on what is a tenet of deep ecology: that unless humans attend to what nature tells them, they will continue to promote a human/nature binarism in which humans determine what is best for nature. When overfishing is identified as the cause of the penguins' predicament, the film shows a collage of world leaders debating how to address this issue. It is noticeable in this sequence that while all such leaders speak in various versions of English for and against a resolution on fishing, the final and decisive statement is made by an authoritarian white man, speaking in American English, who says, 'Hang up the sign: No fishing'. Ecological virtue is thus seen to reside with the Western world, exemplified by mass demonstrations in which humans carry signs such as 'Survival or Denial', 'One struggle, 1 fight', and 'Crisis on ice'.

Most environmental texts for children feature white protagonists and imply Western readers. However, environmental degradation is far more likely to negatively affect Third World than First World populations, who can generally rely on state intervention to alleviate the consequences of global warming. As Carolyn Merchant notes, 'environmental problems in the Third World are rooted in poverty and hunger, population pressure on marginal lands, and unbalanced land distribution, while those in the First World stem from industrial pollution, waste, conspicuous consumption, and planned obsolescence' (1992: p. 25). In the next section we consider how environmental discourses in children's books imply a unified white environmental subject and privilege Western systems of environmental knowledge.

Postcolonial readings of environmental texts

Tricia Oktober's *Rainforest* (1998) depicts a destructive assault by logging machines on a pristine rain forest. The narrative is built upon an opposition between an implied, virtuous 'we' who observe the rainforest, and the unnamed and evil 'they' whose machines destroy it. The illustrations, showing appealing, helpless animals, birds, and insects looking out of the pages, imply concerned and sympathetic viewers who may be expected to grow into the 'brave people who...fought so hard for this forest to be...PROTECTED WILDERNESS' (1998: p. 30). As is so often the case when discourses of wilderness are deployed, the notion of a pristine, untouched environment precludes reference to Indigenous habitation, so that whiteness is enshrined as the normal and unremarked ground of knowledge and activism. As Fabienne Bayet-Charlton notes, 'The concept of wilderness as nature without any trace of human interaction, dehumanises the Indigenous peoples living within that landscape' (2003: p. 174), erasing Indigenous associations with the use of their ancestral lands over many thousands of years.

A similar effect is evident in a nonfiction work for children, Pat Slater and Steve Parish's *Discover & Learn about Australian Forests and Woodlands* (2002), which commences with a history of the Australian continent heavily weighted toward Western imagery and traditions. The text explains that after the land mass of Gondwana broke up, 'Like a giant Noah's Ark, the new continent carried a cargo of living things' (2002: p. 3). In the conceptual scheme presented by Slater, Indigenous Australians were 'a new crew', boarding the Ark much like the 'European humans' who arrived in 1788. To be sure, Slater notes that this 'new crew' boarded the Ark '60,000 or more years ago', but her focus on the effects of human habitation subsumes Indigenous Australians within the category of 'Australians' who 'have come to realise that the Ark's resources need to be saved' (2002: p. 3). In this densely written book, Indigenous Australians are occasionally named in the 'Facts' N Figures File' which appears at the bottom of some pages, generally in the past tense: 'Acacia bark was used by Aborigines to poison fish.... Aboriginal uses for melaleucas included materials for canoes, shelters, blankets, burial shrouds and bandages' (2002: p. 37). The effect of such references is both to homogenize Indigenous cultures and to consign Indigenous habitation and knowledge to a remote past cordoned off from the body of the text, which organizes environmental concepts in relation to Carl Linnaeus's taxonomic principles,[2] so implying that Western systems of thought are normative.

Advocacy on behalf of endangered species in children's texts, as in broader cultural contexts, is liable to appeal to emotionality through images of attractive (and potentially suffering) individual creatures (Buell, 2001: pp. 201–2). This effect is clear in the images on the cover of Rick Wilkinson's *Endangered!* (2002), where the tiny body, large eyes, and appealing expression of the mountain pygmy-possum construct this animal as a child-like figure 'speaking' to a child audience to a more marked extent than the other featured animals, the Sumatran Tiger, Red Panda, and White Rhinoceros. Such individualization of an endangered (young) animal accords with narrative practices endemic to children's literature, which habitually tracks the growth and development of protagonists, typically from a state of solipsism to an enhanced capacity for empathy. Implied child readers are thus positioned as potential 'friends' or 'saviours' of child-like endangered animals such as the pygmy-possum.

In line with this approach, responsibility for the survival of endangered species is projected in many children's texts onto a single heroic figure or on institutions such as the 'safe havens' celebrated in *Endangered!*: Melbourne Zoo, Healesville Sanctuary, and Werribee Open Range Zoo. These institutional sites, and the individuals who function as their metonyms, are treated as 'naturally' white through representations of knowledge, expertise, and hierarchies; and they imply child readers whose assumptions and ideologies accord with those of adult narrators. One of the animals profiled in *Endangered!* is the tree kangaroo, which survives in small numbers in northern Queensland and Papua New Guinea. The 'discovery' of one species of tree kangaroo is described as follows:

> there is one species [of the 'Tenkile' tree kangaroo], that no scientist knew existed until Australian biologist and explorer Tim Flannery came across it during an expedition through Papua New Guinea in 1989.... Unfortunately, by the time Tim arrived there were probably fewer than 200 Tenkile left. After talking to the local villagers, he realised that if they were not protected the species would soon be extinct. (2002: p. 10)

The narration is then attributed to Gary Slater, of Melbourne Zoo, who offers the following explanation:

> In the past, the villagers have hunted the tree kangaroo for food and for its fur, or to trade for other items. They now understand that soon there may be no Tenkile for their children to see, and they have agreed to stop hunting the animal for two years. We hope it will be longer'. (2002: p. 10)

Here the virtuous white men, Tim Flannery and the zoo staff, are pitted against the ecologically careless villagers, who are disciplined and forced to stop hunting Tenkile. This is a strikingly flattened and schematized representation of the complex social and ecological processes which were set in train by colonialism in Papua New Guinea, and which resulted in deforestation, an increase in human populations, destabilization of traditional practices controlling hunting, and a deficit of sources of protein for Indigenous land-holders.

The incoherence at the heart of the book's explanation about the plight of the Tenkile is apparent in Slater's explanation that 'the local people have very strong feelings for their land and all the animals and plants on it, ... and they will not allow anyone to take even a few of the Tenkile away for a captive breeding program in a zoo in Papua New Guinea or Australia' (2002: p. 10). That is, the local people are prone to excesses of feeling which render them less rational and less strategic than the scientists, who, because of the villagers' emotionality, are obliged to 'build a small research station on government land' for the 'Tenkile Conservation Alliance'. Two photographs accompany the story of the Tenkile: a close-up of the animal, and a picture of 'Melbourne Zoo keeper Matt Vincent and a villager with a Tenkile'. Not only are the heroic zoo keepers rational and organized, capable of saving the Tenkile in the face of the villagers' excesses of emotion, on one hand, and exploitation, on the other, they also have, unlike the villagers, names and identities.

Warren Brim and Anna Eglitis's illustrated book *Creatures of the Rainforest* (2005) presents a strikingly different perspective of cross-cultural perceptions and values, and results from collaboration between an Indigenous (Brim) and non-Indigenous artist (Eglitis). The book's subtitle is 'Two artists explore Djabugay country'.[3] This formulation of co-production is sustained throughout the text, which is organized as an alphabet book, ranging from the green ant to the Zamia palm. Each page opening incorporates two illustrations, one by Brim and the other by Eglitis, so that one image engages in dialogue with the other. For instance, the letter 'G' is represented by Goanna Ganyal, with Eglitis's illustration on one page and Brim's on the other. The captions are in Djabugay, translated into English, and the sense of this arrangement is that the English text is secondary, a translation of the primary text in Djabugay.

The descriptions of flora and fauna were developed through collaboration between Anna Eglitis, Warren Brim, and the Djabugay elder Uncle Roy Banning, who, Eglitis says, provided information about 'the traditional aspect of certain creatures – such as the use of green ants for medicine and the Mosquito Dance' (A. Eglitis, 2006: pers. comm., 3 November). The transliteration of Djabugay language beneath each picture was provided by Michael Quinn, a British anthropologist and linguist who from 1988 worked with Roy Banning and other elders to study and record Djabugay language. The production of the book thus relies not only on the collaboration of Brim and Eglitis but also on histories of collaboration between Indigenous and non-Indigenous artists and scholars.

The paired illustrations of *Creatures of the Rainforest* produce a sense of cross-cultural dialogue, and this is true also of the verbal text. Thus, the description of the goanna reads as follows: 'The scientific name for this species of goanna is *Varanus tristis orientalis,* and in Djabugay country it is seen on the ground, in trees and among rocks' (2005: p. 14). Scientific epistemologies, signalled through the goanna's Latin name, are set alongside Djabugay knowledge, which incorporates cultural and religious significations: 'Goanna and eggs. Goanna dreaming' (2005: p. 15). The verbal text thus refers to different systems of knowledge, brought together through their focus on creatures of the rainforest, just as the illustrations derive from and refer to different traditions of representation and symbolism. Similarly, in the pages showing 'Owl (boobook) Djurrgu' (2005: pp. 30–31), Eglitis's illustration hinges on a domestic and familial style of representation in which the baby owls wait for their food, while Brim's illustration locates the owl in relation to the earthy colours and the forms which refer to Djabugay traditions.

In contrast with Slater and Parish's *Discover & Learn about Australian Forests and Woodlands,* where Indigenous practices and customs are consigned to the precolonial past, *Creatures of the Rainforest* rejects this distinction between an Indigenous past and a white present and future. In the pages 'Mosquito Ngugun' (2005: pp. 26–7), the text describes how Djabugay dancers 'perform the Mosquito Dance in which they remember the old days when their ancestors would cover themselves in mud and use wulmbarra (leafy branches) to wave away the mosquitoes'. Not only does the text insist on the primacy of Djabugay language, but it asserts Indigenous continuity and survival. Brim and Eglitis do not explicitly promote environmental messages or imply that humans are charged with the responsibility of determining what in nature is good and what is not. Rather, they advocate regard for and knowledge of the creatures they represent and model a respectful and dialogical engagement between Western and Djabugay epistemologies and modes of representation. In this way they demonstrate that relations between humans and the natural world are inflected by cultural beliefs and practices, and position readers to negotiate differences and imagine alignments across cultural perspectives.

Gender and Indigeneity in *Princess Mononoke*

Hayao Miyazaki's 1997 anime *Princess Mononoke* is centrally concerned with relations between humans and the natural world in the fourteenth-century setting of the Muromachi period. Rather than the courtly domain of the emperor, in which nature is artfully transformed into landscaped gardens, the film is located in two settings far from the emperor's palace: wild forests and rivers far in the west of Japan; and the fortress city of Tatara ('Iron Town'). As Susan Napier notes, the film 'deals with the loss of a Japan that existed before the patriarchal system, a Japan in which nature, rather than humans, ruled' (2001: p. 176). Instead of the idealized imagery of a unified people governed by an aristocratic and patriarchal ruling class, the film 'offers a vision of cultural dissonance, spiritual loss and environmental apocalypse' (Napier, 2001: p. 176). As Lucy Wright points out, this vision interrogates a crucial aspect of Japan's national mythology by 'problematis[ing] Japan's oft-touted love of nature' (2005), which coexists with high levels of environmental destruction caused by dam construction, marine pollution, and overbuilding (Taylor, 1999: pp. 541–3).

Moreover, the film's protagonists come from groups traditionally excluded from accounts of the Japanese past: women, characters of non-Japanese ethnicity, outcasts, the *kamigami*, the ancient gods of the land, and the *hakemono*, ghostly figures who are implacably opposed to humans. The principal male protagonist, Ashitaka, the last prince of the non-Japanese Emishi minority, functions in large part as the focalizing agent through whose eyes and consciousness we see the Japanese and nonhuman characters of the film. Wounded by the *tatarigami*, a boar-god driven mad by its injuries at the hand of humans, Ashitaka is marked by a spiral-shaped stain on his arm, an injury which will eventually kill him unless the boar's curse is lifted. The boar's suffering is caused by an iron ball lodged within his body and produced by the workers of Tatara, ruled by the powerful Lady Eboshi and dedicated to the production of iron. The opposition between nature and humans is at its most evident in the destruction of the forest around Tatara, to fuel its smelting furnaces, and in the destructive force of iron as it penetrates the bodies of animals and gods. In the last battle of the film, Eboshi shoots the *shishigami*, or great spirit, and severs his head, instigating an environmental cataclysm in which the forests and their spirits are destroyed. But Ashitaka and San together recover the head and restore it to the *shishigami*, who destroys Tatara and transforms its wasted hills into forests.

Princess Mononoke departs from traditional Japanese hero stories most markedly in its depiction of powerful female protagonists: Lady Eboshi, who rules over Tatara; San, a human girl who has been brought up by wolves; and San's 'mother', the wolf god Moro. It is noticeable that the women in the film, including the former brothel workers employed by Eboshi, are outspoken and independent, whereas the men (apart from Ashitaka) are greedy, venal, and cowardly. Nevertheless, the film does not propose a simple opposition between male and female, or between humans and nature. For instance, Eboshi is in league with the emperor's forces in her battle with the forest gods, and although she promises at the end of the film to construct a 'better' Tatara, this undertaking is contingent upon her maintaining her power. Nevertheless, she is at the centre of her community of outcasts, comprising women she has bought from brothel owners, and lepers to whom she provides home and care. She is thus aligned both with the patriarchal and oppressive forces of the emperor, and also with those excluded from society.

Committed to the destruction of the forests in the interests of her iron-mongering enterprise, Eboshi is scarcely an ecofeminist hero; neither is San, whose upbringing as a wolf-girl leaves her with a deep distrust of humans and an incapacity to commit herself to a close relationship with the only human (Ashitaka) with whom she aligns. We first view San's face after she has sucked poison from the gunshot wound sustained by Moro, in the image made famous through its use in trailers and the covers of DVDs. San's youth and human femininity are juxtaposed with the signifiers of her wolfhood: a necklace of teeth, a fur cape. Her cheeks are marked with red slashes, and her mouth, hand, and arm are stained with Moro's blood. This excess of blood suggests menstrual bleeding and hence San's womanhood; it also signals her propensity for killing. The woman/nature connection privileged in many versions of cultural feminism (Merchant, 1992: pp. 193–222) does not fit with San's rejection of humans, just as Eboshi's formation of a community of women in Tatara is at odds (in ecofeminist terms) with her determination to destroy the forest and its gods.

Rather, it is Ashitaka, the male Aboriginal protagonist, who most closely exemplifies an ecofeminist ideal; or at least the style of social ecofeminism proposed by Plumwood, who argues that the reason/nature dualism privileged in Cartesian thought 'divides, devalues and denies the colonised other which is nature' (Plumwood, 1993: p. 192). At the beginning of the film, Ashitaka, wounded by the boar-god, sits before the Emishi wise woman as she consults the gods through divination. Her tools of trade, laid out before her, comprise stones, herbs, bones. Ashitaka, docile and attentive, models a mode of behaviour based on animist beliefs and female traditions of wisdom. Of all the men in the film he is the only one who relates to women – the iron workers, San – without invoking gender hierarchies, telling the scornful Eboshi that he wishes to 'see with eyes unclouded with hate'. At the end of the film when San returns to the forest, Ashitaka remains with Eboshi to help her develop the new community she promises. Disrupting the nature/human divide which governs the other characters and their conceptual frameworks, Ashitaka constitutes a sign, even if a tentative and provisional one, of the possibility of new models of cognition, affect, and behaviour which reject dualism and its consequences.

Conclusion

As we have suggested in our discussions of recent environmental texts for children and young people, the field of ecocriticism is characterized by deep divides which reflect the rifts and tensions in the broader domain of environmentalism. Within individual texts, too, it is common to see a range of environmental positions, often conflicting with one another. Thus, the appealing, tap-dancing penguins of *Happy Feet* (2006) are privileged above all other Antarctic species, attributed with human-like emotions and aspirations while other species are treated as merely objects. The film's depictions of ice shelves cracking and splitting under the strain of global warming are treated as spectacles evoking awe and even admiration, while the practice of overfishing is treated in isolation from the other factors (such as rising sea levels, ozone depletion, and pollution) negatively affecting the Antarctic ecosystem.

Such conceptual and representational inconsistencies are evidence of the peculiar difficulties faced by producers of environmental texts for children. On one hand, it is a truism that today's children will be charged, as adults, with the task of addressing the negative effects of decisions and practices made by preceding generations. On the other hand, most children's books draw back from the pessimistic messages of environmentalists such as James Lovelock, who predicts that most human life is set for destruction in the near future. There exist powerful tensions, too, between the complexities of environmental science and the limitations of life experience and conceptual development in young children. The passions and fears which inform discussions of environmental futures have shaped the development of ecocriticism as a scholarly field, and are inextricably woven into environmental texts for children.

Further Reading

Huggan, G. & Tiffin, H. 2010. *Postcolonial ecocriticism: literature, animals, environment*. Routledge, New York. This book examines relationships between humans, animals, and the environment in postcolonial texts.

Bradford, C., Mallan, K., Stephens, J., & McCallum, R. 2008. 'The struggle to be human in a posthuman world'. In *New world orders in contemporary children's literature: utopian transformations*. Palgrave Macmillan, Houndmills, pp. 79–104.

Themed issues: 'Ecology and the child' ed. Greenway, B. 1994/95. *Children's Literature Association Quarterly*, vol. 19, no. 4. 'Green worlds: nature and ecology' ed. S. Rahn 1995. *The Lion and the Unicorn*, vol. 19, no. 2.

Ingram, A.M.l., Marshall, I., Philippon, D.J., & Sweeting, A. (eds) 2007, *Coming into contact: explorations in ecocritical theory and practice*. University of Georgia Press, Athens, Georgia. The sixteen essays in this collection expand scholarship in the field of ecocriticism established by earlier texts such as *The ecocriticism reader* (Glotfelty & Fromm, 1996).

Notes

1 James Lovelock's Gaia hypothesis, developed in the 1960s, originally proposed that life on Earth works in such a way that it maintains conditions favourable

to life. During Lovelock's long career he has modified this hypothesis, concluding in his 2009 book, *The vanishing face of Gaia,* that an abrupt change in global temperatures in the near future will lead to the collapse of global life and the near-destruction of humanity.

2   The Swedish naturalist Carl Linnaeus established the system of naming and ordering plants and animals, which is still in use today. His *Systema Naturae* is the starting point for modern taxonomies.

3   Djabugay country is the rain forest and tableland country of far north Queensland, Australia, to which the Djabugay people belong.

7
From 'Wizard' to 'Wicked': Adaptation Theory and Young Adult Fiction

David Buchbinder

There is a word game, to which the title of this chapter partly alludes, in which the participants are required, by changing only one letter in each move, to transform an original word into a new, predetermined one of the same number of characters. Setting aside the question of whether it is indeed possible thus to transform 'wizard' into 'wicked' (and if so, in how many moves), this game serves as a useful metaphor when considering the nature of textual adaptation, since the continuing transformations (for which, read 'adaptations') of the word require one to bear in mind its prior transformations as well as the initiating word that functioned as the starting point. Without such recollection, each word in the process becomes simply an independent lexical item – with its own meaning, to be sure. However, what is lost is the sense not only of transformation but also of the transmission of elements in a series which in itself constitutes part of the meaning of each word. We may call this the principle of antecedent seriality.

Adaptation and adaptation theory

In academic circles and among the general public, critical discussion and debate have often centred on the use of previous works to create new ones, whether in the same medium or genre, as well as about the merits of such adaptation. Frequently, therefore, that discussion turns on the issue of whether those adaptations are accurate re-presentations of the original, or are always-already inferior reworkings. However, the more generalized theorization of adaptation *as a practice* is comparatively recent. Below I consider two works, Linda Hutcheon's *A Theory of Adaptation* and Julie Sanders' *Adaptation and Appropriation*, both published in 2006 and both addressing the issues raised by the practice of adaptation as well as surveying some of the key theorizations of adaptation in relation to specific texts, media, and genres.

The sense of antecedent seriality is an essential component in the understanding of adaptation of texts: unless we are aware of the presence of an originary text,[1] even if we have never read or viewed it, we cannot read and understand the text before us *as an adaptation*. Thus, to take as an example Tim Burton's 2010 film *Alice in Wonderland*, a viewer unfamiliar with Carroll's originary work is likely to treat the film hermeneutically, as a sort of closed system of meaning, rather like the single lexical item in the word game described above. By contrast, a viewer who knows the Carroll narrative will understand Burton's film as a more open text, possessing points of convergence with, but also of departures from, the novel. The question of which viewer would arrive at a more complex reading of the film is thus distinct from that of the evaluation of the film as an accurate rendering of the originary text.

Adaptation, especially of literary texts, has not traditionally enjoyed a good press. It has often been seen as belated, secondary, and inferior to the original. 'The movie isn't as good as the book', is the sort of comment frequently heard about adaptation; and while it may be true that, for any number of reasons, one's response to an adaptation may be less enthusiastic than one's recollection of the text that has been adapted, there are two key assumptions in such a statement that need to be teased out and addressed.

In the first place, our fetishization of originality has comparatively recent beginnings, dating back to the Romantics and their adulation of the rustic, the primitive, and the nonurban as articulating more primal truths than were offered by an increasingly sophisticated, industrialized, and urbanized culture. At the same time, the falling away, from the late seventeenth century, of patronage as a way for artists (including writers) to dedicate themselves to their work without needing to worry about day-to-day necessities such as accommodation or food necessarily meant that artists began to sell their work in order to keep body and soul together. One effect of this was the identification of a work of art as the intellectual property of the artist, which in turn brought about an emphasis on originality in works of art.

As a result, the adaptation of an originary text is quite often treated as only a step away from plagiarism. However, much of the literary output of classical Greek culture, for instance, consisted of reworkings of already familiar narratives, as, for example, in the dramatic work of Aeschylus, Sophocles, and Euripides. Even a prominent writer in English literature such as Shakespeare borrowed most if not, indeed, all of his plots from other writers, appropriating from classical antecedents as well as English, French, and Italian contemporaries and near-contemporaries. Such adaptations were often regarded as testifying to the quality of the source material; but it was also how that material was reinflected and reoriented that attracted attention. That is, the 'originality' of Aeschylus, Sophocles, Euripides, Shakespeare, and many others lay in *what they made of the material they borrowed*, not necessarily in the invention of narratives to tell.

In the second place, as the example of Shakespeare illustrates, the identification of adaptations as 'good' or 'bad' *in principle*, not in execution, is
often highly idiosyncratic and selective. For instance, Shakespeare fashioned his tragedy about youthful star-crossed lovers *Romeo and Juliet* – a text
often set on the literature syllabus in high schools – out of material deriv-
ing ultimately from Ovid's *Metamorphoses* (8 AD), via a number of workings
and reworkings of the story ranging from Masuccio Salernitano's tale of
Mariotto and Gianozza, in novel 33 of *Il Novellino* (1476) to the Romeo and
Juliet story in William Painter's *Palace of Pleasure* (1582). Yet one does not
usually hear Shakespeare accused of being a plagiarist or as a mere adapter
of others' works; on the contrary, an entire scholarly industry has grown up
around the study of Shakespeare's sources. Moreover, *Romeo and Juliet* itself
has given rise to further adaptations, including the musical *West Side Story*,
with lyrics by Stephen Sondheim and music by Leonard Bernstein (first
staged in 1957 and made into a film in 1961), which reset the action in New
York City and transformed the feuding Montague and Capulet families into
the rival gangs of the Jets and the Sharks, divided by their ethnicity; or Baz
Luhrmann's *Romeo + Juliet* (1996), which likewise reset the action in the
USA, and transformed the family feud of the originary play into a corporate
battleground. We may include here also Diana Wynne Jones' 1980 children's fantasy *The Magicians of Caprona*, part of her Chrestomanci series. As
in Shakespeare's play, whose action takes place chiefly in the dukedom and
city of Verona, Jones sets the action in the dukedom and city of Caprona
(whose name echoes that of Verona); and, again, as in *Romeo and Juliet*,
the peace and welfare of the city are threatened by the warring of two
houses or families, here the Montana and the Petrocchi. Only through the
friendship and combined efforts of young Tonino Montana and Angela
Petrocchi are peace restored and the feuding brought to an end. Unlike
Shakespeare's tragedy, Jones' narrative ends happily. However, a reader of
this novel unfamiliar with either Shakespeare's play or at least the narrative
outline of *Romeo and Juliet* would fail to notice not only that Jones' work
was an adaptation of Shakespeare's but that the endings of each diverged
significantly.[2]

An 'adaptation of' implies a strong fidelity to the originary text.
Hutcheon points out that there may be many reasons why an adaptation is undertaken, and several of the subheadings of her third chapter,
'Who? Why? (Adapters)', are broadly indicative: 'The Economic Lures', 'The
Legal Constraints', 'Cultural Capital', and 'Personal and Political Motives'
(Hutcheon, 2006: pp. 79–111). The question of the degree of an adaptation's
fidelity to the originary text, therefore, is partly linked to the reason that
particular adaptation is produced. However, she points out that 'One lesson
[to be learned about adaptation] is that to be second is not to be secondary or inferior; likewise, to be first is not to be originary or authoritative'
(Hutcheon, 2006: p. xiii). Hutcheon observes that 'adaptation is a form of

repetition without replication', and therefore 'change is inevitable, even without any conscious updating or alteration of setting. And with change come corresponding modifications in the political valence and even meaning of stories' (Hutcheon, 2006: p. xvi).

Indeed, she argues that adaptation is always-already built into the culture's understanding of narrative and narratives. Citing Walter Benjamin, T.S. Eliot, and Northrop Frye, she remarks that it is a 'truism' that 'art is derived from other art; stories are born of other stories' (Hutcheon, 2006: p. 2). One should, however, be cautious here: though intertextual reference from one text to another may well alter the signification of material referred to—and in that sense adapt it—adaptation proper exceeds individual, local quotation from and/or alteration of a source text. That is, adaptation *transposes* the originary text into a new mode and/or context (even when it is the adaptation of one literary text into another literary text); and that transposition necessarily creates shifts of meaning and understanding for the reader or viewer.

The transposition of a work from one medium, genre, or context into another is capable of generating pleasure and, Hutcheon suggests, 'Part of this pleasure…comes simply from repetition with variation, from the comfort of ritual combined with the piquancy of surprise'. She continues: 'Recognition and remembrance are part of the pleasure (and risk) of experiencing an adaptation; so too is change' (Hutcheon, 2006: p. 4). Accordingly, when we are aware that an adaptation *is* an adaptation, we engage with what Hutcheon calls, borrowing the term from Michael Alexander, the 'palimpsestuousness' of the relationship between originary text and adaptation; that is, adaptations are 'haunted at all times by their adapted texts' (Hutcheon, 2006: p. 6). The term 'palimpsestuous' neatly encapsulates both the idea of an earlier document making its presence felt literally – that is, remaining legible – through the writing over it of a later text,[3] and that of a close, even intimate, yet somehow improper ('incestuous') relationship between the originary and adapted texts. As Hutcheon points out, 'there are manifestly many different possible intentions behind the act of adaptation: the urge to consume and erase the memory of the adapted text or to call it into question is as likely as the desire to pay tribute by copying' (Hutcheon, 2006: p. 7).

The term 'adaptation', as Hutcheon notes, may refer either to the process or the product of adaptation (Hutcheon, 2006: pp. 7–8); and much of the book is given over to distinguishing between the two and exploring each, while at the same time avoiding both too broad and too narrow a conception of adaptation. For example, seeing the adaptation of a work simply as intertextual is too broad: it denies the specificity, in terms of medium, transcoding, audience, and so on, of the adaptation itself. On the other hand, to view the adaptation of a work as a sort of literal translation is to limit radically the possibilities in terms of a new understanding of the originary work as well as the creation of an independent set of meanings in the adaptation itself. (Such an approach, of course, is also to invite judgment of an adaptation on those grounds alone.) Hutcheon cites John Dryden's definition of paraphrase, in his *Examen poeticum* (first published in 1693), as 'translation with latitude' (Hutcheon, 2006: p. 17). Perhaps adaptation, in its most positive aspect, should be understood rather as translation with attitude. It is for this reason that, in the closing chapter of the book, Hutcheon remarks:

> An adaptation is not vampiric: it does not draw the life-blood from its source and leave it dying or dead, nor is it paler than the adapted work. It may, on the contrary, keep that prior work alive, giving it an afterlife it would never have had otherwise. (Hutcheon, 2006: p. 176)

Like Hutcheon, Julie Sanders foregrounds the fact that texts exist in a relationship to one another, both borrowing and changing material; and she too cites T. S. Eliot's essay 'Tradition and the Individual Talent' (1919), in which Eliot argues, 'not blind adherence to precursor texts or ages, an action that would after all be little more than literary plagiarism; his notion of the "individual talent" was that it created new material upon the surface and foundation of the literary past' (Sanders, 2006: p. 8). As the title of Sanders's book suggests, *Adaptation and Appropriation* draws a distinction between adaptation proper and the appropriation of material. She defines adaptation as 'a transpositional practice, casting a specific genre into another generic mode, and act of re-vision in itself'. She continues:

> It can parallel editorial practice in some respects, indulging in the exercise of trimming and pruning; yet it can also be an amplificatory procedure engaged in addition, expansion, accretion, and interpola-tion. ... Adaptation is frequently involved in offering commentary on a sourcetext. This is achieved most often by offering a revised point of view from the 'original,' adding a hypothetical motivation, or voicing the silenced and marginalized. Yet adaptation can also constitute a simpler attempt to make texts 'relevant' or easily comprehensible to new audiences and readerships by the processes of approximation and updating. (Sanders, 2006: pp. 18–19)

Accordingly, she invokes the three categories of adaptation indicated by Deborah Cartmell: transposition, commentary, and analogue. Transposition includes not merely the relocation of a narrative from one genre to another but also potentially the repositioning of that narrative in terms of culture, geography, and temporality/history. The second category, commentary, is 'more culturally loaded,' in that such adaptations 'comment on the politics of the source text, or those of the new *mise-en-scène*, or both, usually by means of alteration or addition'. The final category, analogue, is considerably distanced from the first: 'While it may enrich and deepen our understanding of the new cultural products to be aware of its shaping intertext, it may not be entirely necessary to enjoy the work independently'. She goes on to exemplify 'stand-alone works that are nevertheless deepened when their status as analogue is revealed' by citing the movies *Clueless* (1995; based on Jane Austen's *Emma*), *Apocalypse Now* (1979; based on Conrad's *Heart of Darkness*), and *The Claim* (2001; based on Thomas Hardy's *The Mayor of Casterbridge*) (Sanders, 2006: pp. 20–23).

While 'An adaptation signals a relationship with an informing sourcetext or original', according to Sanders:

> appropriation frequently affects [*sic*] a more decisive journey away from the informing source into a wholly new cultural product and domain. This may or may not involve a generic shift, and it may still require the intellectual juxtaposition of (at least) one text against another that we have suggested is central to the reading and spectating experience of adaptations. But the appropriate contextual texts are not always as clearly signalled or acknowledged as in the adaptive process. (p. 26)

Sanders proposes two categories: embedded texts and sustained appropriations (p. 26). As examples of embedded texts she offers the musicals *West Side Story* and *Kiss Me Kate*, each of which reworks its originary text – *Romeo and Juliet* and *The Taming of the Shrew*, respectively – so that the action is set in modern times, with other issues foregrounded. For example, in *West Side Story*, questions of ethnicity arise which do not play a part in the original Shakespeare play, while in *Kiss Me Kate* – which Sanders describes as both adaptation (the musicalized stage play) and appropriation (the offstage/backstage goings-on) (Sanders, 2006: p. 29) – the chief focus rests on the backstage stories of, and relationships among, performers, with the admixture of a gangster narrative in the presence of two Mafia-like thugs.

Sanders' section on the category of sustained appropriation is subtitled 'Homage or Plagiarism?' (Sanders, 2006: p. 32). Illustrating her argument with a discussion of the relationship between Graham Swift's novel *Last Orders* (1996) and its close relationship to William Faulkner's *As I Lay Dying* (1930), and the accusation that Swift had plagiarized Faulkner's novel, Sanders argues for a 'kinetic vocabulary ... that would be dynamic, moving forward rather than conducting the purely backward-looking search for source or origin' (Sanders, 2006: p. 38). This is also what Hutcheon argues for in relation to adaptation, although she does not discuss appropriation as a form distinct from adaptation. It may be, indeed, that the distinction between these terms is chiefly heuristic; that is, it is an analytic device that may help us to understand subtle discriminations among types of adaptation, but which may not always work in practice with as much clarity as Sanders' argument might suggest.

Appropriation and parody: *Pride and Prejudice and Zombies* and *Witches Abroad*

A recent example that exposes the difficulty of distinguishing neatly between adaptation and appropriation comes from Jane Austen and Seth Grahame-Smith who author jointly (according to the title page) *Pride and Prejudice and Zombies: the classic regency romance – now with violent zombie mayhem* (2009). Grahame-Smith retains the general narrative trajectory of Jane Austen's 1813 novel *Pride and Prejudice*, together with a considerable quantity of the original prose. However, without prior knowledge of the originary text, the reader is unlikely to get most of the jokes in this parody, in which the Bennet daughters have been trained in Ninja-style fighting in the Shaolin Temple in China in order to do battle with the plague of zombies that has infested Britain. (Their Chinese training becomes for Lady Catherine De Bourgh a matter of scorn and contempt, since she is a leading warrior in the fight against the zombies and was herself trained in Japan.) Indeed, the very opening sentence of this novel – 'It is a truth universally acknowledged that a zombie in possession of brains must be in want of more brains' (p. 7) – makes little sense beyond the purely descriptive unless one is aware of the famous opening statement of Austen's novel: 'It is a truth universally acknowledged, that a single man in possession of a good fortune, must be in want of a wife' (Austen, 1972: p. 51). Even the cover design of *Pride and Prejudice and Zombies* is reminiscent of the classic 1972 Penguin English Library edition of Austen's novel.

The question to ask here is whether *Pride and Prejudice and Zombies* is an adaptation or an appropriation of Austen's original novel. On one hand, the outline of the adapted text (to use Hutcheon's term) remains quite visible through Grahame-Smith's treatment of it; moreover, his use of a good deal of Austen's prose likewise links it 'palimpsestuously' to *Pride and Prejudice*. These two aspects of the more recent novel suggest that we are in the presence of an adaptation. However, the introduction of a plague of zombies into the decorous lives of respectable women living in a small town clearly does something to Austen's original. While it is true that this may allow Grahame-Smith to provide a voice or voices different from those heard in Austen's text, and to foreground and rework certain aspects of the latter that Sanders, as we have seen, identifies with adaptation (here, for example, the well-bred helplessness of middle- and upper-class women), the sheer absurdity of this narrative of the Bennet daughters searching for love and marriage in a zombie-infested Regency England might suggest the novel is in fact an appropriation. Nevertheless, it is difficult to determine here where adaptation ceases and appropriation begins.

Grahame-Smith's reworking and send-up of *Pride and Prejudice* may be understood as aimed at a male readership who might dismiss the original novel as 'old' 'chick lit' since it is in essence a romantic narrative. By introducing zombies and Ninja-style fighting, and sexualizing a number of the characters, especially Elizabeth Bennet and her aunt Mrs Phillips, as well as maintaining a tongue-in-cheek tone, Grahame-Smith ostensibly makes *Pride and Prejudice* both accessible and attractive to male, and especially young male, readers. However, as noted above, by retaining so much of the original prose, he also requires the reader to keep in mind Austen's novel, without which much of the humour becomes puerile. Like the film *10 Things I Hate about You*, *Pride and Prejudice and Zombies* falls into at least two of Hutcheon's categories, namely, 'The Economic Lures' and 'Cultural Capital'.

Parody, then, may be thought of as a form of 'adaptation from' an originary text if it is to work *as parody*. Ironically, therefore, it retains a high level of fidelity to that originary text. In the case of Grahame-Smith's iconoclastic work, the transformation has been from print text to print text; and the parodying of Austen's novel has required a minimal level of transcoding in order to capture a particular readership, namely, one familiar with the original text, or possibly male readers who may be unfamiliar with the original. However, adaptations from one medium to another require more elaborate and complex transcodings, not only in order to transfer the originary text from one medium to another – say, novel into film – but also to identify and target a particular audience. A film or TV miniseries of *Pride and Prejudice* (and there have been several of each) will in general be aimed at an audience familiar with and presumably respectful of the novel. Were a film to be made of *Pride and Prejudice and Zombies*, its audience might well be familiar with Austen's novel but would in all likelihood maintain a rather different attitude towards it, an attitude presumably conditioned by differences of age as well as taste. Such a film would no doubt invoke the codes of horror movies, especially those involving zombies, both because the audience would already be familiar with such codes and because, like the book, the film would target those codes for the purpose of parody.

Grahame-Smith's novel clearly indicates that it is not always possible to distinguish adaptation from appropriation. In his novel *Witches Abroad* (1998), part of his Discworld fantasy series, Terry Pratchett raises the interesting question of the possibility for an adaptation to cease to be an adaptation and become something else entirely – that 'more decisive journey away from the informing source into a wholly new cultural product and domain' which Sanders, as we have seen above, identifies as the trajectory of appropriation. In *Witches Abroad*, narrative is described narrative – 'stories' – as 'great flapping ribbons of shaped space-time' which

> etch grooves deep enough for people to follow in the same way that water follows certain paths down a mountainside. And every time fresh actors tread the path of the story, the groove runs deeper.

This, says the narrator, 'is called the theory of narrative causality, and it means that a story, once started, *takes a shape*. It picks up all the vibrations of all the other workings of that story that have ever been' (Pratchett, 1998: pp. 8–9). The plot of this novel turns around the question of adaptation itself. The witches of the title, Granny Weatherwax, Nanny Ogg, and Magrat Garlick, travel to Genua from their home in Lancre. Upon arriving in the vicinity of Genua, the three witches discover that someone – as it turns out, Granny Weatherwax's sister, Lily – is twisting traditional fairy tales so that they become something different. In effect, Lily adapts the narratives to suit her own ends. Lily Weatherwax can be said, therefore, to have attempted the radical appropriation and transformation of the plots of the various fairy tales that she has distorted; and this is clearly marked in the narrative as immoral, both because those tales are – or should be – inviolate, and because Lily's goal has been the accumulation of power for herself. However, that assumption about the inviolability of an original and originary text is precisely what underlies the negative criticism of adaptations of texts and characterizes them as belated and inferior.

Adaptation: inferior or merely different?

An understanding of the adaptation of an originary text, therefore, requires us to compare what each sets out to signify and whether each achieves its goal. A radical difference between these goals does not necessarily mean that the adaptation is inferior to its originary text, though of course it might raise questions as to why the adaptation was undertaken rather than a completely fresh and original text produced. Indeed, it might be useful to think of adaptations as falling into one of two categories: 'adaptations *of*' an originary text and 'adaptations *from*' such a text (the latter idea sometimes phrased, in film credits, as 'based on' or 'inspired by' an originary text). As the above instances suggest, the business of adaptation has a long and complex history: it is certainly not a simple matter of a novel-into-film transformation, as many today seem to assume. For example, whereas, the protagonist in Lewis Carroll's *Alice's Adventures in Wonderland* (1865) encounters the inhabitants of Wonderland for the first time, Burton's film *Alice in Wonderland* (2010) reworks Alice's adventure so that she in fact *revisits* Wonderland, though she has forgotten that experience, recalling it only toward the end of the film narrative. In the film, the Red Queen is a combination (Humpty Dumpty, in Carroll's narrative, might have called it a 'portmanteau' [Carroll, 1971: p. 164]) of the Queen of Hearts in *Alice's Adventures in Wonderland* and the Red Queen in *Through the Looking-Glass* (1871); and the sibling rivalry between the Red and White Queens (played, respectively, by Helena Bonham-Carter and Anne Hathaway) is entirely Burton's invention, as is the representation of the Mad Hatter (Johnny Depp) as a melancholic individual who becomes Alice's love interest. There are, as Hutcheon notes in her book, adaptations from, to, and among print (novel, drama, poem, or comic book, for example), film, television, and electronic game. Such adaptations should not be judged *a priori* as inferior because they are belated and dependent upon an earlier, primary, and 'original' work.

However, the adaptation, especially into film or television, but also into graphic novel or even comic-book form, of a standard literary text represents a point of ethical as well as pedagogical ambivalence or dilemma for many. Nevertheless, there remains the sense of an imperative that young people ought to be familiar with the literary texts that form part of 'their' cultural inheritance and, importantly, form a significant part of the cultural capital available to them. However, the idea of a shared cultural inheritance is part of the dilemma and ambivalence that encircle these texts and potential readers. The adaptation of such texts into television programmes or films, therefore, meets – but maybe only partially satisfies – this need for awareness of that cultural heritage and capital. Such reworkings may be thought to acquaint those unfamiliar with the original texts at least with the latter's bare narrative outlines and their casts of characters. However, as we have seen in the case of Carroll's *Alice's Adventures in Wonderland*, identity (or near-identity) of title does not always guarantee identity of narrative. Those charged with the function of cultural gatekeeper – parents, educators, governments, and the like – nevertheless often remain concerned that members of the culture gain some exposure also to more subtle and nuanced aspects of the originary texts – the latter's uses of language, deployment of narrative devices, historical context, and so on. Perhaps inevitably, therefore, teachers especially will tend to see adaptations as pedagogical short-cuts and therefore as always-already secondary and inferior to the literary text; a necessary evil only, to be invoked chiefly in order to ensure that students at least know the story line. And of course students themselves have often resorted to visual, filmic adaptations of set texts as short-cuts of their own, without necessarily paying attention to the probability that these are *adaptations*, not simple one-to-one transpositions from one medium into another. They therefore may remain unaware of any antecedent seriality and the shifts of meaning and interpretation that this might produce.

It would, therefore, be a better strategy, not only for teachers and students but also for consumers of texts in general, if the adaptation of an originary text into whatever medium were considered first on the merit of what it sets out to do *as a text in its own right*, rather than being viewed simply as always-already a poor imitation of a better original. Equally important is an understanding of the historical tradition and contextual nature of adaptation. As we have seen in the examples of the Greek dramatists and of Shakespeare, originality of material has not always been a prime requisite of quality work; rather, in certain contexts originality of treatment of familiar material has often served as the basis for critical evaluation.

From *The Taming of the Shrew* to *10 Things I Hate About You*

We cannot have a sense of the ways in which the adapted text is different from the originary one without an awareness of antecedent seriality, whether the latter spans merely the originary text and a single adaptation or, as we saw in the case of *Romeo and Juliet*, a long genealogy of textual antecedents. And that difference between originary text and adaptation can be not only substantial, in terms of changes to the *dramatis personae*, the plot, the setting and other aspects of the text, but also significant, in that the focus as well as central motifs or themes may have changed with the adaptation, as indeed also the intended readership or audience. Consider, for example, Shakespeare's *The Taming of the Shrew*, a play about the improbable relationship of the shrew, Katharina – shrewish in part because her father appears to favour her younger sister, Bianca, who has a retinue of suitors while Kate has none – and Petruchio, who pays court to Kate initially only because she comes from a wealthy house. Without our engaging in a detailed history of adaptations of this play, we can infer from several of its transformations – the 1948 Cole Porter stage musical and later, in 1953, the film musical *Kiss Me Kate*; Franco Zeffirelli's 1967 film of the play; and the 1997 Heath Ledger vehicle *10 Things I Hate About You* – not only three different renditions of the original play but also three very different audiences and, speaking in commercial terms, therefore also different markets.

The Zeffirelli film remains close to the original text, though it drops the framing Christopher Sly plot of the originary Shakespeare play, in which a nobleman and his company play a trick on the unfortunate Sly, leading him to believe that he is in fact a lord before whom a company of players enact the comedy that takes up most of the duration of this play. The film *Kiss Me Kate* directs its audience to its originary text by representing its principals as performers in a production of *The Taming of the Shrew* which is, we are informed by the composer 'Cole Porter' (a character who does not appear in the stage version of *Kiss Me, Kate*),[4] a musical version of the original play. The Sly plot is replaced by another concerning the difficult offstage relationship of Lilli Vanessi (the Katharina of the production) and her ex-husband Frederick Graham (the Petruchio), a relationship that bears such strong resemblance to the Kate-Petruchio plot onstage that frequently the performers appear to act out their marital conflicts in the guise of the Shakespeare play. The staged play in this musical adaptation of *The Taming of the Shrew* retains a good deal of the Shakespearean dialogue, though of course much abbreviated. The film *10 Things I Hate About You* provides plenty of cues to the audience about the fact that it is an adaptation of the Shakespearean play, again omitting the Sly subplot. These include not only quotations from *The Taming of the Shrew* and other dramatic works in the Shakespeare *corpus*, but also other broad hints: such as the name of the high school in which it is set, Padua High, the Petruchio character (played by Heath Ledger) called Patrick Verona, and the two sisters (played by Julia Stiles and Larisa Oleynik) who are named Kat and Bianca Stratford. Nevertheless, despite these winks in the direction of the Shakespeare play, if the intended audience – which is likely to be youthful, given the appeal of the male lead, Heath Ledger, and the resetting of the action in a high school – remained uninformed and unaware of the original text, despite the acknowledgment of the originary Shakespearean play in the credits, its members might well have understood the film as simply a variation on the typical teen 'flick', which typically tells the tale of a difficult relationship between a young man and a young woman.

The absence of the Sly subplot in these adaptations of the Shakespeare play changes the meaning significantly. Its presence raises questions of metatheatrical import – about, for instance, the relationship between 'reality' and 'the stage', as well as who views and who is viewed; or whether behaviour is culturally formed or innate. Has Kate merely been playing the part of a shrew, or is she one in reality? After all, Petruchio's brutal behaviour as husband, in order to 'tame' Kate, is avowedly a performance only. And is her public submission at the end of the play to him as her husband simply another role that she plays, or does she mean it? Are both husband and wife complicit in staging a spectacle that they know will amaze and confound the rest of the company present? These questions remain in the Porter musical but are considerably mediated and modified by the onstage/offstage relationship of Fred and Lilli, which limits the questions about metatheatricality to domestic, marital matters. In *10 Things I Hate About You*, issues of performance and the performativity of social roles are constrained still further, in the absence of the Sly subplot or, as in *Kiss Me Kate*, the approximation of one. Those issues are instead centred on other concerns, such as adolescent love and desire, the fear of rejection and ridicule at both the personal and intimate level, and the more general social one.

It might be argued, consequently, that while the movie *10 Things I Hate About You* is undoubtedly intended to capture a particular market and make money from it, it is also an attempt to preserve the cultural capital of Shakespeare's play at a time when Shakespeare's works have come to be viewed as high culture and therefore consumable only by a cultivated elite; when those works are dismissed by younger generations as irrelevant to their own understanding of their lives and cultural context; and when theatre competes bravely but not always successfully with other forms of performance, such as film, television, and electronic games. By situating their adaptation of *The Taming of the Shrew* in a contemporary context and appealing to young viewers especially, the film's makers have avoided the traditional temptation to make a Shakespeare play 'relevant' to a contemporary audience by simply dressing it up in modern costume and embellishing it with such devices as popular music. Rather, this film constructs a narrative that parallels the plot of the originary play – much as does the double plot of *Kiss Me Kate* – without attempting to replicate it exactly. Intertextual allusions to and quotations from the Shakespeare play function then as anchoring hawsers to prevent this adaptation from becoming a different text entirely.[5]

Adapting a (sub-)genre: from *Frankenstein* to *Blood Music*

Not only the plots of narratives but also the (sub-)genres in which narratives are written may become subject to adaptation. Greg Bear's science-fiction novel *Blood Music* (first published as an award-winning short story in 1983) offers an instance of such an appropriative transformation of a generic model of narrative (Bear, 2007). Bear's work is a version or adaptation of the mad scientist story beloved of many makers of horror films, whose ancestor is Mary Shelley's *Frankenstein, or the Modern Prometheus* (1818). Typically in such narratives, the scientist in question must be neutralized or killed; alternatively, as in Shelley's novel, the scientist realizes his folly and seeks to make redress. In Bear's novel, however, the twist is that Vergil Ulam, despite his monomania regarding his 'noocytes' (genetically rearranged lymphocytes that initially show simple intelligence but gradually develop complex and independent ways of thinking and acting) and his self-absorption, actually creates a better world for humans, always provided, of course, that the latter are willing to surrender their present, limited physical existence; in other words, their humanity. In one sense, then, Bear's novel may be understood as seeking to rehabilitate science and the scientist in a culture which has become sceptical, even openly and deeply suspicious, of science's (and scientists') claims not only to know the universe intimately but also to be able to change it for the better. Such scepticism and suspicion are hardly unexpected: after a century of epidemics and science's inability to prevent these, being able only belatedly to find inoculations and cures; a century of wars and the invention of more and more horrifying means of killing people, including the atomic bomb; and a century of science's acting the willing handmaiden to industry and commerce, and with them contributing to the increasing pollution and profound spoliation of the planet in a number of ways. We should not forget, either, that 1983, the original date of the publication of *Blood Music* as a short story, also saw the world reeling in disbelief at the uncovering of the HIV/AIDS epidemic and the implications of this disease for the world. The promise of a healthier, immortal life, such as Vergil's noocytes offer, a life unencumbered and unendangered by viral attack, no doubt seemed an attractive fantasy at the time; and no doubt it still seems so. We might therefore draw from this the important inference that adaptations are not only *of* originary texts but also adaptations *to* the circumstances and conditions obtaining in the culture at the time that the adaptation is produced.

Bear's novel has an idiosyncratic structure: the first part focuses on Vergil's development of the noocytes and the consequences of that development upon him, while the second deals with the global consequences of his work. Vergil himself vanishes to all intents and purposes in the second part, reappearing only as a sort of ghost. The titles of each section – for example, 'Interphase', 'Anaphase', 'Prophase' – refer to the different stages of mitosis, the process by which cells divide and multiply. The terms are therefore significant to the theme of Bear's novel, of which one could argue that its peculiar structure actually *imitates* mitosis, in the process producing an evolutionarily different kind of narrative that nonetheless retains a 'genetic' coherence with its original parent (DNA) story. The narrative strands of the latter part of the novel are not subplots in any conventional sense. Albeit, in a more limited way, they represent new narrative trajectories, rather as recombinations of DNA that produce new strands that in turn produce new life forms. In this sense, then, *Blood Music* may be described as a work that starts out as the adaptation of a particular subgenre of narrative, that of the mad scientist, but concludes as an *appropriation* of that subgenre, not only in its transformation of the typical narrative trajectory of this type of story but also in its revision of traditional narrative structure itself.

From *The Earthsea Chronicles* to *Earthsea*

Other adaptations, however, while announcing their originary texts and thereby laying claim to some fidelity to those texts, may be subject to criticism on precisely the grounds of fidelity to an original. A case in point is Ursula Le Guin's Earthsea Chronicles. The original trilogy, *A Wizard of Earthsea*, *The Tombs of Atuan*, and *The Farthest Shore* (Le Guin, 1968; 1972; 1973), was first published between 1968 and 1973, and was followed in 1990 by *Tehanu* (Le Guin, 1990). Despite the latter's subtitle, *The Last Book of Earthsea*, 2001, saw the publication of *Tales from Earthsea*, a collection of five short stories, and *The Other Wind* (Le Guin, 2001). Set in the Earthsea world of archipelagos and other islands, the entire series traces the story of Sparrowhawk from his days as a goatherd boy on the island of Gont, where he displays a significant talent for magic, to his training at the school for wizards on the island of Roke, to his ascension to Archmage and thence to his old age back on Gont, after he has lost his magic.

There have been two transformations of the Earthsea series into film. The first of these, *Earthsea* (originally titled *Legend of Earthsea*) (Lieberman, 2004), first screened as a television series, draws on the first two volumes, but, in addition to telescoping events radically, kills off Vetch (played by Chris Gauthier), Sparrowhawk's friend from Roke and his companion on his voyage to deal with an evil entity called a *gebbeth*; and inconsistently calls the young Sparrowhawk (Shawn Ashmore) 'Ged' (his everyday name, as opposed to 'Sparrowhawk,' his secret, true name) but retains Vetch's ordinary name (his true name is Estarriol). Further, the film makes Tenar (Kristin Kreuk) a novice priestess caught up in a power struggle between the high priestess Thar (in the novel one of Tenar's tutors, played by Isabella Rossellini) and the priestess Kossil (another less congenial tutor in the novel, played here by Jennifer Calvert). The latter in the film is the lover of the Kargad king Tygath (Sebastian Roché), who seeks eternal life from the Nameless Ones and therefore requires control of the Temple of Atuan. The film ends with Ged and Tenar (who have each had prophetic dreams about one another prior to meeting in person) emerging as potential lovers from the temple.

The film, more of an appropriation than an adaptation of the Earthsea narratives, substitutes for Le Guin's careful delineation of different cultures and the delicate political and social ecology that this implies an adventure-cum-love story with a lot of special effects. While the film was not a great success with audiences, its rendering of Le Guin's originary text implies a good deal about the intended audience and its expectations. For one thing, there appears to be no assumption that the audience – presumably a young one – would be familiar with the Earthsea Chronicles, whose first three volumes appeared from 1968 to 1973. To all intents and purposes, then, for such an audience this is not an adaptation of an originary text but rather an independent text entirely. For another, the film appears to assume, perhaps not entirely incorrectly, that what a young audience desires to see is a story of derring-do and love – after all, these have been a staple of Western narrative from at least as early as the medieval cycle of narratives about King Arthur and the Knights of the Round Table.

The second film is an animated feature-length movie from Japan. *Tales from Earthsea* (*Gedo Senki*) is directed by Goro Miyazaki (Miyazaki, 2006), the son of the renowned *anime* animator Hayao Miyazaki. Visually stunning, this animated film draws on *The Farthest Shore*, *Tehanu* and, to a lesser degree, *The Other Wind*. The narrative begins with Prince Arren killing his father (a deed without foundation in the originary text) and taking flight, meeting on his way with the Archmage Ged (in this film a man of mature years, signalled by his beard and greying temples) and accompanying him in his investigation into why magic-wielders seem to be losing their powers. The renegade wizard Cob, who appears in *The Farthest Shore*, the third of the novel series, is responsible for that loss; however, rather than living in the shadowlands of death as in the novel, the evil wizard instead inhabits a Gothic castle. The film ends with Arren returning to Enlad to face the consequences of his parricide.

There are no doubt important cultural differences inscribed in this Japanese rendition of the American Le Guin's work, though it is not the task of this chapter – and is beyond the competence of its author – to investigate them. It is also quite likely that the younger Miyazaki shares, at least to some degree, the moral concerns with which his father inscribes his own animated feature films. These can be seen in *Tales from Earthsea* in Ged's concern to maintain the Equilibrium, and in the pastoral nature of life on Tenar's farm, as well as in Cob's overweening self-interest and ambition. By contrast, the Ged of *Earthsea* is represented, when a boy, as chafing against his destiny to become a blacksmith like his father, rejoicing in discovering his talent for magic, and irritated with his mage mentor Ogion, whose teaching about nature does not seem at all to be about wielding magic. That is, the Ged in the American-made film is ambitious both for power and for adventure, and no doubt reflects a different ideological stance from that of the Japanese-made movie. Both of these films, then, can be described not so much as adaptations of Le Guin's work than as appropriations of it – indeed, the cover for the DVD copy of *Earthsea* proclaims that it is 'Based on the stunning Earthsea cycle by legendary fantasy writer Ursula K. Le Guin' (Lieberman, 2004), a formula that, as I have suggested above, often indicates a significant departure from an originary text.

From *The Wizard of Oz* to *Wicked*

A more interesting series of adaptations/appropriations of an originary text is to be found in the novels by Gregory Maguire grouped together under the rubric The Wicked Years. At least in his young adult/adult fiction, Maguire is less a teller than a reteller of tales. For example, *Confessions of an Ugly Stepsister* is a reworking of the Cinderella tale, setting it in seventeenth-century Holland and telling the story from the perspective of one of the 'ugly stepsisters', giving the story a very different twist from the traditional tale that many readers would be familiar with (Maguire, 1999). Likewise, *Mirror, Mirror: A Novel* retells the story of Snow White, setting it in sixteenth-century Tuscany, with Lucrezia Borgia as the wicked Queen, though not married to this Snow White's father (Maguire, 2003).

'Cinderella' and 'Snow White' can be ascribed to various authors: for example, the familiar version of 'Cinderella' derives from Perrault's collection of tales *Histoires ou contes du temps passé* (1697) (Opie & Opie, 1980: p. 152), while 'Snow White' (or 'Snow Drop') can be traced back to *German Popular Stories. Translated from the Kinder- und Haus-Märchen, Collected by MM Grimm, from Oral Tradition* (1823) (Opie & Opie, 1980: p. 228); but there are even older antecedents of both stories. The familiar versions, however, have taken on the status of folktales, a status which implies a lack of any author. Maguire's renditions are therefore adaptations not so much of a fixed key originary text as of a familiar childhood tale which one might have heard in various versions. Perhaps, therefore, it would be more accurate to describe these novels as paraphrases of those tales, retaining a high degree of fidelity to the original stories, even though a good deal of the marvellous – such as fairy godmothers – has been rationalized and explained, while the social and historical context of the story lines has been rendered more detailed and is itself situated within an extra-diegetical historical and cultural frame.

In 1995 Maguire embarked on the retelling of a different narrative or set of narratives, this time choosing L. Frank Baum's children's novels about the Land of Oz (Baum, 2005), of which the best known is surely *The Wonderful Wizard of Oz* (1900); and here we return to the title of the present chapter. This is, of course, not the first time this novel has been adapted: Baum himself reworked it and other novels from the series in various media; and there were several film versions of it before the famous 1939 MGM movie, starring the 17-year-old Judy Garland (Fleming, 1939). In 1978 the film adaptation of a stage musical version, *The Wiz*, appeared with an all-black cast (Lumet, 1978).[6] The first of Maguire's novels, *Wicked: The Life and Times of the Wicked Witch of the West*, tells the story of Elphaba, the wicked witch of the title (Maguire, 1995). (Her name is derived from the sounds of the initial letters of L. Frank Baum's name.) Initially an unsympathetic character, with her green skin and sharp teeth, Elphaba gradually wins the reader over. A loner who is an intellectual of a scientific bent, a political radical, and a feminist, Elphaba questions authority, especially that of the oppressive Emperor. Her encounter with Dorothy and her companions, the dog Toto, the Scarecrow, the Tin Man, and the Lion, is by no means charged with the hostility and vengefulness of her avatar in the MGM film. In *Son of a Witch* (Maguire, 2005), the second in Maguire's series, we learn that Elphaba has had a son – or at least the birth of a boy has been attributed to her – who forges his own life in the shadow of his mother, now a notorious and almost mythical figure in Oz. And in *A Lion Among Men* (Maguire, 2008) we follow the story of the Lion, one of the intelligent talking animals of Oz who have been persecuted by the Emperor. (It is unclear whether Maguire plans any further volumes in this series.) Thus, we may say that while *Wicked* is a clear adaptation of an originary text, the two subsequent novels are more properly appropriations of that same text.

Though Maguire refers intertextually to, and quotes from, both the 1939 *Wizard of Oz* and Baum's Oz novels (for example, in Maguire's narratives there are references to tik-toks, a species of domestic robots, which are absent from the film but certainly appear in the novels – there is even one called *The Tik-Tok Man* [Baum, 2005]), his Wicked Years narratives highlight ideological and cultural gaps and weaknesses in both the original novels and the famous MGM film. For example, Elphaba's green skin in the 1939 film marks her envious, evil nature, instead in *Wicked* it signals her difference and otherness, and provides the ground for her marginalization and persecution. (The all-black cast of *The Wiz* likewise foregrounds the whiteness of the 1939 movie, the version of Baum's The *Wonderful Wizard of Oz* with which most people are familiar.) In *Son of a Witch* and *A Lion Among Men*, Liir, Elphaba's putative son, and Brr, the lion of the title, are both represented as queer, in that both have relations with members of both sexes, something that could not have been treated in a serious fashion either by Baum or by the makers of the 1939 movie, although the latter's Cowardly

Lion, played by Bert Lahr, is fairly camp. In other words, Maguire demands that his readers rethink at least the film of *The Wizard of Oz*, despite its ingrained familiarity fostered by frequent reruns both on television and in the cinema, in terms of what it fails to say or what it says only elliptically.

Some questions

Hutcheon remarks, in connection with what she calls 'the showing mode', that is, texts in performance, that

> [i]n a very real sense, every live staging of a printed play could theoretically be considered an adaptation in its performance. The text of the play does not necessarily tell an actor about such matters as the gestures, expressions, and tones of voice to use in converting words on a page into a convincing performance ... it is up to the director and actors to actualize the text and to interpret and then recreate it, thereby in a sense adapting it for the stage. (Hutcheon, 2006: p. 39)

We may add to this the idea that the actors themselves also adapt the text through their individual understandings of their roles and their performances of these. Moreover, since in live theatre each performance of a play is different, even if only infinitesimally, from all others of the same production – because of factors like audience reaction, the general mood of both audience and actors, the physical conditions of the space in which the performance takes place, and the like – we may conclude that each performance is not only an adaptation of a printed text but also of the director's interpretation of the text.

This raises interesting questions about adaptation and interpretation – that is, textual readings – in general. These questions are particularly relevant in a culture in which 'sampling' in popular music (the excerpting of one or more passages of existing recordings in order to resituate them in an entirely separate new work) is now commonplace, as is the cutting and pasting of text, often accomplished electronically, from one document to another. Whether such practices count as inventive post-modern forms of intertextual reference or merely as plagiarism would depend, one assumes, on the nature of the text into which the excerpted material is relocated and how the latter is repurposed. Are those practices adaptations or appropriations? As I have argued with regard to *Pride and Prejudice and Zombies*, they can be both: Grahame-Smith has, in a sense, 'sampled' Austen's novel, but has also reworked the excerpts to create a different kind of text. Perhaps the answer to the question resides in the manner in which the principle of antecedent seriality is foregrounded in the adapted work, as well as the degree to which that principle functions in the reader's or viewer's perception and understanding, which in turn depends on the nature of her or his cultural capital.

Other key questions follow in relation to the matter of adaptation. To what degree is each reader's understanding of a text, even in the case of a reread-ing of it, an *adaptation* of the text? What then might be the relationship between the *interpretation* of a text and its adaptation? What elements of a text might serve to anchor understandings of that text, in order to prevent it from meaning *anything* at all, like a sort of Rorschach inkblot, to a reader? What criteria can we invoke, in adjudicating among understandings of a text, that permit us to qualify some readings as legitimate and others as not, or as eccentric adaptations or even appropriations of that text? It is among these questions about meaning and understanding, about what constraints and permissions govern interpretation and – perhaps above all – *who controls those constraints and permissions* that we may find a partial answer to the question of why adaptation has so consistently been regarded as inferior to the originary text, and why it has been so vociferously dismissed and even condemned. For, if the very notion of adaptation is broadened to include *all* understandings of a text, dominant and official ideologies and discourses may well come to be undermined, ignored, or attacked. That is, approach-ing the question of adaptation as more than a secondary and probably infe-rior reworking of an originary text can bring us to important interrogations of the nature of textual understanding itself.

Further Reading

Cardwell, S. 2002. *Adaptation revisited: television and the classic novel.* Manchester University Press, Manchester. Addresses key issues of the adaptation of novels, with a particular focus on their transformation into television serials.

Cartmell, D. & Whelehan, I. (eds) 1999. *Adaptations: from text to screen, screen to text.* Routledge, London. Considers the difficulties of adaptations from print texts into film, and the reverse: the novelization of filmic texts.

Stam, R. & Raengo, A. (eds) 2005. *Literature and film: a guide to the theory and practice of film adaptation.* Blackwell, Oxford. A collection of essays on the relationship of literature and film, exploring international and independ-ent films as well as Hollywood movies.

Notes

1 In order to avoid reproducing in my discussion a hierarchy of value in which 'original text' dominates as the only positive term, in what follows I will use instead the term 'originary text' – Hutcheon prefers 'adapted text' (Hutcheon, 2006: p. xiii) – which, unlike 'original', with its connotations of an unassailable and unchangeable quality, suggests the generative power of a text to inspire emu-lation and adaptation.

2 One might add here also such musical adaptations of the Shakespeare play as the *Roméo et Juliette* operas by Hector Berlioz (1839) and Charles Gounod (1867), or

the music composed by Sergei Prokofiev in 1935 for the ballet *Romeo and Juliet*, commissioned by the Kirov Ballet, which in its original form had a happy ending. However, consideration of these works lies somewhat outside the scope of the present chapter.

3   The term 'palimpsest' technically refers to a mediaeval manuscript written on parchment or vellum, which has been, to use the contemporary term, recycled by removing earlier inscription by means of a sharp or abrasive implement. However, in a palimpsest a faint trace of the original inscription may still be discerned, whether because vestiges of the original ink remain on the page, or because the quill or other writing instrument used has scored the surface of the page.

4   The title of the stage play correctly and grammatically inserts a comma before 'Kate', whereas the title of the film omits it.

5   It is worth noting that the film *10 Things I hate about you* itself generated in 2009 a spin-off in the form of a TV sitcom series with the same title. A viewer of the series ignorant of the relevant antecedent seriality would see only the connection with the film, making the genealogical connection to *The taming of the shrew* more tenuous and remote.

6   Wikipedia has an entire entry on adaptations of this novel and others in Baum's Oz series –see bibliography.

8
All That Matters: Technoscience, Critical Theory, and Children's Fiction

Kerry Mallan

There has long been an uneasy relationship between the Western discourse of science and critical theory. The differences have centred on the questionable authority and legitimacy of science's perceived inherent attributes of truth, rationality, and value-free methodologies. Critical theory questions such attributes as given or inherent to any discipline or epistemological approach, especially with respect to gender, sexuality, class, race, and ethnicity – concerns that have been at the heart of critical theory. Since the last stages of the twentieth century, critical theory has arguably been moving in some respects beyond these concerns, enquiring into questions of *what matters* in a world characterized by rapid changes in political economy (globalization), wide-ranging social and cultural shifts, the collapse of distinctions between public and private, environmental crises, and continuous advances in technoscience and nanotechnology.

In exploring beyond human limits and limitations, and the postbiological body, technoscience is producing knowledge about bodies, matter, and life as its developments in biotechnologies, information technologies, entertainment and surveillance technologies, and more recently nanobiology redefine the very essence of life. Colin Milburn believes that the developments in the rapidly advancing field of nanotechnology foresee 'a technocultural revolution that will, in a very short time, profoundly alter human life as we know it' (2002: p. 263). Technoscience has prompted shifts in both ontology and epistemology, ushering in ethical challenges and necessitating a rethinking of critical theory's approaches to identity, power, and desire (among other factors that impact on subjectivity, agency, and bodies). Milburn contends that as we have the ability to perform molecular surgery on our bodies and on our environment, this will have irrevocable social, economic, and epistemological effects, changing not only our relation to the world but also what it means to be human. Patricia Ticineto

Clough too sees the new technologies, including those described above, as provoking shifts in thought that impact on all spheres of life:

> in politics, from disciplining to biopolitical control; in economy, from the productivity of human laborers to the circulation of affects; in biophilosophy, from organic life to nonorganic life; in the physical sciences, from the closed system to the complex system under far-from-equilibrium conditions; and in culture, from representation and meaning to information. (Clough, 2004: p. 4)

Many of these conditions or shifts have been, and continue to be, represented in children's fiction, especially science fiction and utopian/dystopian fiction, genres that have traditionally opened up possible futures to their readers. However, the future is already unfolding and many recent fictional speculations register a knowledge that is becoming obsolete with an indecent haste, such is the speed of change in a nanotech era. It is therefore not surprising that as technoscience gives rise to new ways of thinking about the relationships between the computer and 'life', organic and inorganic, reproduction and replication, new narratives are being generated both in science and in fiction, and often the distinction between the real and the fictional is not so clear. Milburn comments on this by noting that critics of nanotechnology's speculations about the future claim that it is 'less a science and more a science fiction' (2002: p. 264).

An in-depth engagement with the shifts that Clough describes is beyond the scope of this chapter; nevertheless, the shifts she nominates inform this chapter's consideration of the interplay between technoscience and children's literature, and how critical theories can assist us in understanding this interplay. In particular, I consider the posthuman condition and the evolving interrelations between the organic and the nonorganic, and the circulation of affects through information-communication technologies and fiction.

The posthuman condition: machines, cyborgs, and bodies

Well before critical theorists turned their attention to the deficits and possibilities of technoscience as a resource or a framework for considering cultural shifts and current social practices, 'science' was regarded as a natural philosophy. In its Latin form *scientia*, science means knowledge, and it was originally used generically to encompass a wide range of knowledges and disciplines including mathematics, chemistry, astronomy, ethics, history, and fine arts. Today, 'the new technology of the computer' (Johnston, 2008: p. 7) is opening up ways in which these disciplines can once again speak to each other, especially in how computerized technology has impacted on nearly all sectors of Western societies. A brief gloss of the past opens the way for thinking of the shifts and challenges that technoscience now poses for twenty-first-century critical theories, especially with respect to bodies, matter, and life.

During the period known as The Enlightenment (eighteenth century), philosophical thought concerned itself with knowledge and reason, and mathematical calculations began to supplant faith in the classical writings that the Humanist movement of the Renaissance period advocated. The early French philosopher René Descartes advanced his argument 'I think, therefore I am' (*cogito, ergo sum*) in the First Meditation to establish a truth of a self-evident, clear, and distinct proposition, and as a consequence he later argued in the Fifth Meditation that mathematics establishes its proposals on similar self-evidence that presents itself to the mind. His argument turned on the idea that mathematical truths are clearly and distinctly perceived, and that our knowledge of them depends on our knowledge of God (Olson, 1988: p. 409). By applying reason and mathematics, he provided 'proof' of the existence of God.[1] Descartes asserted that humans have the unique ability to reason and would therefore always be superior to machines. The uniqueness of human beings, blessed with reason, was the cornerstone of Enlightenment thought, and guaranteed not only humans' superiority over animals and human-made artefacts but promoted a belief in their ability to create a better world. Descartes' idea (known as Cartesian philosophy) that reason was separate from emotion influenced Enlightenment's interest in promoting the rational subject and endorsing the Mind/Body split. With its questioning or discarding of old certainties, and the contesting of boundaries between the natural and the artificial, body and mind, animals and humans, the Enlightenment became a time when thinkers became fascinated with the question of what it is to be human (Vermeir, 2008).

The Industrial Revolution of the nineteenth century confirmed the superiority of the human (at that time, 'man') over machine. However, by the late nineteenth century this perception was beginning to change, as employers, industrialists, and politicians began to regard machines as faster, stronger, and more productive than human labour. By the late twentieth century and continuing into the present, the separation between human and machine became not so distinct. Increasingly, humans depend on technology to enable their access to services, places, information, and entertainments that would otherwise not be possible. We also rely on technology to overcome the limitations or shortcomings tied to the human body through the use of implants, prostheses, artificial joints, artificial retinas, brain chips, and pacemakers.

The cybernetic organism known as the 'cyborg' is a familiar example of the human–machine hybrid. Cyborgs have populated popular culture for children and adults for some time, regularly finding their way into fiction, films, television, comics, manga, anime, and videogames. Claudia Springer argues that the cyborg complicates Cartesian philosophy: 'The idea of a cyborg is simultaneously a culmination of Descartes's separation of reason from emotion and a supersession of that opposition' (1996: p. 19). This paradox is often resolved in cyborg-featured fiction that typically equates machine with reason, and human with emotion, or machine as evil and human as good (Springer, 1996: p. 30). This simple separation is evident in many examples of children's fiction.

The Lunch Lady and the Cyborg Substitute, a graphic novel by Jarrett J. Krosoczka (2009), makes an explicit distinction between evil and good. The amusing story line of the eponymous, cyborg-fighting lunch lady parodies high-tech science fictions that both dazzle with their technological wizardry and extol masculine ingenuity and superhuman physicality. With her fellow lunch lady, Betty, the two women more than compensate for their lack of culinary skills by whipping up effective cyborg-fighting aids from simple kitchen utensils and lunch meal ingredients – spatu-copter, chicken nugget bombs, fish stick nunchucks. After the lunch lady uncovers the plot by 'Mr Edison' (the science teacher) to replace all the teachers at the school with cyborgs, so he can win teacher of the year award, she single-handedly annihilates all the cyborgs and, with the help of Betty and her skill at flinging her hairnet net, captures Edison.

At one level, the story appears to endorse simple reductions between nature/technology, human/cyborg, real/simulated. It also paradoxically extols female ingenuity, courage, and creativity, yet constructs femininity as homely and eccentric. At another level, the text can be understood as complicating simple binaries. The women use the boiler room in the school as their laboratory, equipping it with CCTV and the necessary tools for making their inventions. In this private space, they invent new technologies as well as operate a surveillance system on all the classrooms. Consequently, the story demystifies 'Science' as rarefied knowledge, and depicts the women not as passive bodies on which science and technology act but as active subjects who experiment and use technology for their own purposes. Rather than endorse science as a masculine-based epistemology, the story represents the women as exemplifying a particular kind of female way of knowing, which shifts readers' attention away from science and its products as being solely a historically and culturally male endeavour. The women also defeat the male science teacher at his own game. Furthermore, the women's use of food metaphors to convey threat ('looks like today's special is a knuckle sandwich'), surprise ('cauliflower!'), and success ('justice is served!') follows in the footsteps of popular fiction (e.g., Batman and Robin) by appealing to the assumed popularity of word-play humour with the implied child audience. There is a further correspondence in naming the female duo as the lunch lady and Betty.

We can consider a further double play in the text, in that the puns form a 'language game', which playfully corresponds to the lunch ladies' non-scientific or everyday uses of language as food providores. Extratextually, there is a parodying of the language game that science plays: a game that legitimates its linguistic practices and communications as a metadiscourse of specialized knowledge.[2] At an elementary level, *Lunch Lady and the Cyborg Substitute* illustrates how even 'ordinary' people can come to rely on tools and technology in order to go beyond their personal human limitations. It also offers a liberating narrative that resonates with Donna Haraway's post-modern cyborg, whereby the technologically enabled lunch lady is able to literally use the tools that circumscribe her status to make her mark. This comment paraphrases the point that Haraway makes with respect to cyborg writing that she says 'is about the power to survive, not on the basis of original innocence, but on the basis of seizing the tools to mark the world that marked them as other' (1991: p. 175).

In her widely cited essay, 'Cyborg Manifesto' (1991), Haraway offers an optimistic vision that the cyborg's inherent hybridity (organic and mechanical) will challenge the dichotomy between natural and artificial, promising to free the subject from imposed categories: 'the cyborg is a creature in a post-gender world: it has no truck with bisexuality, pre-Oedipal symbiosis, unalienated labor, or other seductions to organic wholeness' (1991, p. 150). However, despite the liberating cyborg figure that Haraway imagines, more often than not cyborg fictions fail to evade cultural stereotyping, and texts often fall back into clichéd iconography that reproduces conventional gender representations. Furthermore, questions of difference are often framed and resolved from a humanist standpoint, rather than from a posthuman one.[3] Haraway and other feminists interested in post-modern science studies have explained how science is not just a body of unimpeachable facts but one set of discourses and representations among others that construct dominant images and concepts of women, animals, and machines. The cyborg combines the hybrid 'nature-culture' and the 'non-human', defying the notion of core identities or essences sustaining one true 'self'. This non-essentialist view supports the post-modern notion of the subject as a hybrid of different influences (cultural, racial, sexual, historical – real and artificial). Thus the post-modern cyborg illustrates most vividly how subjects and objects are connected in digital societies.

Computerized connections are apparent in David Tomas's classification of cyborgs as 'post-organic, classical ... (hardware-interfaced) cyborg and the postclassical (software-interfaced) transorganic data-based cyborg or personality construct' (quoted in Springer 1996: p. 19). The first type is a hybrid combining organic and nonorganic (implants, prostheses). The second has no organic form, but the human brain is preserved on computer software or is wired so that software can be uploaded. Springer further distinguishes cyborgs from robots and androids, noting that robots are completely mechanical figures and androids, while looking like humans, do not combine organic with nonorganic parts. These cyborgian examples are one form that posthuman bodies can take.

The term posthuman suggests human obsolescence. Springer's paradox mentioned earlier is extended when she notes that the cyborg 'represents the triumph of the intellect' and signifies 'obsolescence for human beings', heralding the dawn of the 'posthuman, post-Enlightenment age' (p. 19). However, in their book *Posthuman Bodies* (1995), Judith Halberstam and Ira Livingston refuse to acknowledge human obsolescence as a consequence of posthumanism. Rather than see the posthuman as representing an evolution or devolution of the human, they argue that the posthuman 'participates in re-distributions of difference and identity' (p. 10). To highlight their point, they describe the posthuman body as 'a technology, a screen, a projected image ... a contaminated body, a deadly body, a techno-body ... a queer body' (p. 3). These widely disparate attributions require unpacking, but at this point we could see them as underscoring the conditions of possibility that have increased dramatically in the decade or more since *Posthuman Bodies* was published. Given the ways in which technology and human 'determine and in-determine each other', as Athena Athanasiou (2005: p. 127) puts it, we are now able to consider the posthuman not as a form of compensatory or alien presence for humans to deploy, invent, or overcome, but as a condition of the human. Katherine Hayles addresses this condition in her book *How We Became Posthuman* (1999), noting that 'a dynamic partnership between humans and intelligent machines replaces the liberal humanist subject's manifest destiny to dominate and control nature' (p. 288). However, Cary Wolfe (2010) is critical of Haraway saying that she represents a humanist way of being posthuman. Wolfe's account of posthumanism considers the human, but not as representing the humanist idea of the autonomous, rational subject. Rather, his notion of the human is that it is aware of its 'embodiment, embeddedness, and materiality, and how these in turn shape and are shaped by consciousness, mind, and so on' (p. 120).

Literary figurations of the posthuman are not a recent invention, as their appearance goes back (at least) to early Greek Myths and the golem stories of early Judaism. Contemporary fictions for children and young adults have expropriated these early posthumans, breathing new life into their ancient bodies. Rick Riordan's Percy Jackson fantasy series gives the early Greek figures a makeover. Percy, a seemingly ordinary teenager living in the contemporary world of the novel, is in reality a hybrid; the dust jacket describes him as 'Half Boy – Half God – All Hero'. As the son of Poseidon, Percy has powers that enable him to defeat an array of Titan monsters including '*dracaena* snake-women, hellhounds, giants, and the humanoid sea-lion demons known as telkhines' (2009: p. 7). These modern day Greek posthumans rely on computers and other technologies as part of their fighting strategy. Riordan inflects the text with humour to convey both the hybridity of the characters and a digital world familiar to the implied readership:

A telkhine was hunched over a console, but he was so involved with his work he didn't notice us. He was about a metre and a half tall, with slick black sea-lion fur and stubby little feet. He had the head of a Dobermann, but his clawed hands were almost human. He growled and muttered as he tapped on his keyboard. Maybe he was messaging his friends on ugly-face.com. (Riordan, 2009: p. 9)

The golem story has been retold in several children's picture books, including David Wisniewski's *Golem* (1996), which won the Caldecott Medal. Golem figures also appear in J.R.R. Tolkein's (1954–5) *The Lord of the Rings* (the transformed hobbit named Gollum) and more recently in *Clay* by David Almond (2005).

Almond's text is of particular interest because its realistic setting and treatment of characters work with, rather than against, the fantasy element that pivots on the eponymous Clay, a golem that two boys create and give life to. This story is centrally concerned with the nature of being, truth, and the boundaries between organic and nonorganic, artificial and natural, reproduction and replication that the preceding discussion raises. Although *Clay* is not about Jewish religion or lore, its golem figure can be traced back to the story of the Rabbi of Prague (15th –16th century) who is said to have created a golem out of clay to protect the Jewish community from Blood Libel[4] and to help them by doing physical labour (because of its superior strength). In a related way, the boys, Stephen and Davie, create a golem out of clay who has the strength to protect them from the village bully, Martin Mould ('Mouldy'). Stephen Rose is cast as a mysterious character from the outset. His arrival in Felling, where Davie lives, is accompanied by stories of his past – his failed attempts to train as a priest as an adolescent, the death of his father, and his 'mad' mother who was taken away to an asylum. The Poor Clares (a religious order) eventually find him a place to live with his aunt, Crazy Mary. By contrast, Davie comes from a conventional and settled family life, where his biggest fear is being beaten up by Mouldy. Stephen has a powerful, mystical hold over Davie.

Well before Clay is created, Stephen muses on the possibility of Mouldy's premature death, even denying him his humanness and thinking of him only in terms of his 'thingness': 'the world'd be a much better place without a thing like Mouldy' (p. 65), and later he laughs: 'Mouldy. That's what he will be when he's dead' (p. 81). According to Jewish lore, one way to bring the golem to life was to write God's name on parchment and to insert this into the golem's body; to 'kill' the golem, the parchment was removed.[5]

Stephen instructs Davie, who is an altar boy, to steal the body and blood of Christ so that they can make their creature. Davie retrieves some crumbs from the Communion wafer and tears a small strip of the linen cloth used by the priest to wipe the chalice of the residue of the Communion wine. As instructed by Stephen, he puts these in a small locket, which is inserted into Clay's belly: ' "We plant him like a garden," Stephen says. "We fill him with the sources of life. And this..." He lifts the locket. "This'll make his soul" '. (p. 176). The boys whisper the words 'Move, my creature. Move and live'

(p. 177), and gradually Clay comes to life. His body is an amalgam of living and nonliving – he moves and speaks, but has sycamore seeds for eyes, ash keys for ears, dried-out hawthorn berries for nostrils, and twigs and grass for hair (p. 176). The 'reality' of the boys' creation is juxtaposed with other internal viewpoints that not only conflict with this reality but also are representative of wider cultural narratives about the possibility of postbiological life. These contradictory narratives about life and truth encircle the events, posing questions without answers alongside the verifiable 'facts':

> [Davie]: 'I wondered, is it only God who can breathe life into the world, only God who can create?' (p. 95)
> [Davie]: 'Flesh and blood. But could you make something that isn't flesh and blood? Could you make something out of clay, and make *that* live?'
> [...]
> 'They say that one day we'll be able to make life in test tubes,' [...] 'We'll be able to create living creatures with chemicals and electricity and nuclear power.'
> [Maria] 'Trouble with that is,' [...] 'mebbe we won't know where to stop.'
> [Davie] 'And we'll make monsters' (p. 115).
>
> And later:
> [Davie] 'It's true. It really worked. We really did make a monster'.
>
> (p. 216)

These instances speak to two cultural narratives: one which sees human beings losing control as silicon life performs what Hans Moravec calls 'a genetic take-over' of carbon life (quoted in Johnston, 2008: p. 12); the other that speaks of a human's capacity to create (indeed, become) a posthuman body. Davie and Stephen inscribe Clay's body with natural materials, which stand in for human organs and body parts. They also command Clay to perform as a human body – move, sleep, respond to commands. Through physical enactment and cognitive response to language, Clay as a posthuman is 'becoming-human' (Deleuze & Guattari, 1987), and when he is unable to kill Davie when Stephen commands, he appears to have an ethical dimension. Almond leaves open the possibility of a future scenario of destruction that Frankenstein's monster embarked upon when, long after Stephen has disappeared (and Clay 'dies' when his locket/soul is removed), Davie ponders the possibility of Stephen still playing God. When he reads of reports of maiming and murder, he awaits the possibility: 'There's no reference to Stephen Rose or a boy like Stephen Rose or to a monster, but I keep on watching, waiting, and at times I'm filled with dread' (p. 294). Yet, alongside this possibility of other (evil) monsters, the remains of (good) Clay slowly return to the earth, and the 'sycamore seeds and the hawthorn berries and ash keys have hatched and a little forest of saplings grows from him. [...] Time goes by. The seasons turn' (p. 293). We can read this as a return to nature and the proper order of (organic) life (death, re-growth), a triumph of nature over culture, and/or, ironically, as the completion of the process of the posthuman 'becoming-organic' (Lenoir, 2002: p. 384).

Literary fascination with the posthuman has parallels with the real world's fascination with toys, which are not exclusive to children. Historically, toys were the province of adults and were only gradually passed on and relegated to children when mass production enabled domestic automata, mechanical figures, and miniatures to become part of domestic amusement and play for families who could afford them.[6] Children's fascination with their toys, treating them as friends and playmates, is a common theme played out in children's literature.

In toy fictions, the artificial object often takes on the persona of a real person, which inverts the natural order of play whereby the child normally 'gives life' to the object through language and actions. In her book, *When Toys Come Alive: Narratives of Animation, Metamorphosis, and Development* (1994), Lois Kuznets writes of the outcome of this narrative invention:

> Toys, when they are shown as inanimate objects developing into live beings, embody human anxiety about what it means to be 'real'– an independent subject or self rather than an object or other submitting to the gaze of the more powerfully real and potentially rejecting live beings'. (p. 2)

From a psychoanalytic perspective, Kuznets's point speaks to the toy as a 'transitional object', a term first used by Donald Winnicott (1951/1953) to designate any material object to which an infant/child attributes a special value. From Winnicott's perspective, the object is the 'first not-me possession' and is located in a zone between subjectivity and objectivity. When the toy incorporates mechanical parts that move or transform the object into yet another 'Other' as in the case of Transformer/Alternator/Binaltech toys (cars that transform into robot warriors), the liminal zone between subject and object (me and not-me) is further blurred. Children (and adults) can manipulate the toys, creating the new object in much the same way that puppeteers manipulate their puppets.

The fascination with a simulated 'being' is not confined to Western culture. Dolls, toys, puppets, and other automata cross cultural boundaries. Christopher Bolton (2002) draws a parallel between early Japanese puppets and puppet theatre (*ningyo joruri*) and anime (e.g., *Ghost in the Shell* [1995]). Working with Haraway's cyborgian imagery, and Western and Japanese critics' readings of the Japanese puppet theatre, Bolton attends to the nature of the performance and its relationship with the audience to engage with Haraway's questions of duality, dichotomy, and ambivalence. For Haraway, cyborgs 'populate worlds ambiguously natural and crafted' (1991: p. 149). In *Ghost in the Shell* (1995), the female action hero, known by her rank as Major, is a cyborg who is an elite officer in Shell Squad, the Section 9 security force. The story is set in a not-too-distant future urban space inhabited by both 'pure' humans and cyborgs. However, the naturalness of any body being without mechanical implant is not known with any certainty, even for the characters themselves: Major's partner Toguse is mostly human with only slight brain augmentation, while her partner Batou is a cyborg.[7] The ethics of neurosurgeons who perform brain transplants and create cyborgs is also questioned at one point, but this is part of the film's exploration of the bigger question – What is life? – a question that continues to be asked in our extratextual world as nanobiology is poised to redefine the very essence of what we refer to as 'life'.

There are obvious parallels with puppets in *Ghost in the Shell* as the Major sets out to defeat the elusive criminal hacker, the Puppet Master. The Puppet Master hacks into the minds of his victims, erasing their memories, making them puppets that live out their existences that are in fact computer-generated simulations. They also unwittingly carry out his crimes. He also killed his own body (shell) to 'dive into' a cyborg body. The Ghost is the name for the soul, the indefinable element of human consciousness which can inhabit a cyborg or human body. Bolton suggests that for many critics the 'puppet represents language and action that are simultaneously embodied and disembodied' (p. 738). Bolton sees the Major's mechanical body as being divided between a desire for a physical body and a desire to transcend that body and 'enter a world of pure data or language' (p. 731). In Western puppet theatre the puppeteer is hidden from the audience, creating an illusion of the puppet as a unified, whole subject that speaks, moves, and feels. This is in contrast to traditional Japanese puppet theatre where the puppet is manipulated by three human puppeteers who remain visible onstage, while a single chanter performs the voices of the puppets. Thus,

> the Western dichotomies that constitute the self as this unified whole – dichotomies such as inside and outside, body and soul, and God and human – are now replaced with new articulations of body, voice, and will that expose the layers of signification and self'. (p. 748)

Major hears 'whispers' from her shell, which seem to come from her Ghost. At times a voice speaks through her, without her mouth moving, making her more like the traditional Western puppet who is given voice by a hidden puppeteer. A dislocation of voice from body occurs in other instances in anime, when technological implants and aids enable characters to speak without moving their mouths when they need to communicate silently and secretly. When Major appears defeated and destroyed by the Puppet Master, he inhabits her body so that the two of them can merge and, as he says, 'create a new and unique entity'. This merged entity initially has the male

Puppet Master not only speaking from within the Major's destroyed body with his own voice, but he is able to converse with her with both male and female voices speaking interchangeably. When Major is 'reborn' and given a new shell (of a young girl), her voice again changes to sound like the young female, but her Ghost or that of the Puppet Master inhabits this shell.

Another aspect of the performing puppet/anime's body is the way in which it is a 'dialectic of mass and speed, heaviness and lightness' (Bolton, 2002: p. 760). Audiences of puppet theatre and animation are used to seeing puppets/characters flying, floating, seemingly liberated from human bodily limits and gravitational restrictions. When the human manipulator's arm or hand is inside the puppet, its 'lightness' is incongruously given weight and bulk. Lightness in *Ghost in the Shell* is more complex. As Bolton explains, the Major is an image drawn on celluloid, but her image 'never had a body behind it', thus it appears luminescent and evanescent, subject to manipulation by the technology. The 'birth' of the Major is shown in the opening credits as a result of computational numbers and codes. She appears as a machine-built body that is submerged and gently turned in a skin bath that not only covers her body with skin and colour but makes her near-perfect, female form complete. From this body, which gently moves within the liquid, emerges the strong, hard, and powerful cyborg commander. When Major flies through the air, skilfully dodging bullets, somersaulting down the stairs, and scaling buildings, she seems to be lightness itself, but her body is the body of a machine (despite the film of skin that encases it). She defies the laws of gravity as she likes to float in the sea, whereas she should sink because of the weight of her mechanical body.

A final point that Bolton raises returns us to Hayles's proposition that we are all posthuman. While audiences become captivated by the magic of the puppet theatre, forgetting that the characters are inanimate objects whose fate is literally at the hands of the manipulator, in viewing anime there is a different kind of subject position vis-à-vis these fictional cyborgs, which, unlike the live puppet theatre, requires 'a prosthesis to see it, a projector, DVD player, or VCR' (Bolton, 2002: p. 767). His point links with Halberstam and Livingston's description earlier that a cyborg is 'a technology, a screen, a projected image'. However, 'the technologies of reproduction implicate us in the loop or the network of high-tech representation that is turning us into cyborgs ourselves' (Bolton, 2002: p. 767). Ironically, it is reproduction, not replication, that the Puppet Master desires so that he can become a 'new born': 'neither the woman known as the Major nor the man who was the Puppet Master'.

This section has considered how technoscience has contributed to shifts in epistemologies as technological innovation and experimentation with bodies, matter, and life produce new forms of knowledge production. It has also discussed how technological advances are taken up or predicted in children's fiction, raising ontological crises about the nature of existence, being, or reality. The discussion now considers how information and communication technologies are intensifying the circulation of affects that occur between individuals.

Affects, becomings, and sensations

As indicated in the discussion of *Clay*, the concept of 'becoming' is a significant element in the work of Gilles Deleuze and Felix Guattari (1987). *Ghost in the Shell* is also about becoming – becoming a cyborg, becoming a newborn. Becoming enables a new understanding of affect as a pleasurable and desirous experience outside more traditional (critical) frameworks of image and representation alone. For instance, feminist theory of classic realistic film and even more recent post-classical, 'feminist' films has focused on text, meaning, the visual, and signification, or how a film is a mode of representation and can be studied for what it 'means' politically in terms of the ways women are represented (see Mulvey, 1975; 1981; Tasker, 1998). The approach that Deleuze (1986; 1989) considers in his work on cinema is not so much concerned with what a film means but what it *does*, switching attention from representation to experience (sensations, desires, pleasures).

Deleuze and Guattari have opened up ways of theorizing the 'body' not in terms of the Cartesian dualisms of mind/body, nature/culture, but as a set of continuous flows, energies, organs, processes, and affects. Deleuzian ideas also provide creative ways of seeing how bodies make interconnections – how they form linkages to other bodies, human and inhuman, animate and inanimate, machinic and nonmachinic. This linkage between bodies is most explicit in *Ghost in the Shell* when Puppet Master and Major merge, and as cyborgs and humans share parts (ghosts, shells, computerized components, or human organs). These linkages are a necessary component for understanding what Lenoir (2002) and others term 'the posthuman techno-scape'. For Deleuze, bodies are not just flesh and blood, but a more complex assemblage, much in the way that Clay is an assemblage, a 'body without organs'. As Barbara Kennedy explains, within Deleuzian conceptualizations: 'Body becomes a more composite, machinic, technologized term, dissolved from any formulaic interpretation based upon biological terms' (2000: p. 98). Because bodies are not stable or fixed units, but elements in an assemblage, which itself is fluid and changeable, the body is a 'space of becoming' (Kennedy, 2000: p. 99).

In the young adult novel *Hero* (Moore, 2007) and the film *Sky High* (2005), becoming posthuman is both a motif shared by the texts and a condition of the male protagonists. Each comes to experience his body as a complex assemblage that supersedes its biological limits. Thom (*Hero*) initially has no knowledge of his (separated) parents' posthuman bodies. His father is a silent, depressed man who is a far cry from his former self, the superhero, crime-fighting Captain Courage. His estranged mother, the former Invisible Lass, too, was once a member of the elite League of superheroes. Thom eventually gains knowledge of his parents' past lives while also discovering his own ability to use his hands to suture and heal wounded bodies. *Sky High* parallels this parent–child posthuman status with the late blooming of a posthuman child. Will discovers as a teenager that he has superhuman strength like his famous parents the legendary Commander and Jetstream (aka a normal couple, Steve and Josie Stronghold). At the school Will attends (the eponymous Sky High), all students and teachers are posthuman, but there is a hierarchy that separates the 'heroes' from the 'sidekicks'. For example, the 'failures' or sidekicks include: Layla who can make plants grow; Zac who glows in the dark; Magenta who is a shape-shifter (but can only turn into a guinea pig); and Ethan, who can melt into a colourful pool of liquid. Consequently, the posthuman body is not depicted as a fixed and universal entity but multiple and mutable. However, it continues to be characterized in binary terms. Similarly, in *Hero* the League has its internal stratification with the misfits: the volatile Miss Scarlett who can burst into flames; Typhoid Larry who makes people sick when they come into contact with him; and an older woman, Ruth, who can see the future. The bodies depicted in both these texts are not fixed entities but fluid, changeable, spaces of becoming, and as such they can be thought of, in Deleuzian terms, as sets of continuous flows, energies, organs, processes, and affects.

Sky High can be theorized as a visual experience that goes beyond the representation of subjects (defined by gender, race, age, and so on) by considering Deleuze's ideas of becoming and sensation in the way the film connects as a set of intensities, speeds, and 'haecceities', which are entire assemblages in their individuated component elements (Deleuze & Guattari, 1987: p. 262). *Sky High* resonates with multiple rhythms and intensities of speed; for example, the force of coach Sonic Boom's voice makes students fly through the air and crash into the walls of the spacious gymnasium; high school senior, Gwen Grayson, transforms within nanoseconds from her human form into the evil posthuman Royal Pain; Penny (Gwen's best friend) can duplicate herself into becoming the entire cheerleading team; skinny Lash is able to stretch his body to extreme limits; while Speed can run at lightning pace. These visual sensations and the film's sound track and music score create a haecceity that is *Sky High,* which exudes dizzying visuals, vibrant soundtrack of popular 1980s music and other aural effects, multiple rhythms, and vibrant colours. These various visual and aural 'affects' function as sensations. The filmic event is therefore constituted by its own affect and the viewer does not passively observe the images but actively engages with them by processing the speed, cuts, breaks, colours, dissolves, time-shifts, and so forth. This internalization of technology is the central trope of the cyborg, and in film we can see how this internalization occurs not through implants or augmentation but through sensory affects.

As a novel, *Hero* produces a different kind of sensation for readers, one that relies on language for both effect and affect. It also provides a more vivid exploration of the destruction of the posthuman body than *Sky High*, which offers visual images of the body morphing, duplicating, stretching, and moving that exceeds the human body's limits. Both texts disrupt the body's boundaries, but *Hero,* in particular, gives graphic destruction of the 'human' form. In her book on Gothic horror, Judith Halberstam notes that human bodies in splatter films are punished beyond human limits and they are marked as 'always stitched, sutured, bloody at the seams, and completely beyond the limits and the reaches of an impotent humanism' (1995: p. 144). In *Ghost in the Shell* there is much violence that results in bodies being blown apart, blood splattered over walls and other surfaces, heads severed and split open to reveal cyborg brains destroyed with broken parts. The Major's body is violently destroyed and her brain sucked from its shell. While the destruction ultimately achieves a physical and social transformation and rebirth, this comes after her body goes through extreme ordeals. In the final showdown with the Puppet Master, the Major lands on top of the armoured tank in which he is hiding. In getting to the tank her body is invisible because of the thermo-optic clothing she wears. However, her body becomes visible and changes to exaggerated proportions as she strains to pry open the tank's hatch. The strain eventually pulls her body apart, with her mechanical parts and wires ripping through her skin, her arms being pulled from their sockets. A similar kind of 'splatter' that Halberstam speaks of occurs in *Hero*. One striking instance occurs in the final showdown between Thom's father (now attempting to prove his mettle in a Captain Courage comeback) and the evil (and ironically named) Justice; here bodies are literally torn asunder:

> Justice shrieked at a pitch that shook the city. We covered our ears, but still my left eardrum popped. Justice was in agony. He clawed large chunks of flesh off his neck and chest and arms, like he'd been poisoned with a topical agent and all that mattered was freeing himself from the prison of his own body.
>
> [...]
>
> He mustered whatever strength he had left and stared at my father. His pupils were now gone, his eyes entirely milky white. Then he squinted and launched two lasers from those cloudy eyes. The beans shot across the room and severed my father's good hand from his arm at the wrist.
>
> [...]
>
> Dad muffled a scream and clutched his forearm above the cauterized stump. He dropped to his knees in pain, and Justice was behind him in a flash. Justice took Dad's arms and yanked them out of the sockets, and tied them behind his back as if they were rope. (pp. 408–9)

The outcome of the contestation occurs when Thom's father straps himself and Justice to a rocket that he then fires into space, exploding 'like a million rounds of spectacular fireworks' (p. 421). This scene and others in the book are both horrifying and enthralling (and reminiscent of the battle between Grendel and Beowulf when Beowulf tears off Grendel's arm).[8] While there is a point of complete annihilation for Captain Courage and Justice who are blasted to smithereens, other bodies are brought back from the edge of obliteration by being auto-regenerated, or repaired by one of the cyborgs.

These instances offer hyperbolic accounts of how the body is made and unmade. This making/unmaking corresponds to medical technologies and procedures such as the percutaneous nephroscope, which allows doctors to blast kidney stones to smithereens with a bombardment of sounds waves.[9] In nanobiology, a similar kind of dual process of making and unmaking bodies is activated through molecular technology: 'even structures that one might feel are permanent, such as bones, are continually disassembled, repaired, and rebuilt' by the bionanomachinery always at work inside the body (Goodsell quoted in Milburn, 2005: p. 291). A further potential of nanotechnology is to reproduce an exact replica of virtually anything (Milburn, 2002: p. 288). While Penny in *Sky High* is able to replicate herself exponentially, another novel, *The Speed of the Dark* (Shearer, 2003) uses nanotechnology to circumvent the laws of physics and biology to replicate exact miniature copies of people (and things) who can continue to survive and live otherwise normal lives inside a miniaturized world of a snow dome. Not only is the dome city 'the ultimate postmodern space, a simulacrum whereby technology has taken mimicry and imitation to the extreme' (Bradford et al., 2008: p. 143), it is also a posthuman space whereby the technology has produced perfect copies which are not just replicants who mimic the original; rather, these nanocopies actually *are* the original, and are able to reproduce. This scenario illustrates Jean Baudrillard's (1994) point that in hyperreality the boundary between the real and the simulacrum collapses.

Ghost in the Shell, Hero, and *Sky High* present the posthuman as always already part of the world of the narrative, and in the *Speed of the Dark* the postbiological condition is the subject matter that shapes the novel's narrative trajectory. The difference is that *Speed of the Dark* and *Ghost in the Shell* consider how the posthuman (as a clone or augmented human body) evolves in conjunction with intelligent machines and human ingenuity. In *Speed of the Dark*, Eckmann's development of miniaturizing technology enables him to replicate in miniaturized form anything he so desires. If, like Eckmann, people could make whatever they desire, a potential that some predict nanotechnology will enable, it would then fulfill the 'dream of information' as a 'realm of plenitude and infinite replenishment' (Hayles, 2005: p. 62).

Information, entropy, and the arrow of time

Hayles argues that the notion of plenitude and replenishment is in sharp contrast to what she terms 'the regime of scarcity', which is based on the fundamental assumption that energy and matter are conserved, a foundational premise for the first and second laws of thermodynamics: the first law is the conservation of energy; and the second law is that in closed systems every exchange tends to result in the loss of energy for useful purposes, moving towards states of higher entropy (Hayles, 2005: p. 62). Hayles sees information as not operating according to the same constraints that govern matter and energy. The Internet, search engines such as Google, software-copying facilities, Web 2.0, email, and other information technologies demonstrate that information can proliferate and change. In the opening moments of *Ghost in the Shell* the following words tell of the reach of information and its potential to erase humanity: 'In the near future – corporate networks reach out to the stars, electrons, light flow throughout the universe. The advance of computerization however has not yet wiped out nations and ethnic groups.'

The concept of information has value for cultural analysis. As Clough proposed earlier in this chapter, there has been a shift in culture from representation to information. This shift is captured in post-modern theory's description of the culture of late capitalism as a culture of floating signifiers, that is of signs that are not anchored in networks of signification. This world out of control, of signs referring only to other signs, constitutes the hyperreality of which Baudrillard speaks. Spatial metaphors (such as 'space of flows' and 'space of places' that Castells [1996] uses in referring to network societies) give the impression that we are barely coping with the changes to everyday life brought about by rapid advances in communication and information technologies, and yet we are becoming technological as we drift and float or drown in a 'sea of semirandom noise' (Terranova, 2004: p. 52). In *Ghost in the Shell* a similar point is made by the Puppet Master who speaks of living entities 'created in the sea of information'. Clough posits that the early work on information theory by Claude Shannon in the 1940s can be understood as providing the shift in 'focus of critical engagement with information technologies away from meaning and interpretation and toward time, labor, and bodily affectivity' (2004: p. 8). While Shannon's work has been criticized (see Hall, 1980), his mathematical theory of communication still offers important insights which can be useful for considering time, labour, and affect. However, a more extended consideration of entropy provides a useful way for considering the element of time and information.

Entropy is 'the measure of the amount of disorder in a physical system' (Greene, 2004: p. 154). High entropy equates with *high disorder*, whereas low entropy means the system is *highly ordered*. Greene explains that the second law of thermodynamics offers us an 'arrow of time' ... 'one that *emerges when physical systems have a large number of constituents*' (p. 157, emphasis in original). A forward in time arrow points in the direction of increasing entropy. For example, in watching a film of a glass of ice water, we can determine which direction is forward in time by check-ing that the ice melts – that the molecules disperse, achieving higher entropy. Thus, the second law of thermodynamics singles out the future as the direction in which entropy increases. These notions of informa-tion and entropy are central tropes in the picture book *The Lost Thing* (Tan, 2000).

The end pages of *The Lost Thing* begin and close the story within a sea of random images of machines, words, and a humanoid figure who emerges subsequently as the focalizer 'Shaun'. Overlaying this chaos of signifiers are ordered rows of bottle tops inscribed with mathematical formulae, sci-entific and technological images, words, phrases, numerals, symbols: signs that appear random and unanchored. However, one bottle top, placed in the centre of the rows, is inscribed with the word 'ENTROPY'. Shannon's definition of information positively correlates with entropy or noise, where information arises out of noise. Rather than see information in opposi-tion to noise, Shannon proposes that the more noise or turbulence, the more uncertainty and the greater the probability for information (Clough, 2004). If we read 'entropy' here in Shannon's terms then it can be under-stood as a random variable among others, a turbulence or noise, that con-tains information and which attempts an order out of the chaos. Shaun is a bottle-top collector who randomly collects bottle tops lying on the ground but who appears to enjoy imposing order on his collection, as indicated by the large book he carries entitled 'What bottle top is that?': a reference to standard scientific classificatory texts such as 'What bird is that?'. The story at its simplest level tells of a boy (Shaun) who finds and befriends a large, pear-shaped, red 'thing' which is an assemblage of mechanical and organic parts. It also enjoys eating and stores or metabolizes nonorganic objects (Christmas decorations and junk) fed through a hatch that opens at the top of its 'body'. The thing moves and human emotions are attrib-uted to it – 'The lost thing made a small sad face' (when it clearly does not have a discernible face). Shaun presumes the thing is lost and sets out to find for it a place to belong. It is in his searching that the text offers a means for exploring information and its relationship to entropy, labour, and affect.

As mentioned previously, the second law of thermodynamics states that as energy systems decrease, their entropy increases: high entropy = low order (or high disorder); low entropy = high order. Clough makes the connection between entropy, labour, and disorder:

> Entropy is defined as energy that can no longer be put to work, no longer can be organized to do something, having become chaotic, like microparticles moving out of order, aimlessly. As such, entropy is the measure of turbulence or disorder in a closed system. (Clough, 2004: p. 9)

We can see how entropy operates in the text when Shaun, contemplating what to do with the thing, comes across an advertisement that begins:

> Are YOU finding that order of day-to-day live is unexpectedly disrupted
> by
> Unclaimed property?
> Troublesome artifacts of unknown origin?
> Things that don't belong?
> Filing cabinets leftovers?
> Objects without names?
>
> (unpaged)

This advertisement explicitly links information to noise or turbulence (entropy) – a surplus of information has resulted in property, artifacts, things, correspondence no longer able to be organized or useful, and the disruption of order has led to disorder whereby these bits of information are now troublesome, no longer belonging, leftover, unclassifiable. But the advertisement offers a solution – The Federal Department of Odds & Ends has a 'pigeon hole' for all this useless surplus of information, its motto 'Sweepus underum carpetae' suggesting that the information is indeed redundant and can be swept under the carpet and forgotten. It can also mean that there is a place after all (a pigeon hole, a space under a carpet), and the advertisement itself is the channel for transmitting the information which Shaun receives, thereby in itself it is not redundant but becomes a useful piece of information.

The advertisement appears in the centre of a newspaper page and is surrounded by other pieces of information, or noise, all of which are concerned with extolling the virtue of a piece of electrical equipment, selling a technological aid or service, classifying electronic parts (diodes), recalling faulty automated gadgets, and giving details of a competition for perpetual-motion ideas. The meaningfulness of these messages is not guaranteed either by the newspaper as a channel of communication or by the implied reader as a potential receiver of information. According to Clough, Shannon defined information as 'the measure of the probability of a message's transmission, regardless of meaning or context' (2004: p. 8). When a piece of information travels from a sender to a receiver, the problem arises concerning the channel of communication. By taking into account Shannon's proposition that the more noise or turbulence (entropy), the more uncertainty and the greater the probability for information, then the information that is communicated on this one page of *The Lost Thing* alone arises out of noise and displays some pattern of redundancy and frequency that enables a reader to apprehend it as information. Thus, entropy 'might be productive of an information surplus' (Clough, 2004: p. 9).

When Shaun is given a 'sign' (a squiggly arrow on a business card), his attempts to follow this entropic arrow are complicated by the profusion of similar-looking signs, other arrows, and squiggly shapes. But out of this profusion of difference (the noise or turbulence) the sign is located on a buzzer which when pressed opens up a big door onto a large space of multiple colonnades and objects, and, for the first time in the book, a blue sky. The space appears chaotic with a proliferation of objects of different shapes and sizes, floating, anchored, assemblages of organic and nonorganic parts, emitting clouds, water, smoke, and other indefinable substances. However, the disorder or high entropy creates many ways for things to coexist in the space, and to go unnoticed. In the high order/low entropy urban space, the thing stands out (at least to the reader). Furthermore, the seemingly high order/low entropy of the government department (which can be read as a satiric comment on bureaucratic 'efficiency'), and the arrow of time that leads to the space of disorder, may serve as a reminder that the future is the direction of increasing entropy.

The urban space is characterized by its repetition of shapes, design, and sombre colour scheme. Rusting, nonfunctioning machines dominate the landscape, and emotionless humans commute in slow-moving, ordered lines. The commuters are dressed as office workers but the buildings appear empty of workers, and the only people who are actually depicted 'working' are three maintenance men in white overalls and a cyborg cleaner (who gives the sign to Shaun). The size, bulk, and red colour of the thing mark its difference. The cyborg cleaner too is different and it is through 'her' gesture that the thing comes to find a space of other machinic assemblages, bodies that are comprised of elements of both living matter and machines, a space of colour, liveliness, and nonuniformity. Whereas the urban space suggests a place that has had its time, one that has grown weary, rusting, and abandoned in parts, the other space (the no-place) is not quite utopian as the inscription on a wall suggests with its spelling – 'UtOqIA' – a place that is in-between. This notion of being in-between, or we could say 'in-formation', opens up the possibility of seeing this space as an open system, one that is dynamic, changeable, energetic, and where bodies have no fixed form but are varied, machinic bodies. Clough describes 'machinic bodies' as 'bodies in the time of becoming, in the time of in-between, of emergence or transformation. They are bodies of virtuality' (2004: p. 11). A comparison occurs with *Ghost in the Shell* where the opening scenes show the Major's machinic body in various stages of becoming amidst the noise and rapid flickering of computer codes, scientific and mathematical drawings. Later, when the Puppet Master's ghost merges with the Major's, he comments that 'all things change in a dynamic environment'.

The Lost Thing is in many ways the real thing, especially in its imaginative depiction of human–technology relations, whereby the human species appears to have lost its asserted mastery over machines and the liberal humanist subject's manifest destiny to dominate and control nature. This text proffers a destination for the Thing, one that is different from the other

world that is depicted in the text; a future perhaps, but one that opens to
the possibility of otherness and disorder. However, even this future appears
destined to nothing other than its own possibility of becoming, and this is
one of the responsibilities of fantasy and science fiction, to make us aware
of the limitations of our present world and to think beyond our own biological lives, and to entertain possible realms of otherness that may yet come or
that may indeed already exist.

Conclusion

As this chapter has demonstrated, technoscience and children's fiction
often proceed hand in hand, with each providing narratives of possible
futures and current realities. In the technoscapes that fiction creates, anything is possible; a similar kind of narrative logic is offered by nanotechnology. In writing about our posthuman futures, the new sciences provide
important material, ideas, and stories, which bring massive biological,
ecological, ethical, corporeal, and cultural considerations. Whether these
stories convey a utopian or apocalyptic vision there is usually an element
of prescience, which forewarns of the possible consequences if care is not
exercised.

The various texts in this chapter carry both warning and celebration. In
reinscribing the logic of life in nonbiological forms, notions of the artificial, the nonorganic, the machinic, and the cyborgian produce new kinds
of entities which are becoming less strange and more familiar. The new
sciences that have produced these evolving and mutating entities are positioned between two perspectives: the metaphysics of life and the history
of technological objects. As the fictional texts in this chapter have shown,
these perspectives are both complex and overlapping, with ontological crises often accompanying technological developments. As science and fiction
continue their reciprocal relationship, they also open up new theoretical
space to explore questions about life, death, and all that matters.

Further Readings

Bradford, C., Mallan, K., Stephens, J., & McCallum, R. 2008. 'The struggle to
be human in a posthuman world'. In *New world orders in contemporary children's literature: utopian transformations*. Palgrave Macmillan, Houndmills.
This chapter's focus is on how children's fiction and film are responding
to the posthuman.
Mallan, K. 2009. 'Gendered cyborgs: the dilemma of technological
"Existenz"'. In *Gender dilemmas in children's fiction*. Palgrave Macmillan,
Houndmills. This chapter examines philosophical notions of existence
and existenz when real and virtual worlds become blurred and the impact
this has on gendered bodies.

Napier, S.J. 2001. 'Doll parts: technology and the body in ghost in the shell in Anime from "Akira" to "Princess Mononoke"'. In *Experiencing contemporary Japanese Animation*. Palgrave, New York. Further reading on the ghost in the shell.

Sawers, N. 2009. 'Capitalism's new handmaiden: the biotechnical world negotiated through children's fiction'. *Children's Literature in Education*, vol. 40, no. 3, pp. 169–79. Considers the ethical implications of scientific practices such as organ transplantation and how children's literature socializes children to accept or challenge the dominant ideologies underpinning organ transplantation.

Notes

1 'Descartes often compares the ontological argument to a geometric demonstration, arguing that necessary existence cannot be excluded from idea of God anymore than the fact that its angles equal two right angles, for example, can be excluded from the idea of a triangle ... God's existence is purported to be as obvious and self-evident as the most basic mathematical truth': http://plato.stanford.edu/entries/descartes-ontological/ (Accessed 12 November 2009)

2 For further information about 'language games' refer to the work of Ludwig Wittgenstein, *Philosophical investigations* (1958).

3 For a discussion of texts that illustrate this point see *Gender dilemmas in children's fiction* (Mallan, 2009), Chapter 3.

4 Blood libels are false accusations against Jews claiming they use human blood in some of their religious rituals.

5 See 'The Golem' by Alden Oreck: http://www.jewishvirtuallibrary.org/jsource/Judaism/Golem.html (Accessed 20 October 2009).

6 Bolter (1984) also offers an example from ancient Greek and Roman mythology, where the master craftsman, Pygmalion, sculpts out of ivory the perfect likeness of a beautiful woman, whom he falls in love with. This theme is repeated with a contemporary twist in the film *Lars and the real girl* (2007). In this story, Lars decides to purchase a life-size doll named Bianca from an online catalogue. He buys clothes for her, talks to her, watches television with her, all the time living out the fantasy of harmonious coupledom and being a loving and devoted partner to Bianca. A similar story is told of Descartes and his female android that he named Francine after his deceased daughter. It is said that Francine accompanied Descartes on all his journeys (Vermeir, 2008).

7 Sometimes spelt Bateau on some DVDs of the film.

8 There are several children's versions of this Anglo-Saxon epic poem (see for example: *Beowulf* retold by Kevin Crossley-Holland, illustrated by Charles Keeping. OUP, 1999). There is also an R rated film *Beowulf & Grendel* (2005).

9 See *Time* report: http://www.time.com/time/magazine/article/0,9171,923286-1,00.html (Accessed 16 October 2009).

Bibliography

Adaptations of the Wizard of Oz. Wikipedia. Accessed 26 September 2009, http://en.wikipedia.org/wiki/The_Wizard_of_Oz_%28adaptations%29.

Aeschylus. *The Oresteia*. 1983 [458 BC]. Trans. R. Fagles. Penguin, Hammondsworth.

Ahlberg, J. & Ahlberg, A. 1987. *The clothes horse and other stories*. Puffin, Harmondsworth.

Alexie, S. 2007. *The absolutely true diary of a part-time Indian*. Andersen Press, London.

Alice in Wonderland. 2010. Motion picture. Walt Disney Studios Motion Pictures, USA.

Alien. 1979. Motion picture. 20th Century Fox, USA.

Aliens. 1986. Motion picture. 20th Century Fox, USA.

Almond, D. 2005. *Clay*. Hodder Children's Books, London.

Anderson, M.T. 2002. *Feed*. Candlewick, Somerville, MA.

Apol, L. 2003. 'Shooting bears, saving butterflies: ideology of the environment in Gibson's *Herm and I* and Klass's *California blue*'. *Children's Literature*, vol. 31, pp. 90–115.

Appadurai, A. 1990. 'Disjuncture and difference in the global cultural economy'. *Theory, Culture and Society*, vol. 7, no. 2–3, pp. 295–310.

Appadurai, A. (ed.) 2001. *Globalization*. Duke University Press, Durham.

Appadurai, A. 1996. *Modernity at large: cultural dimensions of globalization*, Minnesota University Press, Minneapolis.

Ardis, A. 1990. *New woman, new novels: feminism and early modernism*. Rutgers University Press, New Brunswick.

Ashcroft, B. 2001. *Post-colonial transformation*. Routledge, London.

Ashcroft, B., Griffiths, G., & Tiffin, H. 1989. *The empire writes back: theory and practice in Post-colonial Literatures*. Routledge, London.

Athanasiou, A. 2005. 'Technologies of humanness, aporias of biopolitics, and the cut body of humanity'. *Differences: a Journal of Feminist Cultural Studies*, vol. 14, no. 1, pp. 126–62.

Auge, M. 1995. *Non-places: introduction to an anthropology of supermodernity*. Verso, London.

Austen, J. 1972. *Pride and prejudice*. Penguin, London.

Austen, J. & Grahame-Smith, S. 2009. *Pride and prejudice and zombies: the classic regency romance—now with ultraviolent zombie mayhem*. Quirk Books, Philadelphia.

Auty, S. & Lewis, C. 2004. 'The "delicious paradox": preconscious processing of product placements by children'. In L.J. Shrum (ed.), *The psychology of entertainment media: blurring the lines between entertainment and persuasion*. Lawrence Erlbaum Associates, New Jersey, pp. 117–33.

Babcock, J. 2006. *The boys and the bees*. Carroll & Graff, New York.

Baccolini, R. 2007. 'Finding utopia in dystopia: feminism, memory, nostalgia, and hope'. In T. Moylan & R Baccolini (eds), *Utopia method vision: the use value of social dreaming*. Peter Lang, Oxford, pp. 159–89.

Baccolini, R. & Moylan, T. (eds) 2003. *Dark horizons: science fiction and the dystopian imagination*. Routledge, New York.

Bachofen, J. 2005 [1861]. *An English translation of Bachofen's Mutterrecht (mother right): a study of the religious and juridical aspects of gynocracy in the ancient world*, trans. D Partenheimer. Edwin Mellen Press, Lewiston, NY.

Baggett, D. & Klein, S. 2004. *Harry Potter and philosophy: if Aristotle ran Hogwarts.* Open Court, Peru, IL.

Baillie, A. & Magerl, C. 2005. *Castles.* Penguin/Viking, Camberwell, Vic.

Baillie, A. & Wu, D. 1996. *Old magic.* Random House Australia, Milsons Point, NSW.

Ball, J.C. 1997. 'Max's colonial fantasy: rereading Sendak's *Where the wild things* are'. *Ariel: A Review of International English Literature*, vol. 28, no. 1, pp. 16–79.

Barber, B.R. 1996. *Jihad vs McWorld.* Ballantine Books, New York.

Barber, B.R. 2002. 'Jihad vs McWorld'. In G. Ritzer (ed.), *McDonaldization: the reader.* Pine Forge Press, Thousand Oaks, pp. 191–98.

Barry, P. 2002. *Beginning theory: an introduction to literary and cultural theory.* Manchester University Press, Manchester.

Base, G. 2006. *Uno's garden.* Viking, Camberwell, Victoria.

Baudrillard, J. 1994. *Simulacra and simulation*, trans. S.F. Glaser. University of Michigan Press, Ann Abor.

Baum, L.F. 2005. *15 Books in 1: L. Frank Baum's original 'Oz' series.* Ships and Shoes and Sealing Wax, UK.

Bauman, Z. 2000. *Liquid modernity.* Polity Press, Cambridge.

Bauman, Z. 1998. 'Tourists and vagabonds'. In Z Bauman (ed.), *Globalization: the human consequences.* Columbia University Press, New York, pp. 77–102.

Bayet-Charlton, F. 2003. 'Overturning the doctrine: Indigenous people and wilderness—being Aboriginal in the environmental movement'. In M Grossman (ed.), *Blacklines: contemporary critical writing by Indigenous Australians.* Melbourne University Press, Carlton, pp. 171–80.

Bear, G. 2007. *Blood music.* Gollancz-Orion, London.

Beck, U. 2000. *What is globalization?*, trans. P. Camiller. Polity Press, Cambridge.

Bell, E., Haas, L., & Sells, L. (eds) 1995. *From mouse to mermaid: the politics of film, gender and culture.* Indian University Press, Bloomington.

Benjamin, J. 1998. *The shadow of the other: intersubjectivity and gender in psychoanalysis.* Routledge, New York.

Benjamin, W. 1992. 'Theses on the philosophy of history', trans. H. Zohn. *Illuminations*, Fontana, London, pp. 245–55.

Beowulf & Grendel. 2005. Motion picture. Movision, UK.

Bhabha, J. 1998. ' "Get back to where you once belonged": identity, citizenship, and exclusion in Europe'. *Human Rights Quarterly*, vol. 20, no. 3, pp. 592–627.

Blackman, M. 2001. *Noughts & crosses.* Random House, London.

Bloch, E. 1986. *The principle of hope* (3 vols). MIT Press, Cambridge, MA.

Bloch, R.H. 1991. *Medieval misogyny and the invention of western romantic love.* University of Chicago Press, Chicago.

Bolter, D.J. 1984. *Turing's man.* University of North Carolina Press, Chapel Hill.

Bolton, C. 2002. 'From wooden cyborgs to celluloid souls: mechanical bodies in anime and Japanese puppet theater'. *Positions: east asia cultures critique*, vol. 10, no. 3, pp. 729–71.

Botting, F. 2002. 'Aftergothic: consumption, machines, and black holes'. In J.E. Hogle (ed.), *The Cambridge companion to gothic fiction.* Cambridge University Press, Cambridge, pp. 277–300.

Bradford, C. 2006. 'Multiculturalism and children's books'. In *The Oxford encyclopedia of children's literature*, vol. 3. Oxford University Press, New York, pp. 113–18.

Bradford, C. 2001. *Reading race: Aboriginality in Australian children's literature.* Melbourne University Press, Carton, Vic.

Bradford, C. 2003. 'The sky is falling: children as environmental subjects in contemporary picture books'. In R McGillis (ed.), *Children's literature and the fin de siècle.* Praeger, Westport, CT, pp. 111–20.

Bradford, C. 2007. *Unsettling narratives: postcolonial readings of children's literature.* Wilfrid Laurier University Press, Waterloo, Ontario.

Bradford, C., Mallan, K., Stephens, J., & McCallum, R. 2008. *New world orders in contemporary children's literature: utopian transformations.* Palgrave Macmillan, Basingstoke.

Branch, M.P., Johnson, R., Slovic S., & Patterson, D. (eds) 1998. *Reading the earth: new directions in the study of Literature and the environment.* University of Idaho Press, Moscow, ID.

Brim, W. & Egilitis, A. 2005. *Creatures of the rain forest: two artists explore Djabugay Country.* Magabala Books, Broome.

Brown, S. 2006. 'Monster house'. *Sight and Sound,* vol. 16, no. 9, pp. 60–2.

Browne, A. 1993. *The big baby: a little joke.* Julia MacRae, London.

Buckingham, D. 1995. 'On the impossibility of children's television: the case of Timmy Mellett'. In C. Bazalgette & D. Buckingham (eds), *In front of the children: screen entertainment and young audiences.* British Film Institute, London, pp. 47–61.

Buell, L. 2005. *The future of environmental criticism.* Blackwell, Malden, MA.

Buell, L. 2001. *Writing for an endangered world: literature, culture, and environment in the US and beyond.* Harvard University Press, London.

Bugs life. 1998. Animation. Pixar Animation Studios, USA.

Burningham, J. 1977. *Come away from the water, Shirley.* Jonathan Cape, London.

Butler, C. 2008. 'Experimental girls: feminist and transgender discourses in *Bill's new frock* and *Marvin Redpost: is he a girl?'. Children's Literature Association Quarterly,* vol. 34, no. 1, pp. 3–20.

Butler, J. 1993. *Bodies that matter: on the discursive limits of 'sex'.* Routledge, New York.

Butler, J. 1999. *Gender trouble.* Routledge, New York.

Butler, J. 2004. *Undoing gender.* Routledge, New York.

Calcutt, L., Woodward, I., & Skrbis, Z. 2009. 'Conceptualizing otherness'. *Journal of Sociology,* vol. 45, no. 2, pp. 169–86.

Carter, P. 1987. *The road to Botany Bay: an essay in spatial* history. Faber & Faber, London.

Castells, M. 1996. *The rise of the network society. The information age: economy, society and culture vol. 1.* Blackwell Publishers, Malden, MA.

Cheney, J. 1989. 'Postmodern environmental ethics: ethics as bioregional narrative'. *Environmental Ethics,* vol. 11, no. 2, pp. 117–35.

Clough, P.T. 2004. 'Technoscience, global politics, and cultural criticism'. *Future Matters,* vol. 80, no. 22, pp. 1–23.

Clover, C. 1992. *Men, women and chainsaws: gender in the modern horror film.* British Film Institute, London.

Coats, K. 2008. 'Between horror, humour, and hope: Neil Gaiman and the psychic work of the gothic'. In A. Jackson, K. Coats, & R. McGillis (eds), *The gothic in children's literature: haunting the borders.* Routledge, New York, pp. 77–92.

Coats, K. 2004. *Looking glasses and Neverlands: Lacan, desire and subjectivity in children's literature.* University of Iowa Press, Iowa City.

Cohen, M.P. 2004. 'Blues in the green: ecocriticism under critique'. *Environmental History,* vol. 9, no. 1, pp. 9–36.

Commoner, B. 1971. *The closing circle: nature, man, and technology.* Knopf, New York.

Cooper, M. 2007. *The rage of sheep.* Random House Australia, North Sydney.

Creed, B. 2004. 'Horror and the monstrous-feminine: an imaginary abjection'. In F. Botting & D. Townshend (eds), *Gothic: critical concepts in literary and cultural theory*, vol. 4. Routledge, London, pp. 244–72.

Creed, B. 2002 [1993]. *The monstrous-feminine: film, feminism, psychoanalysis.* Routledge, London.

Crossley-Holland, K. 1999. *Beowulf*, illust. C Keeping. Oxford University Press, Oxford.

Culler, J. 2007. *The literary in theory.* Stanford University Press, Stanford.

Cunningham, V. 2002. *Reading after theory.* Blackwell, Oxford.

Dawson, L. 2005. 'Menstruation, misogyny, and the cure for love'. *Women's Studies*, vol. 34, pp. 461–84.

De Lauretis, T. 1991. 'Queer theory: lesbian and gay sexualities'. *Difference: A Journal of Feminist Cultural Studies*, vol. 3, no. 2, pp. Iii–xvii.

De Man, P. 1986. *Resistance to theory.* University of Minnesota Press, Minneapolis.

Delany, S.R. 1991. 'Reading modern American science fiction'. In R Kostelanetz (ed), *American writing today.* Whitston, Troy, NY, pp. 517–28.

Deleuze, G. 1986. *Cinema 1: the movement-image*, trans. H. Tomlinson & B. Habberjam. University of Minnesota Press, Minneapolis.

Deleuze, G. 1989. *Cinema 2: the time-image*, trans. H. Tomlinson & R. Galeta. Athlone, London.

Deleuze, G. & Guattari, F. 1987. *A thousand plateaus: capitalism and schizophrenia*, trans. B Massumi. University of Minnesota Press, Minneapolis.

Dijkstra, B. 1996. *Evil sisters: the threat of female sexuality and the cult of manhood.* Alfred A. Knopf, New York.

Dijkstra, B. 1986. *Idols of perversity: fantasies of feminine evil in fin-de-siécle culture.* Oxford University Press, New York.

Dixon, B. 1977. *Catching them young: sex, race and class in children's fiction.* Pluto Press, London.

Dryzek, J.S. 2005. *The politics of the earth*, 2nd edn. Oxford University Press, Oxford.

Duncan, A. 2003. *Sushi central.* University of Queensland Press, St Lucia.

Eagleton, T. 2003. *After theory.* Penguin, London.

Eakin, E. 2002. 'The latest theory is that theory doesn't matter'. *New York Times*, 19 April, accessed 16 September 2009, http://www9.georgetown.edu/faculty/ irvinem/theory/NYT-TheoryDoesntMatter-04-19-03.html.

Earthsea. 2004. DVD. Hallmark Entertainment, USA.

Easterlin, N. 2004. 'Loving ourselves best of all: ecocriticism and the adapted mind'. *Mosaic: A Journal for the Interdisciplinary Study of Literature*, vol. 37, no. 3, pp. 1–18.

Escobar, A. 2001. 'Culture sits in places: reflections on globalism and subaltern strategies of localization'. *Political Geography*, vol. 20, no. 2, pp. 139–74.

Estok, S.C. 2001. 'A report card on ecocriticism'. *AUMLA: The Journal of the Australasian Universities Language and Literature Association*, vol. 96, pp. 220–38.

Falk, R.A. 1999. *Predatory globalization: a critique.* Polity Press, Cambridge.

Fiedler, L. 1982. *Love and death in the American novel.* Stein & Day, New York.

Finding Nemo. 2003. Animation. Pixar Animation Studios, USA.

Flanagan, V. 2007. *Into the closet: cross-dressing and the gendered body in children's literature and film.* Routledge, New York.

Fleenor, J. (ed.) 1983. *The female gothic.* Eden Press, Montreal.

Foucault, M. 1972. *The archaeology of knowledge and the discourse on language*, trans. A.M. Sheridan Smith. Pantheon Books, New York.

Foucault, M. 1977. *Discipline and punish: the birth of the prison*, trans. A.M. Sheridan. Pantheon Books, New York.

Foucault, M. 1967. *Madness and civilization: a history of insanity in the age of reason*, trans. R. Howard. Tavistock, London.

Galeano, E. 2006. *Las palabras andantes*, accessed 27 February 2010, http://www. patriagrande.net/uruguay/eduardo.galeano/las.palabras.andantes/ventana.sobre. la.utopia.htm.

Gallese, V. 2003. 'Intersubjectivity'. *Psychopathology*, vol. 36, pp. 171–80.

Gantz, K. 2000. ' "Not that there's anything wrong with that": reading the queer in Seinfield'. In C. Thomas (ed.), *Straight with a twist: queer theory and the subject of heterosexuality*. University of Illinois Press, Chicago, pp. 165–90.

Ghost in the Shell. 1995. Animation. Bandai Visual Company, Japan.

Gibbs, R.W. Jr. 2003. 'Prototypes in dynamic meaning construal'. In J. Gavins & G. Steen (eds), *Cognitive poetics in practice*. Routledge, London.

Giddens, A. 1990. *The consequences of modernity*. Polity Press, Cambridge.

Gilmore, D. 2001. *Misogyny: the male malady*. University of Pennsylvania Press, Philadelphia.

Giroux, H. 1995. 'Memory and pedagogy in the "wonderful world of Disney": beyond the politics of innocence'. In E. Bell, L. Haas, & L. Sells (eds), *From mouse to mermaid: the politics of film, gender and culture*. Indiana University Press, Bloomington, pp. 43–61.

Glotfelty, C. 1996. 'Introduction: literary studies in an age of environmental crisis'. In C. Glotfelty & H. Fromm (eds), *The ecocriticism reader: landmarks in literary ecology*. University of Georgia Press, Athens, Georgia, pp. xv–xxxvii.

Goldberg, J. 1993. 'Sodomy in the new world: anthropologies old and new'. In M. Warner (ed.), *Fear of a queer planet: queer politics and social theory*. University of Minnesota Press, Minneapolis, pp. 3–18.

Gray, D.J. (ed.) 1971. *Alice in Wonderland/Lewis Carroll: authoritative texts of Alice's adventures in Wonderland, Through the looking-glass, The hunting of the snark, backgrounds, essays in criticism*. W.W. Norton and Company, New York.

Greder, A. 2002. *Die insel. Eine tägliche geschichte*. Sauerländer, Aarau, Frankfurt am Main.

Greder, A. 2007. *The island 2007*. Allen & Unwin, Crows Nest.

Greene, B. 2004. *The fabric of the cosmos*. Penguin, London.

Gupta, S. 2005. 'Sociological speculations on the professions of children's literature'. *The Lion and the Unicorn*, vol. 29, no. 3, pp. 299–323.

Gupta, A. & Ferguson, J. 1992. 'Beyond "culture": space, identity, and the politics of difference'. *Cultural Anthropology*, vol. 7, no. 1, pp. 6–23.

Gutierrez, A.K. 2009. '*Mga kwento ni Lola Basyang*: a tradition of reconfiguring the Filipino child'. *International Research in Children's* Literature, vol. 2, no. 2, pp. 159–76.

Halberstam, J. 2004. 'Oh bondage up yours! Female masculinity and the tomboy'. In S. Bruhm & N. Hurley (eds), *Curiouser: on the queerness of children*. University of Minnesota Press, Minneapolis, pp. 191–214.

Halberstam, J. 1995. *Skin shows: gothic horror and the technology of monsters*. Duke University Press, Durham.

Halberstam, J. & Livingston, I. (eds) 1995. *Posthuman bodies*. Indiana University Press, Bloomington.

Hall, S. 1980. 'Encoding/decoding'. In S. Hall, D. Hobson, A. Lowe, & P. Willis (eds), *Culture, media, language*. Hutchinson, London, pp. 107–16.

Hall, S. 1995. 'New cultures for old'. In D. Massey & P. Jess (eds), *A place in the world? Places, cultures and globalization*. Oxford University Press, Oxford, pp. 175–213.

Hanke, R. 1992. 'Redesigning men: hegemonic masculinity in transition'. In S Craig (ed.), *Men, masculinity and the media*. Sage, Newbury Park, CA, pp. 185–98.

Happy feet. 2006. Kennedy-Miller Productions & Animal Logic Films, Australia.

Haraway, D. 1991. 'A cyborg manifesto: science, technology, and socialist-feminism in the late twentieth century'. In *Simians, cyborgs and women: the reinvention of nature*. Routledge, New York, pp. 149–81.

Harmer, W. 2009. *I lost my mobile at the mall: teenager on the edge of a technological breakdown*. Random House, North Sydney.

Harré, R., Brockmeier, J., & Mühlhäusler, P. 1999. *Greenspeak: a study of environmental discourse*. Sage, London.

Harris, A. 2003. 'Misogyny: hatred at close range'. In D. Moss (ed.), *Hating in the first person plural: psychoanalytic essays on racism, homophobia, misogyny, and terror*. Other Press, New York, pp. 249–78.

Hartmann, D. 2009. 'Space construction as cultural practice: reading William Gibson's *Neuromancer* with respect to postmodern concepts of space'. In R. Pordzik (ed.) *Futurescapes: space in utopian and science fiction discourses*. Rodopi, Amsterdam, pp. 275–99.

Harvey, D. 1990. *The condition of postmodernity*. Blackwell, Oxford.

Harvey, D. 1989. *The condition of postmodernity*. Oxford University Press, Oxford.

Harvey, D. 2000. *Spaces of hope*. University of California Press, Berkeley, CA.

Hay, P. 2002. *Main currents in western environmental thought*. University Press, Bloomington, Indiana.

Hayles, K.N. 1999. *How we became posthuman: virtual bodies in cybernetics: literature and informatics*. University of Chicago Press, Chicago.

Hayles, K.N. 2005. *My mother was a computer: digital subjects and literary texts*. Chicago University Press, Chicago.

Heiland, D. 2004. *Gothic and gender: an introduction*. Blackwell, Malden, MA.

Herman, D. 2004. *Story logic*. University of Nebraska Press, Lincoln, NE.

Hinkins, J. 2007. '"Biting the hand that feeds": consumerism, ideology and recent animated film for children'. *Papers: Explorations into Children's Literature*, vol. 17, no. 1, pp. 43–50.

Hogle, J. (ed.) 2002. *The Cambridge companion to gothic fiction*. Cambridge University Press, Cambridge.

Holmes, D. 2001. 'Virtual globalization—an introduction'. In D. Holmes (ed.), *Virtual globalization: virtual spaces/tourist spaces*. Routledge, London, pp. 1–54.

Holston, J. & Appadurai, A. 1996. 'Cities and citizenship'. *Public Culture*, vol. 8, no. 2, pp. 187–204.

Honeyman, S. 2006. 'Manufactured agency and the playthings who dream it for us'. *Children's Literature Association Quarterly*, vol. 31, no. 2, pp. 109–31.

Hopkins, J. 2004. *Shrek: from the swamp to the screen*. Harry N Abrams, New York.

Howarth, W. 1996. 'Some principles of ecocriticism'. In C. Glofelty & H. Fromm (eds), *The ecocriticism reader: landmarks in literary ecology*. University of Georgia Press, Athens, Georgia, pp. 92–104.

Huber, H. 2004. Review of *Die insel. Eine tägliche geschichte*, accessed 19 October 2009, http://www.lesekost.de/deutsch/kinder/HHLDK04.htm.

Huet, M-H. 1993. *Monstrous imagination*. Harvard University Press, Cambridge, MA.

Huggan, G. 2007. *Australian literature: postcolonialism, racism, transnationalism.* Oxford University Press, Oxford.

Huggan, G. 2004. ' "Greening" postcolonialism: ecocritical perspectives'. *Modern Fiction Studies*, vol. 50, no. 3, pp. 701–33.

Hunt, P. 1990. *Children's literature: the development of criticism.* Routledge, London.

Hurley, K. 1996. *The gothic body: sexuality, materialism, and degeneration at the fin de siècle.* Cambridge University Press, Cambridge.

Hutcheon, L. 2008. 'Harry Potter and the novice's confession'. *The Lion and the Unicorn*, vol. 32, no. 2, pp. 169–79.

Hutcheon, L. 2006. *A theory of adaptation.* Routledge, London.

The Incredibles. 2004. Animation. Pixar Animation Studios, USA.

Jackson, A., Coates, K., & McGillis, R. (eds) 2008. *The gothic in children's literature: haunting the borders.* Routledge, New York.

Jameson, F. 2007. *Archaeologies of the future: the desire called utopia and other science fictions.* Verso, London.

Johnston, J. 2008. *The allure of machinic life: cybernetics, artificial life, and the new AI.* MIT Press, Cambridge, MA.

Jones, D.W. 1980. *The magicians of Caprona.* Macmillan, London.

Kahane, C. 2004. 'Gothic mirrors and feminine identity'. In F. Botting & D. Townshend (eds), *Gothic: critical concepts in literary and cultural theory*, vol. 1. Routledge, London, pp. 276–92.

Kalman, B. 2009. *What is culture?.* Crabtree Publishing, Ontario.

Kennedy, B. 2000. *Deleuze and cinema: the aesthetics of sensation.* Edinburgh University Press, Edingburgh.

Kenway, J. & Bullen, E. 2001. *Consuming children: education-entertainment-advertising.* Open University Press, Buckingham.

Kermode, F. 2003. 'Value after theory'. In M. Payne & J. Schad (eds), *Life after theory.* Continuum, London, pp. 52–77.

Kerridge, R. & Sammells, N. (eds) 1998. *Writing the environment: ecocriticism and literature.* Zed Books, New York.

Khorana, M.G. 2006. 'India'. In J. Zipes (ed.), *The Oxford encyclopedia of children's literature.* Oxford University Press, Oxford, pp. 282–5.

Kidd, K. 1998. 'Gay and lesbian children's literature'. *Children's Literature Association Quarterly*, Special Issue, vol. 23, no. 3, pp. 114–19.

Kincaid, J. 2004. 'Producing erotic children'. In S. Bruhm & N. Hurley (eds), *Curiouser: on the queerness of children.* University of Minnesota Press, Minneapolis, pp. 3–16.

Kiss me, Kate. 2003. PBS broadcast. Image Entertainment, USA.

Kiss Me Kate. 1953. Motion picture. MGM, USA.

Klein, N. 2000. *No logo.* Flamingo, London.

Knox, J. 2009. 'Mirror neurons and embodied simulation in the development of archetypes and self-agency'. *Journal of Analytical Psychology*, vol. 54, pp. 307–23.

Kolodny, A. 1996. 'Unearthing herstory: an introduction'. In C. Glotfelty & H. Fromm (eds), *The ecocriticism reader: landmarks in literary ecology.* University of Athens Press, Athens, Georgia, pp. 170–81.

Kristeva, J. 1982. *Powers of horror: an essay on abjection,* trans. L.S. Rondiez. Columbia University Press, New York.

Krosoczka, J.J. 2009. *Lunch lady and the cyborg substitute.* Alfred A. Knopf, New York.

Kutzer, M.D. 1996. *Writers of multicultural fiction for young adults.* Greenwood Press, Westport, CT.

Kuznets, L. 1994. *When toys come alive: narratives of animation, metamorphosis, and development*. Yale University Press, New Haven.

Kymlicka, W. 2007. *Multicultural odysseys: navigating the new international politics of diversity*. Oxford University Press, Oxford.

Laird, E. 2003. *The garbage king*. Macmillan, London.

Lakoff, G. & Johnson, M. 1980. *Metaphors we live by*. University of Chicago Press, Chicago.

Langer, B. 2002. 'Commodified enchantment: children and consumer capitalism'. *Thesis Eleven*, vol. 69, pp. 67–81.

Lars and the real girl. 2007. Motion picture. Kimmel Entertainment, Canada.

Lee, M. J. 1993. *Consumer Culture Reborn: The Cultural Politics of Consumption*. Routledge, London.

Le Guin, U.K. 1973. *The farthest shore*. Puffin-Penguin, Harmondsworth.

Le Guin, U.K. 2001. *Tales from Earthsea and The other wind*. Science Fiction Book Club, Camp Hill, PA.

Le Guin, U.K. 1990. *Tehanu: the last book of Earthsea*. Puffin-Penguin, London.

Le Guin, U.K. 1972. *The tombs of Atuan*. Puffin-Penguin, Harmondswoth.

Le Guin, U.K. 1968. *A wizard of Earthsea*. Puffin-Penguin, Harmondsworth.

Lefebvre, H. 1971. *Everyday life in the modern world,* trans. S. Rabinovitch. Allen Lane, London.

Lehr, S. 2001. *Beauty brains and brawn: the construction of gender in children's literature*. Heinemann, Portsmouth, NH.

Lenoir, T. 2002. 'Makeover: writing the body into the posthuman technoscape. Part two: corporeal axiomatics'. *Configurations*, vol. 10, pp. 373–85.

Levey, G.B. 2009. 'What is living and what is dead in multiculturalism'. *Ethnicities*, vol. 9, no. 1, pp. 75–96.

Levin, J. 2002. 'Beyond nature? Recent work in ecocriticism'. *Contemporary Literature*, vol. 43, no. 1, pp. 171–86.

Levitas, R. 2010. *The concept of utopía*. Peter Lang, Oxford.

Levitas, R. 2007. 'The imaginary reconstitution of society: utopia as method'. In T. Moylan & R. Baccolini (eds), *Utopia method vision: the use value of social dreaming*. Peter Lang, Oxford, pp. 47–68.

Levithan, D. 2006. *Boy meets boy*. HarperCollins, London.

Lewis, M. 1973 [1796]. *The monk: a romance*. Oxford University Press, London.

Lofthouse, L. & Ingpen, R. 2007. *Ziba came on a boat*. Viking, Camberwell, Vic.

Lombroso, C. & Ferrero, G. 2004 [1893]. *Criminal woman, the prostitute, and the normal woman*, trans. N.H. Rafter & M. Gibson. Duke University Press, Durham.

Love, G.A. 2003. *Practical ecocriticism: literature, biology, and the environment*. University of Virginia Press, Charlottesville.

Lovelock, J. 2009. *The vanishing face of Gaia: a final warning*. Allen Lane, London.

Lowry, L. 1992. *The giver*. Houghton Mifflin, Boston, MA.

Ma vie en rose. 1997. Motion picture. Sony Pictures Classics, France

MacKenzie, E. 1994. *Privatopia: homeowner associations and the rise of residential private government*. Yale University Press, New Haven.

MacLeod, D. 2003. *Tumble turn*. Penguin Group, Victoria.

MacLeod, G. & Ward, K. 2002. 'Spaces of utopia and dystopia: landscaping the contemporary city'. *Geografiska Annaler*, vol. 84, no. 3–4, pp. 153–70.

Madagascar. 2005. Animation. DreamWorks, USA.

Madagascar: escape 2 Africa. 2008. Animation. Dreamworks, USA.

Maddox, G. 2006. 'The Pixar principle'. *The Sunday Age*, May 28, pp. 6–7.

Maguire, G. 1999. *Confessions of an ugly stepsister: a novel*. Harper-HarperCollins, New York.

Maguire, G. 2008. *A lion among men: volume three in the wicked years*. William Morrow-HarperCollins, New York.

Maguire, G. 2003. *Mirror, mirror: a novel*. Harper-HarperCollins, New York.

Maguire, G. 2005. *Son of a witch: volume two in the wicked years*. Harper-HarperCollins, New York.

Maguire, G. 1995. *Wicked: the life and times of the Wicked Witch of the West: a novel*. ReganBooks-HarperCollins, New York.

Mallan, K. 2009. *Gender dilemmas in children's fiction*. Palgrave Macmillan, Basingstoke.

Mandler, J.M. 1992. 'How to build a baby: II. Conceptual primitives'. *Psychological Review*, vol. 99, no. 4, pp. 587–604.

Maras, A. 2005. *Azadi*. Short film. South Australian Film Corporation, Australia.

Massey, D. 1999. 'Spaces of politics'. In D. Massey, J. Allen, & P. Sarre (eds), *Human geography today*. Polity Press, Cambridge, pp. 279–94.

Massey, D. 1995. *Spatial divisions of labour: social structures and the geography of production*. Macmillan, Basingstoke.

Masso, A. 2009. 'A readiness to accept immigrants in Europe? Individual and country-level characteristics'. *Journal of Ethnic and Migration Studies*, vol. 35, no. 2, pp. 251–70.

McCallum, R. 1999. *Ideologies of identity in adolescent fiction: the dialogic construction of subjectivity*. Garland, New York.

McEachern, M. 2006. 'This old house: Imageworks uses performance capture and hand animation to create "dollhouse" realism'. *Computer Graphics World*, vol. 29, no. 7, pp. 28–48.

McGillis, R. 1996. *The nimble reader*. Twayne Publishers, New York.

McGillis, R. 1999. *Voices of the other: children's literature and the postcolonial context*. Routledge, New York.

'Medicine: Blasting to Smithereens'. 1983. *Time*, 10 January, accessed 16 October 2009, http://www.time.com/time/magazine/article/0,9171,923286-1,00.html.

Merchant, C. 1992. *Radical ecology: the search for a liveable world*. Routledge, Chapman & Hall, London.

Mercier, S. 1999 [1771]. *L'an 2440*, ed. C Cave & C Mercandier-Colard. La Découverte, Paris.

Milburn, C. 2005. 'Nano/splatter: disintegrating the postbiological body'. *New Literary History*, vol. 36, no. 2, pp. 283–311.

Milburn, C. 2002. 'Nanotechnology in the age of posthuman engineering: science fiction as science'. *Configurations*, vol. 10, no. 2, pp. 261–95.

Miller, S. & Rode, G. 1995. 'The movie you see, the movie you don't: how Disney do's that old time division'. In E. Bell, L. Haas, & L. Sells (eds), *From mouse to mermaid: the politics of film, gender and culture*. Indiana University Press, Bloomington, pp. 86–103.

Ministerial Council on Education, Training and Youth Affairs. 2008. *Melbourne declaration on educational goals for young Australians*. Melbourne.

Misson R. & Morgan W. 2006. *Critical literacy and the aesthetic: transforming the English classroom*. National Council of Teachers of English, Urbana, IL.

Miyake, O. 2006. 'Eastern Asia'. In J Zipes (ed.), *The Oxford encyclopedia of children's literature*. Oxford University Press, Oxford, pp. 9–11.

Mobile social networking set to increase ten-fold in Latam and Africa. 2009. Colibria, accessed 4 December 2009, http://colibria.com/media/press-releases/2818.

Moers, E. 1977. *Literary women*. Anchor Books, New York.

Monster house. 2006. Animation. Columbia Pictures, USA.

Monsters Inc. 2001. Animation. Pixar Animation Studios, USA.

Moore, P. 2007. *Hero*. Random House Children's Books, London.

More, T. 2003 [1516]. *Utopia*. Penguin, London.

Moylan, T. 2008. 'Making the present impossible: on the vocation of utopian science fiction'. *Arena*, vol. 31, pp. 79–109.

Mühlhäusler, P. & Peace, A. 2006. 'Environmental discourses'. *Annual Review of Anthropology*, vol. 35, pp. 457–79.

Mulvey, L. 1981. 'Afterthoughts on "visual pleasure and narrative cinema" inspired by King Vidor's *Duel in the sun*'. In *Visual and other pleasures*. Macmillan, London, pp. 2–6.

Mulvey, L. 1975. 'Visual pleasure and narrative cinema'. *Screen*, vol. 16, no. 3, pp. 6–18.

Naess, A. 1989. *Ecology, community, and lifestyle*, ed. and trans. D. Rothenberg. Cambridge University Press, Cambridge.

Napier, S. 2001. *Anime from Akira to Princess Mononoke: experiencing contemporary Japanese animation*. Palgrave, New York.

Nodelman, P. 2008. *The hidden adult: defining children's literature*. The Johns Hopkins University Press, Baltimore, MD.

Nolan, L. 2006. 'Descartes' ontological argument'. *Stanford encyclopedia of philosophy*, accessed 12 November 2009, http://plato.stanford.edu/entries/descartes-ontological/.

Norton, J. 1999. 'Transchildren and the discipline of children's literature'. *The Lion and the Unicorn*, vol. 23, no. 3, pp. 415–36.

Nosferatu. 1922. Moving picture. Film Arts Guild, Germany.

Oktober, T. 1998. *Rainforest*. Hodder, Sydney.

Olson, M.A. 1988. 'Descartes' first meditation: mathematics and the laws of logic'. *Journal of the History of Philosophy*, vol. 26, no. 3, pp. 407–38.

Opie, I. & Opie, P. (eds) 1980. *The classic fairy tales*. Granada, London.

Oreck, A. 'The golem'. *Jewish virtual library*, accessed 20 October 2009, http://www.jewishvirtuallibrary.org/jsource/Judaism/Golem.html.

Over the hedge. 2006. Animation. DreamWorks, USA.

Peters, J-A. 2004. *Luna*. Littlebrown and Company, New York.

Phillips, D. 2003. *The truth of ecology: nature, culture, and literature in America*. Oxford University Press, Oxford.

Plumwood, V. 1993. *Feminism and the mastery of nature*. Routledge, London.

Pordzik, R. 2009. 'Introduction'. In R. Pordzik (ed.), *Futurescapes: space in utopian and science fiction discourses*. Rodopi, Amsterdam, pp. 17–21.

Pratchett, T. 1998. *Witches abroad*. Corgi, London.

Prince, S. 1996. 'Psychoanalytic film theory and the problem of the missing spectator'. In D. Bordwell & N. Carroll (eds), *Post-theory: reconstructing film studies*. University of Wisconsin Press, Madison, pp. 71–86.

Princess Mononoke. 1997. Studio Ghibli, Japan.

Psycho. 1960. Moving picture. Paramount, USA.

Punter, D. & Byron, G. 2004. *The gothic*. Blackwell, Malden, MA.

Rabinowitz, R. 2004. 'Messy new freedoms: queer theory and children's literature'. In S. Chapelau (ed.), *New voices in children's literature*. Pied Piper Publishing, Litchfield, pp. 19–28.

Raschke, J. 2005. 'Who's knocking now? The rise and fall of "multicultural" literature'. *Overland*, vol. 180, pp. 21–26.

Reeve, P. 2001. *Mortal engines*. Scholastic, London.

Reynolds, K. 2007. *Radical children's literature: future visions and aesthetic transformations in juvenile fiction*. Palgrave Macmillan, Basignstoke.

Riddle, T. 1997. *The great escape from city zoo*. HarperCollins Publishers, Sydney.

Riddle, T. 2000. *The singing hat*. Viking, Ringwood, Victoria.

Riordan, R. 2009. *Percy Jackson and the last olympian*. Penguin Books, London.

Ritzer, G. 1993. *The McDonaldization of society: an investigation into the changing character of social life*. Pine Forge Press, Thousand Oaks.

Robertson, R. 1992. *Globalization: social theory and global culture*. Sage, London.

Robertson, R. 1995. 'Glocalization'. In M. Featherstone, S. Lash, & R. Robertson (eds), *Global modernities*. Sage, London, pp. 23–44.

Robertson, R. & White, K.E. 2008. 'What is globalization?'. In G. Ritzer (ed.), *The Blackwell companion to globalization*. Wiley-Blackwell, Oxford, pp. 54–66.

Romeo + Juliet. 1996. Motion picture. Twentieth Century Fox Film Corporation, USA.

Rose, J. 1992. *The case of Peter Pan or the impossibility of children's fiction*. The University of Pennsylvania Press, Philadelphia, PA.

Rosen, M. & Graham, B. 1996. *This is our house*. Walker Books Ltd, London.

Russell, E. 2000. *A is for Aunty*. ABC Books, Sydney.

Said, E. 1993. *Culture and imperialism*. Chatto & Windus, London.

Said, E. 1978. *Orientalism*. Pantheon Books, New York.

Sanders, J. 2006. *Adaptation and appropriation*. Routledge, London.

Sargent, L.T. 2007. 'Choosing utopia: utopianism as an essential element in political thought and action'. In T. Moylan & R. Baccolini (eds), *Utopia method vision: the use value of social dreaming*. Peter Lang, Oxford, pp. 301–17.

Sargent, L.T. 1994. 'The three faces of utopianism revisited'. *Utopian Studies*, vol. 5, no. 1, pp.1–37.

Schank, R. & Abelson, R. 1977. *Scripts, plans, goals and understanding: an inquiry into human knowledge structures*. Lawrence Erlbaum Associates, Hillsdale, NJ.

Sedgwick, E.K. 1992. *Between men: English literature and male homosexual desire*. Columbia University Press, New York.

Sedgwick, E.K. 1990. *Epistemology of the closet*. University of California Press, Berkeley.

Sedgwick, E.K. 1998. 'How to bring your kids up gay'. In S. Jenkins (ed.), *The children's culture reader*. New York University Press, New York, pp. 231–40.

Sedgwick, E.K. 1993. *Tendencies*. Duke University Press, Durham, NC.

Seidman, S. 2004. 'Identity and politics in a "postmodern" gay culture: some historical and conceptual notes'. In M. Warner (ed.), *Fear of a queer planet: queer politics and social theory*. University of Minnesota Press, Minneapolis, pp. 105–41.

Selvadurai, S. 1995. *Funny boy: a novel in six stories*. Vintage, London.

Sendak, M. 1963. *Where the wild things are*. Harper & Row, New York.

Shakespeare, W. 1980. *Romeo and Juliet*. Methuen, London.

Shakespeare, W. 1969. *The taming of the shrew*. In R. Hosley (ed.), *William Shakespeare: the complete works*. Penguin, Baltimore.

Shearer, A. 2003. *The speed of the dark*. Macmillan Children's Books, London.

Shelley, M. 1980 [1818]. *Frankenstein, or the Modern Prometheus*. Oxford University Press, Oxford.

Shome, R. 2006. 'Transnational feminism and communication studies'. *The Communication Review*, vol. 9, no. 4, pp. 255–67.

Shrek. 2001. Animation. Dreamworks, USA.

Sky High. 2005. Motion picture. Max Stronghold Productions, USA.

Slater, P. & Parish, P. (Illus.) 2002. *Discover and learn about Australian forests and woodlands.* Steve Parish Publishing, Archerfield, Qld.

Soper, K. 2000. 'Naturalized woman and feminized nature'. In L. Coupe (ed.), *The green studies reader: from romanticism to ecocriticism.* Routledge, London, pp. 139–43.

Springer, C. 1996. *Electronic eros: bodies and desire in the postindustrial age.* University of Texas Press, Austin.

Steger, M.B. 2005. *Globalism: market ideology meets terrorism,* 2nd ed. Rowman and Littlefield, Lanham, MD.

Stein, K. 1983. 'Monsters and madwomen: changing female gothic'. In J. Fleenor (ed.), *The female gothic.* Eden Press, Montreal, pp. 123–37.

Stephens, J. 1992. *Language and ideology in children's fiction.* Longman, London.

Stephens, J. (ed.) 2002. *Ways of being male: representing masculinities in children's literature and film.* Routledge, New York.

Stephens, J. 1995. 'Writing *by* children, writing *for* children: schema theory, narrative discourse and ideology'. *Revue Belge de Philologie et d'Histoire,* vol. 73, no. 3, pp. 853–63 (revised and reprinted in Bull, G. & Anstey, M. (eds) 2002, *Crossing the boundaries.* Prentice Hall, French's Forest, NSW, pp. 237–48).

Stephens, J. & McCallum, R. 2009. 'Positioning otherness: (post-)multiculturalism and point of view in Australian young adult fiction'. In U. Garde & A-R. Meyer (eds), *Belonging and exclusion: case studies in recent Australian and German literature, film and theatre.* Cambridge Scholars Publishing, Newcastle, pp. 129–42.

Stephens, J. & McGillis, R. 2006. 'Critical approaches to children's literature'. In J. Zipes (ed.), *The Oxford encyclopedia of children's literature volume 1.* Oxford University Press, New York, pp. 364–7.

Stoker, B. 1997 [1897]. *Dracula.* Norton, New York.

Suvin, D. 1979. *Metamorphosis of science fiction: on the poetics and history of a literary genre.* Yale University Press, New Haven.

Takolander, M. & McCooey, D. 2005. ' "You can't say no to *The Beauty and the Beast*": *Shrek* and ideology'. *Papers: Explorations into Children's Literature,* vol. 14, no. 1, pp. 5–14.

Tales from Earthsea. 2006. Animation. Buena Vista Home Entertainment, Japan.

The taming of the shrew. 1967. Motion picture. Columbia Pictures, USA.

Tan, S. 2000. *The lost thing.* Lothian, Port Melbourne.

Tasker, Y. 1998. *Working girls: gender and sexuality in popular cinema.* Routledge, London.

Taylor, J. 1999. 'Japan's global environmentalism: rhetoric and reality'. *Political Geography,* vol. 18, pp. 535–62.

10 things I hate about you. 1999. Motion picture. Buena Vista Pictures, USA.

10 things I hate about you. 2009. Television program. ABC Family, USA.

Terranova, T. 2004. 'Communication beyond meaning: on the cultural politics of information'. *Social Text,* vol. 22, no. 3, pp. 51–73.

Thomas, G.T. 2008. 'Globalization: the major players'. In G. Ritzer (ed.), *The Blackwell companion to globalization.* Wiley-Blackwell, Oxford, pp. 84–102.

Tolkein, J.R.R. 1954–5. *The lord of the rings.* George Allen & Unwin, London.

Tomlinson, J. 1999. *Globalization and culture.* Polity Press, Cambridge.

Townshend, D. 2008. 'The Haunted Nursery: 1764–1830'. In A. Jackson, K. Coats, & R. McGillis (eds), *The gothic in children's literature: haunting the borders.* Routledge, New York, pp. 15–38.

Townshend, D. 2007. *The orders of the gothic: Foucault, Lacan, and the subject of gothic writing 1764–1820*. AMS Press, New York.
Toy story. 1995. Animation. Pixar Animation Studios, USA.
Toy story 2. 1999. Animation. Pixar Animation Studios, USA.
Trites, R.S. 1997. *Waking Sleeping Beauty: feminist voices in children's novels*. University of Iowa Press, Iowa City.
Tsukioka, I. & Stephens, J. 2003. 'Reading development across linked stories: Anna Fienberg's *Tashi* series and *The magnificent nose and other marvels*'. *The Lion and the Unicorn*, vol. 27, no. 2, pp. 185–98.
Turner, M. 1996. *The literary mind*. Oxford University Press, New York.
United Nations Environment Program. 2007. *Global environment outlook*, accessed 20 August 2010, http://www.unep.org/geo/geo4/report/ GEO-4_Report_Full_en.pdf.
Urry, J. 1995. *Consuming places*. Routledge, London.
Vautier, E. 2009. 'Playing the "Race Card": White Anxieties and the Expression and Repression of Popular Racisms in the 1997 UK Election'. *Patterns of Prejudice*, vol. 43, no. 2, pp. 122–41.
Verkuyten, M. 2009. 'Support for Multiculturalism and Minority Rights: The Role of National Identification and Out-group Threat'. *Social Justice Research*, vol. 22, no.1, pp. 31–52.
Vermeir, K. 2008. 'RoboCop dissected: man-machine and mind-body in the enlightenment'. *E-Technology and Culture*, vol. 49, no. 4, accessed 12 November 2009, http://etc.technologyandculture.net/2008/12/robocop-dissected-man-machine-and-mind-body-in-the-enlightenment/.
Warren, K.J. 1998. 'Ecofeminism: introduction'. In M.E. Zimmerman & J.B. Callicott (eds), *Environmental philosophy: from animal rights to radical ecology*, 2nd edn. Prentice Hall, Upper Saddle River, New Jersey, pp. 263–76.
Warren, K.J. 1995. 'Feminism and ecology: making connections'. In M.H. MacKinnon & M. McIntyre (eds), *Ecology and feminist theology*. Sheed & Ward, Kansas City, MO, pp. 105–23.
Waters, M. 2002. 'The global culture of consumption'. In G. Ritzer (ed), *McDonaldization: the reader*. Pine Forge Press, Thousand Oaks, pp. 213–21.
Wegner, P.E. 2002. *Imaginary communities: utopia, the nation, and the spatial histories of modernity*. University of California Press, Berkeley.
Weiten, W. 2001. *Psychology: Themes and Variations*. Wadsworth: Stamford.
West side story. 1961. Motion picture. United Artists, USA.
Westerfeld, S. 2004. *So yesterday*. Penguin, Camberwell.
Wilkie-Stibbs, C. 2002. *The feminine subject in children's literature*. Routledge, New York.
Wilkinson, R. 2002. *Endangered: working to save animals at risk*. Allen & Unwin, Melbourne.
Winnicott, D.W. 1971. *Playing and reality*. Routledge, New York.
Winnicott, D.W. 1951/1953. 'Transitional objects and transitional phenomena: a study of the first not-me possession'. *International Journal of Psycho-Analysis*, vol. 34, pp. 89–97.
Winter, K. 1992. 'Sexual/textual politics of terror: writing and rewriting the gothic genre in the 1790s'. In K.A. Ackley (ed.), *Misogyny in literature: an essay collection*. Garland, New York, pp. 89–103.
Wisniewski, D. 1996. *Golem*. Clarion Books, New York.
Wittgenstein, L. 1958. *Philosophical investigations*. Blackwell, Oxford.
The Wiz. 1978. Motion picture. Universal Pictures, USA.
The Wizard of Oz. 1939. Motion picture. MGM, USA.

Wolfe, C. 2010. *What is posthumanism?*. University of Minnesota Press, Minneapolis.

Wood, N. 2004. '(Em)bracing icy mothers: ideology, identity, and environment in children's fantasy'. In S.I. Dobrin & K.B. Kidd (eds), *Wild things: children's culture and ecocriticism*. Wayne State University Press, Detroit, pp.198–214.

Wood, N. 1995. 'A (sea) green Victorian: Charles Kingsley and *The Water-Babies*'. *The Lion and the Unicorn*, vol. 19, no. 2, pp. 233–52.

The World Commission on Environment and Development. 1987. *Our common future*. Oxford University Press, Oxford.

Wortley, E. 2009. '"The world of television microwave dinners, air-conditioning and Have a Nice Day": representations of globalization in two young adult novels'. *International Research in Children's Literature*, vol. 2, no. 2, pp. 278–290.

Wright, L. 2005. 'Forest spirits, giant insects and world trees: the nature vision of Hayao Miyazaki'. *Journal of Religion and Popular Culture*, vol. 10, accessed 22 August 2010, http://www.usask.ca/relst/jrpc/art10-mitazaki.html.

Yoshimura, K. and Hardin, C.D. 2009. 'Cognitive Salience of Subjugation and the Ideological Justification of U.S. Geopolitical Dominance in Japan.' *Social Justice Research*, vol. 22, pp. 298–311.

Zeavin, L. 2003. 'As useless as tits on a bull?: psychoanalytic reflections on misogyny'. In D. Moss (ed.), *Hating in the first person plural: psychoanalytic essays on racism, homophobia, misogyny, and terror*. Other Press, New York, pp. 227–48.

Zipes, J. 1995. 'Once upon a time beyond Disney: contemporary fairy-tale films for children'. In C. Bazalgette & D. Buckingham (eds), *In front of the children: screen entertainment and young audiences*. British Film Institute, London, pp. 109–26.

Zoolander. 2001. Motion picture. Paramount Pictures, USA.

Index